Of Many Houses

Of Many Houses

A YOUNG WOMAN'S JOURNEY
FROM THE THIRD REICH TO
THE NEW WORLD

To Bee,

Looking forward
to a great new
friendship.

Felicia

FELICIA ALTMAN GILBERT

Feb. 2017
Felicia will be 100 on April 22nd

To order additional copies of this book, contact:
Xlibris Corporation
1-888-795-4274
www.Xlibris.com
Orders@Xlibris.com
23523

Dedication

I wrote this book for my children and their wives, Eric,
✗ <u>Ralph</u> and Mary, Bruce and Lex, and for their children,
my grandchildren Noah, Zac, Isabel, and Leah.

I dedicate it to the memory of my dear husband Gil,
whose keen interest and support kept me at my task when I
faltered off and on. He had me read each chapter to him as it
grew and, with a big smile and a nod of his head, sent me back
to my desk. And even when he was so very ill during his last
days he'd call, "Read to me." Did he really hear me? His eyes
were closed, but I heard a murmured, "That's good."
How I wish he could see the completion of my effort.

✗ He's at GSU (Art) + Knows my son,
Eddy (Prof. of Philosophy) very well.

CONTENTS

ACKNOWLEDGMENTS

I do want to thank many people, but foremost my son Ralph, my chief supporter and editor, who worked for many hours to correct flawed punctuation and occasional Germanic sentence structure in spite of his crowded schedule.

The knowledgeable and kind advice of James McKean at the Iowa Writer's Workshop, and Melanie Bishop of Prescott College was extremely helpful. Carol Lee Lorenzo at Callenwold and Megan Sexton of Georgia State University also deserve my thanks.

Thanks to Lepska Warren, Sophia and Mael Melvin, Diane and Morrie Seidler, Mara and Walter Kohn, and all of my good friends of the Santa Barbara Book Club for their loving interest and relentless nudging through the years to read to them as my writing progressed.

Thanks to Marjorie Kellogg and Sylvia Short, whose help and friendship has meant so much.

My thanks also go to Nancy Cooley in Atlanta who gave me invaluable support, advice and friendship when I was in great need of it.

I am grateful to the Hedgebrook Retreat for Women Writers that granted to me the incredible gift of a six-week stay at their estate on Whidbey Island. I had a little house all to myself on the beautiful wooded grounds, solitude to write undisturbed, I was fed and pampered, and had the chance to enjoy the stimulating company of other writers at the end of the day. The time there was validating, encouraging and provided just the push I needed at a critical time.

Felicia Altman Gilbert, Atlanta, 2004

CHAPTER ONE

The First House and Its People

No one about. Here was my chance.

It was a little scary at first, climbing up from the second floor, the children's quarters, to the third story of the big house and then even higher up a narrow stairway to the attic. I had to use judgment to accomplish this quickly and silently in order not to arouse the attention of either Nanny or one of the maids. Surely they'd say I was too independent, as usual. The dusty attic was unhealthy, it was an unsuitable undertaking, altogether senseless, and anyway, just plain forbidden. A few sounds came up from the downstairs kitchen, the muffled ringing of the doorbell, someone laughed, a dog barked for a moment, then it was quiet.

Careful, careful, no noise. One landing, another one, and another. The last narrow stairway lay ahead and I stopped. My heart was beating hurriedly and I swallowed hard. The comfort of the hallway, the daylight coming in through the brightly polished windowpanes lay behind me. The banister and even the carpet covering the staircase had come to an end and the raw wooden steps in front of me led upwards in dim and ever dimmer light to a small door at the top of the landing. And I tiptoed slowly, slowly not to arouse—whom? I did not know who or what might be lurking in this passage. Behind me lay the world of everyday, of grown-ups, of being scolded, of lessons, and taking baths—but up there, behind the door, lay my secret world where no one thought to look for me.

As always, the door stuck a little; I had to tug hard to open it. I slipped in quickly and closed it quietly behind me. I sighed with satisfaction. In spite of the large size of the room, stretching nearly across the whole expanse of the house, and even with only a small amount of light filtering in through the two little windows, I felt safe and protected.

The walls of the gabled roof slanted steeply down to the floor, like all-enfolding wings around me. In the shadowy corners of half-partitions and supporting posts, chests of drawers, cardboard boxes, stacked-up pieces of small furniture, all kinds of nondescript bundles were stored. There were suitcases, shipping labels still attached. A big laundry basket was filled with old toys, waiting to be donated to some charity for next year's Christmas drive.

Over on one side stood a huge upright chest, its elaborately carved doors had mirrors set into them, sending any reflected image back with amber-colored blotches and crackly black lines like spider tracks. I had to stretch to turn the key with both hands and swing the heavy panels open, revealing the treasures within. The acrid vapor of mothballs stung my eyes and I crinkled my nose. On the left side hung my father's heavy winter coat, but there, on the right, encased in special cotton bags, my mother's costumes were stored, nostalgic witnesses to a past career on the stage.

I had been up there before. I had parted the overlapping folds of the bags and my probing hands let the slippery silks, the soft velvets, the scratchy brocades, and filmy laces slip though my fingers. But this time a brightly colored sleeve came dangling loose, and I had to pull it out a little, and a little more, and all at once out they tumbled, the wrappings and trappings of storybook and fantasy, all landing in a glorious heap at my feet. Fear and worry were forgotten. I reached and lifted this piece up, spread that one, smoothing out the wrinkles, draped a large fringed shawl around my shoulders, held a peasant skirt up to my waist.

Here was a gauzy pink ballet costume. I slipped my dress off and tried it on. The skirt stood around my small frame like a tent. The shoulder straps kept slipping down, and the bodice parts, where the adult dancer's bosom was supposed to be encased, hung like two pouches under my armpits. I held them up with my thumbs and turned and twirled, remembering the fairies of the Nutcracker performance at Christmas.

And here was a costume in purple velvet. For a grown-up, the ballooning pants were to be fastened under the knees, adorned with loosely floating golden braids, and the matching, long-sleeved, high-collared jacket was meant to have a broad leather belt tied around its waist holding a scabbard and sword. I did not know, of course, that this was a page's costume from a Shakespeare play. I tried it on. I hooked the fastener of the heavy jacket in front instead of the back, where it was supposed to be. I tried to hitch the sleeves up and struggled to hold the pants together at the waist.

And then I found the hat, a purple velvet beret with a long, white, somewhat dilapidated plume on its broad brim. I stepped in front of the mirror and gazed at my ghostly, small figure in the plumed hat through the amber blotches and black spider tracks. An arrow-thin stream of sunlight had stolen through the small window behind me and quivered eerily through the image in the glass.

I turned away and the pants fell off and the jacket got to be too hot and heavy, but I kept the hat on. Looming dark and commanding beyond the thin stream of sunlight stood a large rocking horse. It was the size of a real-life pony and may even have been one in its, let us say, better days. Its dusty brown hide showed bare spots on the flanks, and it was not wise to pull his mane or tail too hard; you'd end up with some hair in your hand. Its nostrils were bright black and its large glass eyes shone golden brown under human-looking eyelids. My father had owned this horse as a boy and my older brother had played with it.

"It's not for girls!" I was told, but I loved it.

Along the walls under the slanting roof I now walked and there was my real dreamland. On table-high shelves stood row upon row of small, three-dimensional models of various stage sets that were designed for plays my father had directed. Each was encased on three sides by boxes with little electric lights that could be switched on individually. And each one in turn, when lit, became a small glowing world of its own within the darkness of the walls.

There were scenes of blooming gardens with paths and pergolas in them. There were villages with snowy mountains in the backgrounds. There were castles and formidable bridges, elegant modern drawing rooms, foreboding prison interiors, forests with huge tree trunks and rocks, and shore scenes with ocean and ships. In front of each of them I could sit on an old stool I had found in a corner, my elbows propped on the shelf, dreaming myself into every one.

I made up stories: I hid in the forests, scaled the mountains, and walked about the castle courts. I found a witch in the medieval village. There was one stage set I liked especially well. It was a street, quite like my own, with houses, trees and gardens. There were flags waving, and a circus wagon was painted on the backdrop.

But the scene next to this one I hated. There was a house with the roof ripped open showing walls torn down and windows shattered. Flames leapt all around it, and a dark, dismal street lead away into empty space. Only once had I switched this one on. The lighting was not bright, but red and dull. I had turned it off, not wanting to look too closely.

But today my hand found the switch again, and I stared and shuddered. What happened? Who made it break, who made it burn? Who had lived in this house, where had they gone? This house, any house—could be *my* house.

I ran to the little window, dragging a stool, and climbed on it and reached the sill, just high enough to stick my nose above it. I saw the houses across the street, the crowns of trees, a cloud or two. The sun was shining. *There* was the real world.

My hand ran down the rough wall planks, my feet gave a dull little thud, hitting the floor when I jumped off my perch. The wood felt so solid, nothing shook.

I climbed on my horse. The rough hide scratched my bare legs. I wrapped my arms around his sturdy neck, stared across to the dull little red light and the fallen house, my chin in the horse's mane, and I rocked back and forth, stared and rocked and rocked and rocked.

The purple hat had fallen to the floor.

Berlin-Dahlem, Wildenow Strasse 44.

Solid, seemingly indestructible, it was beyond a child's understanding that it might not always be there. The tall, gray, stuccoed house, three stories high with wide windows and lush green ivy climbing up its walls contained the essence of my early childhood.

Dahlem was a quiet suburb of Berlin. One part of it consisted of large one-family homes surrounded by well-kept gardens that, like ours, stood on broad tree-shaded streets that ended in a long stretch of fields. Beyond the fields was a small farm, beyond that a village where the only paving ran along the main road and was flanked by squat houses. Market day was held once a week along the little village road, and sometimes I was allowed to accompany the cook on her long trek across the fields to shop for fresh fruits and vegetables.

We would pass the farm where several buildings were arranged in a half circle around the cobblestone-paved yard, eyeing the large compost heap and the scratching and clucking chickens. There was a well with a pump and a bucket on a chain. I always wanted to walk right across the big bumpy stones of the pavement, open those heavy-looking double gates to the barn and peek in, but the grim-looking man stomping about in high, black, mud-caked boots scared me.

Stalls, buckets and huge baskets lined the village street on both sides. Fruit, vegetables, chickens, bread and eggs, aprons, brooms and shovels were to be had. Our cook and, sometimes, even Mother would wander up and down filling the baskets on their arms. The air smelled of apples and cabbages. Blotches of sunlight came through the trees as though carelessly splashed by someone's brush, highlighting the red kerchief on a woman's hair, a flowery skirt, a green umbrella. I was given a small apple or a few dusty strawberries, and they tasted wonderful.

A little beyond the village lay the Lyceum, the girls' school that I attended from age eight on, until we moved to Hannover. When I was six and seven, in 1926 and 1927, I was taught at home by a Herr Erdmann, who was weighed down by a sizable beer belly and smelled of stale cigar smoke. As a young man, he had been one of my father's boyhood teachers and now was quite elderly. Mother considered me too frail to go to public school for the first two years and was prone to keep me in bed when it rained, and I had sneezed more than twice.

When I was finally allowed to walk to school without my nanny it was most often in the company of other girls. Sometimes it happened that my brother, who was eight years older than I, took off to his classes at the big-boys' school, the Gymnasium, at the same time I left for the Lyceum, and then, oh joy, he let me ride on the handlebars of his bicycle when the coast was clear, which meant that Mother was not watching.

Beyond the two schools loomed the large imposing Berlin Voelkerkunde Museum (Ethnic Culture and Art Museum), surrounded by bare fields and wide stretches of unoccupied

land. It was here that my father's uncle, James Simon, l
donated important art objects, paintings, as well as antique
sculpture, whose excavations he had financed, among them
the famous head of the Egyptian queen, Nefertiti. Of course,
these things formed only a small part of the museum's vast
and varied collection, but to my mind the whole building
belonged to Uncle James.

On the way home from school my girlfriends and I
would stop at the village candy store quite regularly. For a
few pennies we could buy a small corked glass vial that
contained Love Pearls, tiny colored sugar-balls that you
crunched between your teeth very slowly, one by one. On
some such occasion I might mention quite casually that next
Sunday I was going to visit my uncle's museum with my
father. Wide eyes and reverent silence from my audience
would follow such an announcement, and I'd fish another
Love Pearl from the glass.

Another favorite treat, although it cost one penny more,
was a marshmallow cone that was covered by a thin skin
of chocolate. It was called a Black Kiss. A special ritual had
to be followed to attack this delicacy: First, you carefully
nibbled off the dark coating all around without marring
the shape of the snow-white mound inside. Then you could
suck the cone from its tip down to the cookie at its base,
shaping it carefully with your tongue as it grew smaller
and smaller until nothing was left except the sticky mess
on your fingers.

I see myself on a dreary autumn day returning from a
walk with Seusa, my Nanny. I am bundled up to my chin and
a woolen cap is covering my ears. We go down the quiet street
with its large chestnut trees and well-tended gardens behind
low brick walls or tall wrought-iron fences. I am dragging my
feet. The high-laced boots with their posture correcting inserts,
which my mother insisted I wear, are quite cumbersome, but

I cannot resist the mounds of fallen leaves banked against the sidewalk curbs. Into them I run, up and around they whirl, yellow, red, brown, and green, dust and old papers join in, and my Nanny protests in pursuit.

The rosebushes lining our garden path are bare now. The scraggly branches of the lilacs beyond the lawn make one long for summer and their majestic growth and clouds of blue and white blossoms. The sandbox is wet and the swing unhooked. Down the graveled garden path we go and up the high divided staircase to the door.

Now I stand in our dim front hall that is dominated by a large oil painting of a late paternal grandfather in all his dignity and carefully groomed mustaches. He holds a gold-knobbed cane in one hand and the other rests on a leather-covered tome of, no doubt, great significance. I often gaze up to this imposing presence in the heavy gold frame that towers over me, slightly abashed and feeling very small, which, of course, I am. When one of the connecting doors to the living room or kitchen is opened suddenly, it seems as if the imposing gentleman would wrap the gold frame around his shoulders, pick up his cane, and descend upon me in the sudden flash of intruding light.

I do not like the hall.

I walk through the dining room, the center of the house, with its great long table. The sideboards are filled with heavy silver utensils and crystal glassware, and the light that shines through the high windows makes everything gleam. Here the family dinners are served by Martha, a tall young woman from East Prussia who stayed with us for many years. Here also, big elaborate dinner parties take place. They naturally excluded me, but the preparations for them were always exciting. The whole staff, Martha, Louise, the cook, my Nanny Seusa, and Anton the chauffeur will gather around the dining table and polish all of the silverware, the serving bowls, the goblets, the pitchers—everything will shine. Sometimes I am allowed to help. I do not know that whatever I rub with great effort is secretly shoved back into the assembly line and redone.

From the dining room I walk into the Herren Zimmer (the Gentlemen's Room) where I sometimes curl up on one of the deep upholstered chairs circling a round oak table that has been especially designed for my father to hold a turquoise Pompeian tile frieze set into its top. Passing Father's library with its thousands of books and its huge desk, I come to my favorite room of all, which, to my great sorrow, is declared "off limits to children," especially me.

This is the Biedermeier room, named for the early 19th century, blond, flamed-birch furniture of that period, a corner room with many high lace-curtained windows and a grand piano in the alcove.

I stand on the threshold peeking into this room and as always the sun is filtering in through the leaves of the birch trees in front of the window and then through the lacy curtains. I carefully listen for approaching steps or voices in the vicinity and then, if all is quiet, I tiptoe in.

I sit on the sofa. It is really quite uncomfortable, stiff and thinly upholstered in silk with green stripes and little flowers on a black background. On the top of each armrest, a hinged cover can be raised, and I never tire of investigating whether the hollow space underneath might contain an unexpected treasure. But no, there are no chocolates, not even a pretty button or some crayons or a notepad to draw on. Occasionally, a dust cloth appears inside, forgotten by one of the maids, or a bunch of keys of unexplained origin, always a disappointment. I lean on one of the hard round side bolsters and dangle my feet that won't reach the floor. Two high-backed grandfather chairs, headrests decorated with colorful beadwork shimmering against black upholstery, flank the round table in front of me. Upon the table is a large, ornate, silver bowl that is always full of fresh flowers. Everything in this room is framed by the glow of the golden wood.

There on my right stands a graceful glass-enclosed cabinet. I slip off my seat and gaze at the wonders on the long narrow shelves behind its locked doors. There are delicate porcelain cups lined up like jewels on a string, each of different shape, size, and design. I was told that many come from other countries, not only from Germany but also from France, Italy and England, but really that means nothing to me yet. I just adore looking at the painted scenes showing ladies in flowing gowns and naked babies with wings on their shoulders, like butterflies. One cup has a whole landscape on it with a boat on water and a windmill. Others have flowers and leaf designs. Some are dark blue or wine-colored with lines of lacy gold. Only once was I allowed to hold my favorite cup, just for a moment, under the anxious eye of my Mother. It was very small, light green with white and gold scrolls and stripes, delicate and transparent like an eggshell.

Now I turn and there under my feet lies a black woven throw rug. Large leaves and flowers in glowing, burning colors are embroidered all over it. I kneel and then lie down and spread my arms wide to gather all of this beauty around me and sink into it, my face pressed against the woolly warmth, trying to dig into the reds and greens and purples.

I turn on my back. A large secretary desk is looming above me on the other wall. My parents' guest book lies on its fold-down writing top and a porcelain candlestick with two white and gold doves for handles keeps watch over it.

The tall grandfather clock near the window is about to chime. I get up and turn the handle on its housing door to take a quick peek at the bright, round pendulum that swings back and forth, back and forth, forever a mystery. What makes it go?

Next, I admiringly stroke the silk and brocade of the antique Mandarin coat that is spread across the top of the grand piano and then slip out of the room, not feeling guilty but rather pleased with myself.

I go back to the dining room and from there through a pair of double doors that open to the so-called Wintergarden, a glass-enclosed room with potted palms, ferns, and other plants. It always smells damp and earthy. It has wicker furniture that sometimes scratches my bare legs. Another door leads out to the open veranda, where lunch and afternoon coffee are served when the weather is agreeable.

In a photograph from that time the whole family sits around the table on the terrace of the Wintergarden: Father, short, plump, dignified, but smiling benevolently, proud of his family. He is neatly dressed, jacket and tie, even at home. Mother, elegant, pearl-necklaced, sweetly domineering. Leaning against her are her earnest sailor-suited twelve-year-old son and I, her four-year-old daughter, whose strands of long hair are carefully brushed around a broomstick every morning to make them curl. Two widowed Grandmothers reign decorously from either side of the table, emitting little sparks of animosity toward each other, that seem to emanate even from the paper of the photograph. Oma Hall, my mother's mother, is comfortably heavy-set and high-bosomed, her sparse gray hair in a knot on top of her head, its volume discreetly enhanced by a wad of cotton stuffed under it. She smiles tentatively. Oma Marta, my father's mother on the other side of the table, does not smile. Oh no, she is stern, regal, sharp-faced, and corseted in body and soul. Around her neck are pearls on top of a broad pink band of sturdy ribbon, disguising and holding the folds of her aging throat.

A visitor coming up the stairs to the second story hallway would have been amazed, confronted by a giant floor-to-ceiling cage next to the door that leads to my brother's and my rooms. Here Max and Moritz, two red squirrels, romped and raced up and down the trunk and branches of a large artificial tree, fastening their shiny, black, raisin eyes on anybody who came near. With their big, bushy red tails and pointy tufted ears poised full of attention and curiosity, they hoped for a little token of friendship from every passerby.

I cannot recall my own room at all, except for the windows. They were equipped with double frames and double panes of glass to keep the cold out in winter. Long, narrow, white oilcloth-covered bolsters rested on the sills between the two frames to keep the draft out. When my friend Irmi came to visit, these bolsters were turned into hobbyhorses. Straddling them, we galloped around the room and up and down the hall and staircases as bold adventurers, encountering dangers of all kinds. Or they ended up on the floor in various shapes and arrangements to provide rooms and playgrounds for dolls and teddy bears. They were also used for walloping pillow fights, which probably did not add to their longevity.

Irmi, Irmgard Weiss, was the daughter of a janitor who lived in the basement of the house next door to us. We met one day, eyeing each other shyly on opposite sides of the wrought iron fence, each pushing our doll carriage. I was four then and did not have friends of my own age. My mother was convinced that the best way to keep me from illness and accidents was to isolate me from all dangerous encounters, including the world outside the safety of our home. Mother, succumbing to my never ending begging, carefully inspected the girl and gave her a clean bill of health. Irmi was skinny, tall, one year older than I was, neat and polite, and was finally allowed to come over to play. We became great friends and stayed close for many years. When Irmi's parents moved away, she came and stayed with us on many a weekend. Even my mother was fond of her.

When there were no rehearsals or other engagements that kept her away from home, Mother could be found reclining on the chaise lounge in her sitting room. On chilly evenings she might wear a white shawl of fine light wool around her shoulders, red and pink roses woven into it. Sometimes I crept under its folds, nestling under Mother's arm, snuggling as tight as I could.

About twice a year, in spring and early fall, representatives of one of the finest dress shops in Berlin would come to the house and then my mother's room was turned into a veritable showroom. The full-length mirror at the center of the dark mahogany dressing table became the focal point of the room so Madam could choose her wardrobe for the season in the latest fashions. At those times I was shooed out of the way, to my intense annoyance.

My parents' bedroom was next door to mother's domain and the only special features I recall are the twin brass beds placed side by side, flanked by nightstands, each hiding a big porcelain chamber pot, comfortably broad-brimmed, flowers painted overall, perhaps to suggest the sweet smell of spring.

Oma Hall, my mother's mother, had two rooms on the third floor of our house. They were musty-smelling rooms, stuffed full of furniture and presided over by Laura, the parrot, cocking her shimmering green head to one side, glaring malevolently and screeching LAURA! LAURA! while not crunching sunflower seeds with her vicious beak and spitting them heedlessly through the rungs of her cage.

Oma Hall was born Susan Ida Thurston in Jersey City, New Jersey, in the United States. I was about six years old when she died. I remember a fairly tall, corpulent woman, her face white and puffy. She went to church every Sunday, if not more often. I always thought that her speach was most peculiar as she scrambled her words in a funny way that made me laugh. She never lost her American accent and never fully conquered the German language or her dislike of it.

I do not know where in America her husband, my grandfather, Charles Henry Hall, was born. It has been stated that *his* father was a mill builder, who also owned a sawmill in a forest. His son grew up at the sawmill and at an early age showed unusual mechanical abilities by implementing numerous small adjustments and improvements to the workings of his father's mill.

At twelve years of age he became bored and restless and ran away from home. He had a hard time roaming about the country finding occasional work in other mills and on sugar plantations. The civil war broke out and Henry, in spite of his youth, served as engineer in Admiral Faragut's fleet. At the end of the war, having been promoted to chief engineer, he went to New York. There he obtained a scientific and a general education, to which he'd had no access to in his early youth. After many experiments he invented the Magic Pump. It was a steam-driven pump system that was based on the action of the human heart. It later became known as the pulsometer.

From 1869 to 1873 Charles Henry Hall took out twenty-seven patents in America and in England. On August 30 of 1873, the *Scientific American journal* in New York ran an illustrated article with detailed descriptions about the workings of Mr. Hall's pulsometer. A report about an 1877 lecture and demonstration given to a scientific society in Berlin stated that it was amazing to see how a fairly small, unassuming-looking contraption was able to throw a tremendous stream of water without the aid of any other mechanical instruments through a firmly inserted steam pipe the size of a finger.

In 1874 Charles Henry Hall married Susan Ida Thurston, on the twenty first of November, in the First Baptist Church in Jersey City. Further information about my grandfather is scarce. He was called to Germany by the Krupp Manufacturing Company to install and supervise the fabrication of his pulsometer for European distribution.

He left the United States and went to Germany with his wife and small child, the boy Charles Percival. It seems they lived in Silesia in a place called Wilhelmshuette, near Sprottau, where the testing and fabrication of his invention took place. Eventually they moved to Berlin. In 1878 a daughter, Florence, was born and eight years later in 1886 my mother, Alice, came into the world. Percy died of pneumonia, probably around 1880 at the age of four or five.

His mission completed, Charles Henry's restlessness set in.

"Susan," he said, "We now have money. Let's go around the world."

She was horrified. "How can I do that with two small children?"

"Then I'll go alone," he said, and he did.

He was never seen or heard from again. For a short time a rumor circulated that he had hanged himself somewhere in the South Seas. This was never confirmed.

Susan was left alone with very little money, two daughters to rear, and a very poor command of the German language. She became a night nurse so she could take care of her children during the day. Almost from the day my parents married they took care of her, and she lived with us until she died.

Oma Marta, my paternal grandmother, had her quarters at the front of the house on the second floor. She stayed with us for several months of the year when not traveling, and then certainly made her presence known. There was always strife when Oma Marta was present. Demands for extra service and critical remarks concerning the household's affairs and inhabitants were distributed freely.

Her husband, Grandfather Eugene Altman, was born in Rochester, New York, in 1849. His Father, Joseph, had immigrated to the United States in 1846 from the little town of Niederstetten in the south of Germany, and eventually became a prosperous banker.

As a young man his son, Eugene, my Grandfather, was sent to Germany to establish a branch of the American Altman-Levy bank. He married Franziska Marta Simon, the daughter of a Jewish shopkeeper from Pyritz in Pomerania and she became our Oma Marta.

Oma Marta was no beauty, but she always carried herself with such unassailable poise that she gave the impression of being handsome. I tried several times to get her to talk about her youth, but all she ever mentioned was that it was she who had to pull the gates across her father's storefront every night. I surmised that since she had become a fiercely dignified and elegant lady, the wife of a rich banker, those times were preferably forgotten. What a pity.

She had three sons. George, my Father, was the oldest, then came Ernst, who gave up his American citizenship in order to join Germany's forces during World War One.

"I owe it to the country where I was born," he said. He died in combat on the eighteenth of October, 1916.

Fritz, the youngest, succumbed to leukemia as a small child.

My grandfather Eugene died when my father was fourteen.

I do not know where or when she met him, but five years later, Franziska Marta Altman was married again, this time to a Catholic Hungarian Count with the impressive name of Ladislaus Antonius von Kovach, Count of Kisczeteny, who became Opa Laszlo to us.

He was slim, delicate, had bright blue eyes, and a gray mustache. He wore a high, stiff collar under a light gray suit. A gray derby felt hat, gray spats with black buttons and a silver-tipped cane completed the picture. And always, but always, there was a carnation in his buttonhole. He was devoted to his wife.

From the age of maybe five or six, I can picture my grandmother dressed in a dark red velvet jacket over a high-necked silk blouse, a plumed, broad-brimmed velvet hat on her iron-gray hair. She is sitting decorously on a stiff, high-backed chair and, her husband is kneeling gracefully on one knee in front of her buttoning her high leather shoes with a buttoning hook. She was very strong willed, this grandmother of mine, often tactlessly outspoken and in a bad mood, but it seemed gentle Uncle Laszlo's influence had a softening effect on her. The poor man must have felt sorely tried, though, when he took her to Hungary to meet his family.

Upon arrival, her first act was to vehemently forbid the servants to kiss her hands. She was then horrified to discover that they were required to sleep on the floor in front of her bedroom at night, and she made her objections known in no uncertain terms. Doubtless, her new relatives were scandalized.

After she was widowed a second time she traveled extensively, spending time in Switzerland, in German and Austrian Spas, and also living with us for months at a time Her presence was not to the delight of my dear mother, who was keenly aware of her initial refusal to accept a lowly actress as her son's wife. The sparring between these two antagonists tended to escalate from time to time into verbal duels, accompanied by outraged screams and the slamming of doors.

At the end of the hall lay the entrance to my brother's room, a room that never lost its fascination for me.

My Brother Ralph was a very important person in my life. He was eight years older then I was. When I was small he was an adult as far as I was concerned, but not the omnipotent, patronizing kind: He was in my league; he was concerned, loving, and protective.

He could also tease a little, off and on. Seeing me munching too much cake or candy he might say, "Sure, sure, just pamper yourself, my little chicken. Get nice and fat, and we'll cook you!" I would pout and, he'd grab my long hair and pull it over my face and, we would both laugh.

"Come on, Chick," he'd say, "Time to study your animals again."

I was seven years old, he fifteen, the big brother I adored. We sat together on one of the broad, overstuffed chairs in his room, an encyclopedia of animal engravings on our knees. One by one, page by page, he covered the descriptive titles with his hand, and I had to name each animal depicted. The domestic and well-known ones we had finished some time ago. Now we worked on the exotic ones. Patiently but relentlessly he made me memorize their names: the cormorant, the manatee, the anteater, the platypus, the armadillo.

Never, but never, will I forget the Platypus and the Armadillo!

On the walls hung display boxes containing collections of exotic bugs and butterflies. From above the bookcase the stuffed Ibis pointed his long curved beak straight down at me, and the sunny room shone in his glass eyes, liquid and golden. I always wanted to stroke his white feathers, if only I could have reached him. Other stuffed birds stood on shelves and in a glass case. There was even a stuffed Lion cub. There were antlers, rocks, fossils, shells, and an aquarium with carefully tended tropical fish. A table held small creatures preserved in jars of alcohol, a pig's fetus among them that always appalled me in its deathly white nakedness. And the huge python skin on the wall did not much please me.

The story often told in my family was when Ralph was about thirteen years old and the cook came running upstairs to my mother, ringing her hands, breathless and horrified. "Frau Doctor, come to the kitchen. It's awful, awful!"

They found the boy bent over the kitchen table, carefully dabbing at the bones of a small white skeleton with a damask linen napkin. Next to it laid a still slightly steaming little heap of cooked flesh and fur.

Ralph looked up. "I found a dead mouse and look what was inside her!"

Beaming with excitement, he held up an already capped jar of alcohol for inspection. In it floated three tiny fetuses extracted from the mouse's belly before he boiled her to obtain the skeleton.

"I had to change the water a few times," he said apologetically, following the two women's horrified stares at the array of pots and pans scattered on the sink and stove.

It was then that my Mother decided that her son was going to be a physician. A few years later, he was drawn to the study of archeology and anthropology, but that did not faze her at all. There was no reason that a medical man could not have a hobby on the side, she proclaimed.

When he was sixteen Ralph came home from school one day full of excitement and enthusiasm. The performance of a play was being planned. It was to be the crowning event at the graduation ceremony of his class. The chosen play was *Antigone* by Aeschylus and he, Ralph, was to have the title role. The gymnasium, the equivalent of high school in Germany, at that time admitted boys only. Girls went to the lyceum. Girls did not study Greek and Latin. So Ralph was to play the female part, in Greek no less.

For many weeks we heard him pacing up and down in his room, practicing his lines. I remember tip-toeing down the hall so as not to disturb him and listening in awe to the sometimes murmured, sometimes vehemently shouted sentences that emanated through his closed doors, repeated again and again and making no sense to me at all.

When finally the great event took place the whole family sat in the school auditorium. I do not remember the performance, but do remember the dramatic ending when we went backstage to congratulate the performers.

Here my Brother met us. He looked strange to me, brown makeup on his face and black lining around his eyes. A turban-like shawl was wound around his head, and he was clad in a long flowing gown that looked like a nightshirt to me. He was beaming and excited from all the applause.

My father just said, "Well, well!" and patted him on the back. But my mother, bubbling over with hilarious laughter, rushed toward him with dramatically outstretched arms and pulled him to her chest, getting grease paint on her blouse and leaving his headgear in disarray. "Thank God," she gasped, "You'll never be an actor."

This was a crushing blow he never forgot.

As far as my mother was concerned, my brother's future profession was decided. She was eventually successful in bullying him and convincing him to study medicine and become a doctor, causing him no end of hardships and, more importantly, emotional problems.

I doubt that Mother had any plans for me except for attempting to make an attractive, fashionable, and charmingly outgoing young lady out of a brooding introvert who hated little lace collars, pink bows, and hats of any kind.

"You can't go in those pants and that sweater," she would say. "We are invited for tea by the Wassermanns.

It's at the Grand Hotel. You have to look nice. I want to be proud of my daughter."

"I'll be bored to tears. Oh, please don't make me go. I hate those people."

"You'll wear your white dress with the pink sash and the white hat and no argument."

"Ursel and Lotti are going to play at Gerda's house. I promised that I'd come. They are waiting for me."

Mother rose from her chair, thunder clouds gathering on her brow. "You are getting dressed. Now!" Slowly she advanced, the hated dress in hand.

"No, I won't." I knew what was coming. Chin thrust out and eyes narrowed, I met the onslaught with cold resolve. Stinging slaps on both cheeks burned my face.

In blazing fury she threw the despised dress at my feet. "All right, I will not speak to you ever again!" This promise she kept for at least a week, if not longer.

I was a rebel and, no doubt, a great disappointment to her. Many fights resulted in painful silent treatments, signaling to me that I was really a very miserable and utterly worthless creature.

When I was about twelve, it was my brother to whom my squeamish mother assigned the task of educating me to the causes and effects of undertakings between men and women that resulted in the birth of a child. After all, she reasoned, he was the medical student, so she was spared a very unpleasant task. Little did she know that my knowledge was already somewhat broader than expected, for in my brother's absence I had eagerly searched his library for information. In addition to anatomy books I had discovered the *Decamaron of Bocaccio* and the tales of *Aretino*, complete with illustrations.

My mother supplemented these initial lessons by admonishing me never to let a man get the better of me and to wait for *The Right One*, who of course had to have enough money to take good care of me. The impression she gave me was that sex was a degrading enterprise and, as she often repeated, that men were all pigs waiting to take advantage.

How these views, bequeathed to her daughter, could come from a beautiful, admired actress who could be flirty, vivacious and full of laughter is hard to understand. Maybe these teachings belonged to a scenario she created solely for the benefit of her daughter, to save her from future dangers and missteps.

So I grew up scared and confused for many years, but at the same time quite determined to find my own way and make my own discoveries.

Ralph never fought. He was his mother's pride, the golden boy, and the handsome, sweet-natured son who could be led and who showed much promise. She did not realize that he knew how to counteract her wishes by seeming to comply then going his own way. He learned to be a diplomat out of self defense. I wish he had continued to resist later on. The road to complete independence was long and hard for him.

My mother talked about her childhood with a sense of drama befitting her profession. "We were so poor," she would say, "Mother became a night nurse so she could take care of us during the day. Often we would wake up during the night and cry because we were afraid to be alone. There were times when we had potatoes to eat and nothing else."

Nevertheless, when Alice showed a talent and liking for music, there appeared a piano in their small cramped apartment, and she received a scholarship with a renowned teacher who was intent on grooming her for the concert stage. She practiced daily before and after school for many hours, full of ambition and relentless energy. Finally, she became ill, suffered from nervous strain and sleeplessness, and the medical verdict came down on her: No More Piano.

Sleeping pills were prescribed. As her system got used to one pill, another was tried. She obtained one prescription after another. She never went to sleep without pills, not for the rest of her life.

Robbed of her goal of becoming a concert pianist, she still dreamt of being on the stage. She was almost fifteen when the Marie Seebach School of Acting, affiliated with the Royal Theater in Berlin, announced that a scholarship competition was going to be held for young ladies. The minimum age for application was sixteen.

She told me the story.

"The stage. That's where I wanted to be. I had just turned fifteen. I lied," she said. "I told them I was sixteen." By her smile I could tell she was still proud of having done so. Out of over a hundred applicants she was one of a few who were chosen. Three years later the theater critic at the *German Times*, a newspaper in New York, wrote this report:

All unknown to her countrymen and countrywomen in Berlin, a charming little 18-year-old American girl has achieved a splendid triumph upon the stage of the Royal Theater in Berlin and after two years of successful work there has just been engaged to play leading roles at the Koenigliches Deutsches Landes Theater in Prague, Bohemia. The young woman, who had given evidence since childhood of remarkable elocutionary talent, entered the Marie Seebach School of Acting, an institution affiliated with the Schaupielhaus in Berlin and eventually was the only one out of a class of 180 who was awarded a coveted position in the Schaupielhaus Company. She has played a great number of leading parts in plays by Shakespeare and Goethe, Ibsen and Gerhart Hauptmann, and is credited as having given some of the best portrayals ever seen in Germany. Last year

Miss Hall was honored with an invitation from Emperor and Empress William to play at the Palace at Potsdam, upon which occasion she was congratulated by all the members of the Royal family.

Miss Hall is a brunette of slender willowy type and of medium stature. She has a most unaffected and engaging personality and a sweetly pitched voice, which bespeaks the actress even in conversation. Her career in Austria will be watched with sympathetic interest by Americans who take a pardonable pride in the achievements of their compatriots in foreign lands. Her mother and sister, with whom she has been living in Berlin, will accompany her to Prague.

As she herself told me, her mother and sister never left her unaccompanied. At the theater one or the other would sit in her dressing room during rehearsals and performances. They chaperoned her practically until the day of her marriage.

My Father played a less prominent role in my earliest childhood. He was gone so much. His mornings were spent with rehearsals at the theater. He came home for the family's main meal at two o'clock and then retired to his library for more work. Often, early evenings and late nights he again spent at the theater, unless one of the innumerable social functions that were connected to his position had to be attended. So for me, when I was small, he was a figure behind the scenes. I knew he was there but he was not very visible, except on special occasions like birthdays, holidays, and summer vacations.

Occasionally, his presence made itself known when the house shook from his yelling. There could be fury and aggravation at my mother, the servants, or displeasing unforeseen happenings of one sort or another. My mother would reply in kind. It always ended by his slamming the library door in defeat and always, later, as I was told, he would apologize and be as sweet and loving as he really was. He idolized his wife, and in most instances it was she who swung the scepter, made the decisions, and laid down the law.

He had a sense of humor and a distinct dislike of what he considered unnecessary rules and regulations. A policeman stopped him once. "Sir, I am going to cite you for jaywalking."

Father was indignant. "I just crossed the street. There is no car in sight anywhere."

He was sternly admonished. "It is against the law. Name, address and profession."

Father pulled himself up as far as his corpulent stature would allow. "I am a philosopher," he said, eyeing the man before him with regal dignity.

Perplexed, the defender of the law stared at him, thoroughly puzzled. At last he closed his book and put his pencil away. "Oh, go on," he said, "But learn to obey the law."

Father returned home in triumph, chuckling merrily. When the law made no sense, he felt it had to be challenged.

There was a time in my early teens when I resented him. I saw my mother leading every phase of our lives—running the household, the finances, travel plans, decisions about her children's education, and what car to buy, all this in addition to giving guest performances in other cities.

What kind of man is he? I thought. Not the kind of husband I would want. He is weak.

Weak? Oh, no. He was a man passionately involved in his art. He was one of the best-known theater directors in

Germany. He led his theater with an iron hand, fair and
decent always, but there was no doubt that he was at the
helm. There was no doubt that he was the master at
rehearsals.

Several times I had occasion to observe him at work
when I was older. He jumped like a rubber ball, stout and
short as he was, from the stage to the back of the auditorium
to observe the scene and back again to change the actors'
positions, like pawns in a chess game. He demonstrated
facial expressions relevant to certain characters in the play
or made the exact meaning and delivery of certain words
clear. The company admired his strength and erudition.
From most of them he had love and respect.

I can only guess what my father's childhood was like
from his mother's remarks and his own musings when the
occasion arose. He grew up in a rich, formal household
presided over by a strict and overbearing mother who was
very conscious of her elevated social standing. She was not
much inclined to engender a warm and loving family
atmosphere, so his life could not have been easy; it was run
by servants and protocol. Nannies, valets, and then tutors
shaped his development.

Early childhood photos, which show him in little Lord
Fauntleroy outfits with white lace collars over velvet suits
and flowing shoulder-length locks, betray no childhood
gayety, not a trace of a smile. Years later he and his brother
Ernest are shown in sailor suits, pudgy boys in straw hats
standing next to their bicycles, a Governess stiffly in
attendance. Again, no sign of merriment, not even a smile.
Playing tennis, a sport he pursued from early youth until
old age, must have given him pleasure, though it did not
curb his appetite or reduce his weight, which remained
considerably higher then it should have been throughout
his life.

In my father's day, a family's wealth was often
measured by the corporeal dimensions of its offspring. A

skinny child? Not enough money to feed him properly? Clearly you are low on the social ladder.

For some reason George's mother entertained the notion that children's rooms should be spare, empty of decoration or extra comfort of any kind. A bed, a wardrobe, a table and chairs; that was enough. No pictures, no frills. How strange a contrast to the opulence of the rest of the house. Art, music, and literature did not play much of a role in his early life, except maybe what one or another tutor managed to smuggle into the prescribed curriculum, which at least served to whet his appetite for further study later on.

History, French, Greek and Latin were taught at the gymnasium, but it was expected that eventually both my father and his brother would enter the banking business like their father. How amazing that both brothers, once exposed to life at their respective universities, blossomed and discovered a richness in the world they had never known. They refused to have anything to do with the world of finance.

A short time after George arrived at the University in Jena, he began to emancipate himself from his mother's yoke. She had commandeered a personal valet to accompany him to school. This faithful man returned a few days later bringing the message that the young gentleman had no need for his services. Mama was appalled.

Here I include a few excerpts from Father's own diary:

As soon as my graduation from the gymnasium was behind me, I went to see professor Meyer, whose book on German literature of the nineteenth century I had admired. I wanted advice on further studies and told him that I wanted to specialize in theater history.

"That does not exist," I was told. "Nobody teaches that."

"Well, then I suppose I will have to take the history of literature."

"That is not taught either. You have to take Germanistic."

That meant I had to take Medieval German poets like Walter von der Vogelweide instead of Shakespeare and Molière. Professor Meyer inclined his head. I was discouraged. I decided to go to the University of Heidelberg instead, without a fixed study plan.

It was the summer of nineteen hundred and two. I signed up for a course on Spinoza, one on Art History and another one on the history of Literature. Lo and behold it was available here!

The following winter I decided to study the theater in Berlin and signed up immediately for membership in the Academic Drama Society that was sponsored by the only professor at the university who was interested in the theater. Already when I was a senior this man was instrumental in bringing classical performances to our gymnasium with famous performers as well as young actors who volunteered to play for us. One of them was Max Reinhardt. We saw Oedipus Rex, Antigone, *and the* Oresteia.

Later, studying in Munich I instigated the first ever performance of Arthur Schnitzler's Dialogue Series, "Merry-Go-Round." (The Dialogue Series was considered extremely immoral and sexually risqué at that time.) It was played by professional actors for an invited audience. The critics were outraged and so was the general public, but at the same time I earned an excellent reputation in professional circles.

Subsequently father became a student of Max Reinhardt's and then his assistant director. At the end of 1907 he was the first student ever to receive his doctorate in the Science of Theater History at the University of Jena and became the assistant director of the theater in Mannheim. A young actress by the name of Alice Hall had also been hired there.

In my father's files I found the following letter.

January 24, 1907:

Highly esteemed Miss Hall,

I am unexpectedly required to be at the theater tonight and will consequently not be able to keep our dinner engagement. Therefore I would like to be able to ask for your forgiveness this afternoon, be it while taking a walk with you or by meeting at a café.

Please send me a few lines back via this messenger as to whether and when I may ring your doorbell.

Another short note:

February 19, 1908:

Good morning, my overtired little darling!
Ten o'clock, Rose-garden.

On May 30, 1908 the marriage license follows, naming the Prince of Mannheim's Court-Dramatist, Dr. George Joseph Altman and the Court-Actress, Edith Alice Emmilie Hall, as man and wife.

My brother Ralph was born in June 1909. When it was that the family moved to Berlin I do not know.

My mother, the actress Alice Hall in 1908, the year of her marriage

Mother as Viola in Shakespeare's "As You Like It" in 1911, the costume in the attic

My father, Dr. George Altman, theater director

The family on the veranda.
From left: Oma Marta, Ralph, Father, me, Mother, Oma Hall, 1921

Mother in the Biedermeier room, 1919

Father in his library, 1919

Our house in Berlin-Dahlem

My playhouse. I am 3, Ralph 11, 1921

Ralph, age 10, in his room with his guinea pig and collections, 1920

At the sandbox, age 5, 1923

With Irmi, age 9, 1927

Our house after the Second World War

CHAPTER TWO

The Years in Hanover

My quiet rural life changed when I was ten years old and we moved from Berlin to Hannover. A sad goodbye to my friend Irmi did not blunt the excitement of the first upheaval in my life.

During the next five years we lived in three different houses, having rented our Dahlem home to acquaintances. Father was now the director of the big city-owned theatre in Hannover.

Right across the street from our first home on Kant Platz sprawled a park, which really must have been the remnant of a large forest, for it consisted only of footpaths that wound their way through dense growths of leafy trees and tall conifers. I do not know how deep into the terrain they led, for I never reached the other side.

Winter was cold in the north of Germany and deep snow covered trees and roads for weeks on end. There was a small embankment that led from the surface of the street down to the edge of the forest. This was a favorite playground for my friends and me. With woolen caps, mittens and shawls wrapped around necks, chins, and noses we zoomed down the gentle slopes on our sleds with what we considered reckless speed. Snowball fights broke out, soon to be interrupted by a voice yelling from an upstairs window of my home across the street.

"That's enough! You're getting too wild. Come inside right now."

I remember walking along the forest paths after a spring rain in early May. The air smelled fresh and woodsy with maybe a trace of mold added to it. I held a piece of chocolate in my hand. It was in the shape of a bug, and I had just bitten its head off, and the hollow body started to crumble in my palm. It was at a time of holiday from school, a time of celebration for the feast of Pentecost. Like getting presents of rabbits and eggs for Easter, Pentecost, occurring a few weeks later, brought us chocolate maybugs. Their bodies were made from dark chocolate and their wings from light milk chocolate. They had legs and feelers made out of wire and lacquered cardboard. What bugs had to do with the feast of Pentecost is not clear to me, but to this day the aroma of leaves and mold and earthiness is the maybug smell in my mind.

I had a whole group of friends then, girls from many different social levels. I went to a public school. At least Mother used good judgment by not enrolling me in an elite private situation. Every Saturday afternoon we would gather, imitating the custom of many ladies at that time, who would get together once a week for a sewing circle or a so-called "coffee klatch." We would serve cocoa or lemonade and cookies and gossip a little about teachers and parents and other girls who were not considered worthy of our company. Sometimes we would read books to each other, but most of the time the girls pulled out their knitting or crochet projects. Some did embroidery and so did I, but instead of carefully following printed patterns like the others did, I drew freehand, willy-nilly with my needle and thread, stitching all kinds of imaginary plants and animals onto the muslin stretched over my embroidery hoop. I was just about to adorn an impossible looking frog with a crooked golden crown on his pea-green head when Hannelore got up and came over to look at what I was up to.

"How do you do that?" Now they all crowded around me.

"Miss Weber said to do cross-stitch." She gazed down at my work, screwing up her pug nose, as if she smelled something bad.

"Fe never does what she's supposed to do. You should know that by now." It sounded more like admiration then rebuke, and my best friend Ursula Zech put her arm around my shoulder.

Ursel, as we called her, was half a head taller then I and almost a year older, a strong-boned, slightly slavic-looking girl with straight, light brown, shoulder-length hair that was always brushed neatly back from her face, and tied at the base of her neck. Even-tempered, robust, and often serious, sometimes almost with a light touch of sadness, she could, nevertheless, laugh and romp about like the rest of her friends.

We did our homework after school one day, just the two of us We sat in the small city apartment she shared with her mother, our books spread out over the carpet-covered round table in the middle of the living room.

"Will your mother be home soon?" I asked.

I liked her mother; I liked her kind broad face, her bustling in the kitchen, tidying the rest of the rooms when she came home from work. I liked the sense of solidity, order, and caring that surrounded her. She was heavy-set and in upper middle age. She was so different from my own vivacious Mama, who seemed forever young, floating about, directing and managing her family even from afar, unless she zeroed in for retribution or sudden stifling embraces of overwhelming love and emotion.

Ursel looked at me. "She is working late today," said.

After a pause she added, "Can I tell you something tha. nobody else knows?"

I nodded. What could that be? Maybe Charlotte had cheated in class again. Or a new plot of troublemaking by those rabble rousers in Munich was discovered. Oh no, everyone would have heard of that.

"My mother," Ursel said and seemed to swallow hard, "She is not my mother."

How could that be? I stared at her. What seemed so real a moment ago was not.

"I do not know my parents," she continued. "My Father owns a large farming estate somewhere near the Polish border. He is married and has other children. My mother worked on the farm. He got her pregnant and I was born. They threw her out and gave me away. So there you have the whole story."

This last sentence was delivered with a clear and determined voice, matter of fact, with her chin stuck out in utter defiance.

"Frau Zech adopted me and I call her Mother. She has mothered me with all her heart and soul and I love her dearly. She told me everything a year ago and I love her even more for it."

"Will you try and find your parents one day?" I could not fully grasp this situation.

"Why should I? They did not want me. I sure don't want them."

At this news I was shaken to the core.

Our large all-girls public school stood gray and forbidding alongside a busy city street, surrounded by a tall wrought iron fence. Gray and forbidding was the demeanor of some of the teachers within its walls as well.

Most of them were formidable authority figures eliciting fear and demanding respect and absolute obedience. I cannot say for sure whether all German teachers were operating under a particular code of behavior towards the young people under their care, but all those I met kept their distance and avoided any personal contact with their students. We were to perform our duties. There was lots of homework and grading. Grades ranged from ones to fours. Should you ever receive a five, you were absolutely at the rock bottom of humanity.

I do not know why many of the lady teachers had greasy hair. Maybe they were too busy to wash. Frau Loehrer certainly belonged in that category. Blousy, with skin the color of pale tea, she did not warm our hearts when she first appeared in the classroom door. She did not look at us. She waddled to her desk, adjusted the cream-colored lace jabot under her chin, opened her book and proceeded to read a poem by the German poet Johann Wolfgang von Goethe with a voice that sang and lifted us almost out of our seats.

It was the first real encounter with poetry for most of us. Thank you, Frau Loehrer! We worshiped her from then on, but always from a distance. She never outwardly recognized us as individuals.

And then there was the geography teacher. I do not recall his name. He was not very tall, but he was sturdy. He had a big head crowned by a lion's mane of white hair that seemed to sink into his broad shoulders; there was not much of a neck to prevent that. We feared him. He smiled and chuckled at his own mean jokes and sarcastic innuendos, whether the targets were the inhabitants of other countries, the German government, or his own pupils. The budding signs of puberty in some of my twelve and thirteen year old friends caused him especially great amusement. Poor Elsie fled the room one day in tears, folding her arms tightly across her already quite pronounced breasts following one

of his smirking sidelong glances in her direction
comparing hills in the Irish landscape to certain f_
human anatomy.

His bulldog head slightly inclined and his mean little
eyes bore down at me from the height of the teacher's
podium. He snarled at me, "Well, well, forgot your
homework again. No wonder." He turned to the class,
"There you have your careless, artsy folk." This was meant
as a slap in the direction of my parents' profession,
pronounced in utter disdain.

Herr Wohlenberg was our homeroom teacher and while
not particularly chummy, he was approachable. He was
reasonable and fair, and we felt sure that he liked us. A
trim man with a small, sandy-colored mustache and an
expression of contained energy on his even-featured face,
one could easily imagine him as a soldier in uniform. As a
matter of fact, I learned in later years that he was killed
fighting during the war. He taught German and literature.
We had to write long essays and stories. The best were read
to the class, and I admit that mine were always among
them. Had it not been for the consistent grade of one I got
in German I would have flunked promotion to a higher
class year after year because of the equally consistent grades
of four I earned in math.

I was twelve or thirteen when we moved again. This
time it was out to the country, near a small village with the
fairy tale name of Kraehenwinkel (Crow's Nook). It took
thirty minutes for a rattling little train to take us to the
bustling, smoky train station in Hannover. From there I had
to take the streetcar to school. Father of course had himself
driven to the theater. By this time we had a car and a
chauffeur again.

Ours was a big, solid two-story house that was meant
to speak of belonging and permanence. Especially in winter

it felt like an impenetrable fortress against storms, snow and freezing cold. It stood all alone in the landscape. You gazed across flat land, fields and heather and not another house could be seen. Even the small village was hidden around a stretch of forest just out of view. It took at least thirty minutes to reach it on foot, passing a low-slung hut that had the word Kraehenwinkel painted on a huge white-washed beam that was laid across its brittle roof like a big man's hand pressing a small boy's shoulder. It was a worrisome sight, but, nevertheless, it was the stopping place for the commuter train that took me to school every morning. I usually caught it in the very last minute, racing madly down the mud-caked road along the tracks, hair and coat flying and my schoolbooks precariously clutched under my arms. The conductor, who had gotten to know me, poked his head out of the window, waved me on and blew his whistle. I have no idea by what whim my parents decided to transfer their substantial household to this solitude, but I loved it.

There was a pond in front of the house and a wooden bridge that led to a tiny island. A small, round garden house sat in the middle of it. No one seemed to have a use for it, so I made it my own. It had windows all around it and a continuous bench circling the wall beneath their sills. On weekends and holidays when there was no school this was my retreat. I piled up blankets, pillows and stacks of books there and read for hours. I read the German translations of Shakespeare's *Romeo and Juliet* and *A Midsummer Night's Dream* and also Dickens's *Oliver Twist* and *Cimarron* by Edna Ferber. I poured over the entire *Leatherstocking Tales* by James Fennimore Cooper.

I had a portable windup gramophone. I played *Blue Skies* and *Tea For Two* and fox trotted or did the Charleston all by myself when I knew that nobody could see me. I listened to Tchaikovsky's emotional outpourings or Fritz Kreisler's violin, singing about love.

I watched the surface of the pond from season to season, from reflecting little growing reeds and grasses in spring to turning into a shining sheet of ice in winter, decorated here and there with little scratch marks made by birds, squirrels or rats.

Summer heat laid a carpet of greenish, glistening algae across the water and tiny insects danced above it. Dragonflies swooped about and frogs sang under my open windows.

Some of my schoolmates from the city came to visit me once in a while and it was always a great excursion for them. If anybody had been inclined to call us Young Ladies at that time they would have been surprised to find us transformed into Indian braves and trappers, hiding and racing around in the wild undergrowth of the large, untended garden surrounding the house. There was always an argument about who got to be Hawkeye the Leatherstocking, the pioneer scout, and who his faithful Indian companion. Toward evening when it started to get dark and my parents were away, we made a fire way back in the garden where it bordered the fields and roasted potatoes that we had stolen from the kitchen. They were the most wonderful potatoes in the world.

To my great sorrow my parents decided to move back to the city after barely two years. The long trip to town got to be too much for them.

The new house stood on Schleiermacher Street. In it we had to abandon one way of life and were launched on a bewildering search for another.

CHAPTER THREE

The Big Upheaval

W e got a letter from Ralph, who was by then studying medicine at the university in Berlin:

March 28, 1932

Dear Family,

The mood in Berlin is unpleasant. Political rallies, riots, shootings and no newspaper mentions any of it. Yesterday my friend Collins and I happened to get caught in a mob of Nazis who had just left a big party rally. They taunted and snarled at us and we moved quickly onto a side street.

It looks very serious and worrisome here. Maybe I can still prove to you that it is advisable to leave Germany for a while before Election Day on April 10. Just now the radio announced giant riots in Fuerstenwalde. The army was confronting the K.P.D. (the communist party). Doesn't that sound like civil war?

Your
Ralph

By 1933 my father had led the city-owned theatre in Hannover for six years with great success. It was clear that Hitler was coming to power. Germany held its breath. Hope and anger, waves of restlessness and foreboding surged beneath the surface of daily life at this time.

Father led many performances of Goethe's plays in commemoration of his death one hundred years prior. The performance of *Faust*, his most famous play, made a tremendous impression on me again. I had seen it before when I was younger. Both my brother and I, in our own time and manner, had made drawings and paintings illustrating the plays we saw on Father's stage, and Faust and Gretchen, with their devil and angels, had been one of our favorite subjects. Now, at fifteen, the impact of the message of this work, the desire for greater knowledge, the price of sacrificing loved ones for selfish gains, was great. The fairytale became a lesson and the music of its poetry was a revelation

We went to movies to lighten the tensions of the time. I must say, though, that I was not fully aware of what was going on. I remember Greta Garbo in *The Shanghai Express* and Johnny Weissmueller's *Tarzan*. The French films of Renee Clair were a delight. We sang *Night And Day You Are The One*. We saw one of the first American musicals ever shown in Germany, *Broadway Melody*. My friends and I played our records and strutted and kicked our legs in the air like the chorus girls in the films.

It was early in March, in 1933.

Our front door was shut audibly one day announcing the return of the master of the house in a thundering mood.

"Resign? Me? They want me to resign?" he roared. "Resign in the middle of rehearsals? First night for *King Lear* is in two weeks; it still needs a lot of work. I am the director. What would they do without me? My actors will not stand for it!"

I was fifteen, and by now used to Father's occasional rages, but this time the outbreak was not the result of simple anger or frustration. This time there was the sound of fear, fury, and defiance in this small man's voice.

"George," my mother said quietly, "I was shopping downtown yesterday, and there, walking towards me arm in arm, were Friedel Mumme and Theodor Becker, actors in your own company. They saw me, stopped and crossed the street, without as much as a nod in my direction. These are the same people who could not smile or compliment me enough just very recently: 'Frau Director' here and 'Frau Director' there, and 'you look beautiful today, dear Frau Director.' George, don't you see what is happening?"

I wrote in my diary:

March 7, 1933

Daily, we hear of this actor, that director, that stage designer being dismissed in Berlin, Hamburg, Dresden, Stuttgart, one after another. And we wonder, when will it be our turn?

Yesterday our neighbor, Fritz Jakob, took a walk with his dog, Heini. Everyone knows that Heini detests uniforms of any kind, especially the mailman's, but any shiny boots will raise his ire. So when two young Nazi hopefuls came marching along, bristling in new uniforms and equally newfound self-importance, Heini, although held by the leash, tried to charge, and barked his most vehement dislike. Fritz Jacob returned home with blood streaming from his broken nose and all of his front teeth knocked out. The next day he took poor Heini to the vet, who delivered him of all his earthly trials and tribulations. There are no uniforms in dog heaven."

A letter from Ralph in Berlin

March 12, 1933

Dear Parents,

I am so infected by the general tensions and nervousness here; the conditions are so awful that I would rather be out of the country by election day. People claim even seriously that there will not be any election at all. Did you read about Hitler's threat that he will arm his people? I would like to go to Belgium and stay there until I can meet up with you at the Haag or somewhere else in Holland. It is supposedly very cheap to live in Brussels.

The Rembrandt exhibit is open until September. At the Haag they are showing the Dutch section from the Colonial Exhibit in Paris. That would be particularly great for me to see, because that is the part of the show that interests me most, apart from India. The more I get acquainted with Indian cultures, the surer I am that I will have to visit their country. This wish is far beyond the stimulation of my childhood's adventure books. Am curious as to where I am finally going to live. In Paris? In Siam?

Yesterday I had a terrible migraine, as usual when the climate changes. So maybe this letter does not sound as nice as it was meant to be.

Ralph.

"Mother, what on earth are you doing?" I gazed at her in utter amazement. Here she was, sitting in front of the dressing table mirror, clad in her silken robe, engaged in a most astonishing enterprise. She had various containers of her cosmetics lined up in front of her. She was armed with a knife, scissors and a spoon and at that moment had scooped her face cream into a soup bowl. She held up the emptied jar for me, and there I saw her diamond brooch incongruously embedded in pink salve. Back she ladled the face cream on top and screwed the lid on as tight as she could.

"There!" she said with an impish grin, and proceeded to decapitate a talcum powder shaker, pouring its contents into another formerly empty one she had outfitted with a false bottom. And on she worked, cutting, fitting, gluing. Jewelry, money, documents were all cunningly disguised and packaged away.

I was frightened. "What if they search us?" I said. She looked at me with narrowed eyes.

"They won't," she said.

The next day, March 23, 1933, the mayor of the city, whose theater my father lead, called him to his office. "Dear friend," he said, "I am powerless. The bastards came this morning and announced that they will get you unless you are gone from the theatre by noon today."

Father returned home in midmorning, leaving the rehearsal for good. Quietly he went to his library and closed the door, this time without slamming it.

Louise, the maid, served the midday meal red-eyed and pale and nobody spoke.

Late that evening a quiet knock on the door, avoiding the shrill sound of the doorbell. It was Otto Graf, one of Father's star actors whom I secretly adored. Here was Romeo, Brutus, Oberon in a long black trench coat with the collar turned up, a slouch hat pulled down to hide his face. "Herr Direktor, I can't stay, I don't dare, but I had to come. Many of us are so sorry. We just had to let you know. Maybe it will pass quickly, maybe we'll have you back. Keep well!" A handshake and he was gone.

A letter arrived in the early morning hours, furtively slipped under our front door. Another actor of Father's repertory group clothed his words in careful language, to avoid possible Nazi recriminations, if discovered.

March 24, 1933

Dear Dr. Altman,

I cannot say too much in this situation because it might turn out to sound sentimental, which is not intended.

One thing I wish to say: Driven by feelings of compassion, I am trying to deal with justified anger at the threat to the concept of value and dignity.

I want to tell you that I thought of you yesterday morning as of a man suddenly thrown off his track. That could happen to all of us, therefore we like to know that somebody, somewhere thinks of us.

Permit me to give a good wish to you and your lady on your way!

Your devoted Herbach.

My friends met at the schoolyard at lunchtime. "Are we meeting at your house on Saturday?" I asked Hannelore.

"Sure. That is . . . no, not you. Just some of us."

She looked away and her pretty pink face grew even pinker. Her eyes shifted back at me looking sorry and embarrassed. She shrugged her shoulders and ran off. No word of explanation.

I took my lunch bag to one of the wooden picnic tables. My friends Gerda and Anneliese were there among others. Every one was chatting happily and laughing. I approached and all talk stopped. Gerda scooped her sandwich up and wiped her mouth.

"I guess I've had enough," she said and left.

Two other girls followed her. Anneliese hesitated, but when everyone else had gone she too departed, murmuring something about going to the bathroom.

I was not hungry anymore.

I sat alone on the bench, my fingers tightly locked around the wrapped contents of my lunch.

Two days later I was to be confirmed in the Lutheran church with most of my classmates, who, by this time, having been informed of my inferior racial status, either out of fear or conviction did not speak to me anymore. Ursula was the only one of all of my friends who stood steadfastly by my side.

Oma Martha wrote to me from a trip to France:

March 29, 1933

There are only a few days left until your confirmation, a meaningful event that signals the end of your childhood. I wish for your future life that the sun will always shine for you and you will be spared from all hardships and sadness. You can imagine how hard it is not to be with you, your dear parents and Ralph. My thoughts are with you and will accompany you. Please write to me about that day that is of such great significance for you.

I embrace you with all my heart, my dear.

Many loving greetings,
Your Oma Marta

Was that my same grouchy Grandmother? What a nice letter. But a meaningful event? I sneered. Are you sure this is of great significance, dear Oma? What significance?

"You do not have to go through with it, you know," said my mother, whose Christian background and whose desire to please her own mother had been the reason for my having been baptized. "They would not want you there anyway."

I bristled. "They can't tell me what to do! I'll go, I'll show them."

The large city church. Maybe it was brightly lit, maybe it was dim. There were candles, maybe, but I know there were crowds of parents, other relatives and friends of the girls who excitedly wriggled and whispered on the benches next to me.

I turned and looked at strange faces, unfamiliar and remote. The vast church interior, organ music seemingly coming from far away. A feeling of unreality engulfed me, a sense of floating, without connection to anything.

And then there was the pastor, and I kneeled before him and all was a dark void around me, except when looking up at him I saw his fat face oozing patronizingly down on me, and his eyes were saying, "You poor little creature, how I pity you."

I felt a surge of hatred such as I had never experienced before. In a fog I left, vaguely seeing Ursula's bright eyes smiling and waving at me from the audience, trying to reach me through the crowd.

That night and again the next boots tromped down the street, torches aflame, their fiery light snaking through the trees. We stood and peered down on them, hidden by the curtains, the curtains shutting out the sunlight by day and shielding us from view by night. We used to love the sun and thought we had nothing to hide. We slept little.

Several nights later, on April the third, the thumping of the hordes receded, the last sounds of the "Horst Wessel Lied," their favorite anthem, stopped reverberating against the house fronts and we fell asleep.

Suddenly my mother sat bolt upright in her bed. The last week's tensions had finally worn down even her iron will and resistance. She panicked. She banged on our doors. "Out!" she called. "Pack up, we are leaving!" After hastily throwing a few necessary belongings in suitcases, we piled in our car and, securing our little American flag to the windshield, drove all night.

As far as the Nazi hordes and the rabble in the streets were concerned, that little flag was no protection, but it allowed us to cross the border into Belgium at Liege and then to Brussels—my parents, my brother Ralph, who had joined us a few days earlier, Bella, and I.

Now Bella, a miniature poodle, was my mother's dog and therefore had principles. She required a lawn on which to perform her business. A well tended lawn, mind you, not just grass. So here we were in the middle of the night, wandering through the streets of Brussels, upset and worn out, looking desperately for a stretch of lawn.

"She'll get sick," my mother wailed. "She'll burst!"

"She'll just pee," I said.

But no, she didn't. Up one street she dragged us, down another, sniffing, sniffing. Concrete pavement, tall, dark, ancient houses, a cobble-stoned city square. Chairs and tables were tipped leaning against each other in front of a silent café.

Oh, but there, a heavenly sight. We had found a patch of grass behind a tall, wrought iron fence. "In you go," I said, one hand under Bella's chest, the other hand compressing her front paws, then ducking her head through, and in she went between the iron rungs.

"But it isn't lawn," my mother moaned. Never mind. Even Bella recognized that these times called for sacrifices. There she squatted, a small white fluff in the moonlight, and we all broke out in hysterical laughter.

The sky was gray the next morning, as cold and gray as we felt, huddling at one little table of the many outdoor cafes on the great square, the Grand Place of Brussels. Facing us, the magnificence of the Grand Palais loomed like the apparition of a world removed from us. There was no connection to time, present or future.

Silently we had our café au lait and croissants, until my brother asked the question we had not yet faced.

"Where do we go from here?"

My father shook his head. He was not ready to make plans.

My mother put Bella off her lap, straightened herself up in her skinny wrought-iron chair, opened her purse, extracted her make-up kit and examined her face in the mirror. A bit of powder and lipstick and she was ready for action again.

"The most important thing," she said to my brother, "is your medical degree. You must finish your studies. You have three more years to go. You are an American citizen; you are not a well-known person in Berlin, as your father is in Hanover. You will not be harmed if you keep a low profile. Go back, finish your studies and later go to America. Your father and I will go back, dissolve the household and pack up. Your sister . . ." Here she looked at me with worried eyes. "No, I don't want her to go through all that upset again. We'll find a good school for her in Switzerland."

So I won't be underfoot, either, I thought. "Why can't I come and help?" I did not want to be left.

"You must not stop your education, either." And that was that.

A second round of café au lait. Brooding silence around the table, except for the rustling of the newspaper Father had procured from the restaurant, drowning himself not in world and political news, as one might expect, but checking the theater announcements to see what plays he could see on the Belgian stage. Nothing was more important for him, except his family. Not even Hitler could compete.

It was April, but springtime had not found us. Men and women of the town, used to gray and chilly days, filed by, some with coats unbuttoned, some with mufflers hanging loose around their necks and some with berets. Some ambled, some hurried to their destinations, all wrapped in their private concerns, not yet troubled by the menace lurking so close across the border. Not yet.

Ralph wrote to the secretary of the University of Berlin:

April 17,1933

May I ask you for the courtesy of an answer to the following questions: I am intending to present myself for the States Examination upon completing my studies of medicine, having received my entire schooling in Germany. Are there any new laws that would prevent me from being accepted, since I am a citizen of the United States and of the Jewish race, and will I, upon passing the examination, receive my degree of Doctor of Medicine without difficulties?

In hopes that it will be possible for you to respond soon,

Sincerely,
Ralph C. Altman, cand. med

No answer was received, no examination date either.

Sitting on my bed in a cold Belgian hotel room, I sadly thought of my friend Ursula in Hanover. I could not talk to her, but I could write.

Dear Ursel,

I know you looked for me at school, probably called at our house and wondered where I was. Well, we left the country and were frightened and it all happened so fast, I could not let you know.

Do you realize the hostilities my dad encountered, being a Jew, the awful attacks against his play directions in the newspapers, the threats he received that culminated in his termination from the theater? We had to be wary of every word we spoke in public, lest it be misconstrued and turned against us.

Turning the radio on, a hate-filled voice would scream something about Jewish pigs, which, one heard in amazement, had been responsible for the First World War. Turning to another station, one was informed that the Jew was a cross between horse and donkey, namely a mule, a Maulesel, a stupid ass with a big mouth.

Hitler claims other nations are lying or are being lied to about atrocities being committed. Is it not atrocious when a 70-year-old lawyer of our acquaintance gets beaten in court, when a Jewish couple gets abducted, driven to a remote field, stripped naked, beaten senseless and abandoned? Even though on paper we are not German nationals, thank God, emotionally and practically, we might as well be.

The anxieties took their toll on my parents' health, and I, too, am very upset. I only need to hear a few people hollering in the street, or a truck passing by and I jump, my heart starts to beat, and in my mind's eye I see the long rows of brown shirts, like they so often marched past our house, their flags billowing above their heads like bloody pieces of cloth flapping in the wind. In the ghostly, fiery torchlight glare they went along the parkland rim and masses of people marched along on the sidewalks, tramping with the sound of trumpets and drums. The stamping of feet lingers on for a long time and the nightmare remains.

One week has passed since we left Germany. We are already breathing a little easier. Thank God! When will I see you again, Ursel? I miss you!

This letter was, wisely, never sent. By this time most mail was opened and censored and could have caused harm to my friend.

We were restless, footloose, searching for a place to settle, to get a hold of our lives again. Ten days we spent exploring Brussels, the city, the parks, the palaces and exhibits. Father needed considerable time at a museum that contained a vast collection of masks and artifacts from the Belgian Congo. Tribal arts and ceremonies were for him the purest forms of theatre. Theatre was more than show; it was a language of human thought, feeling and endeavor. His interests and his studies could not be disrupted by world events.

Soon, the first of our many trips through Europe began. We headed north from Brussels to Ostende, hoping for a time of quiet recuperation at the seashore. We stopped in Ghent on the way. I can still see myself standing there in the church of St. Bavo, the wonder and magnificence of the Van Eyck altarpiece spread out before me. It was still bitter cold at the North Sea when we got there, so we drove inland again and stopped at a place called Le Coque. Albert Einstein lived there in those days. Father had known him for many years and decided to pay him a short visit.

I distinctly remember that afternoon, on April 16, 1933, to be exact, sitting in a car for over an hour all by myself in front of Einstein's house in Le Coque. "We can't just all intrude on him," my mother had said. I was fuming mad. I must admit to still being a little resentful even at this late date. A once-in-a-lifetime opportunity to meet Albert Einstein was nothing to sneeze at. At sixteen I was not too young.

We returned to Brügge, and I fell in love with this small town, it's storybook houses and winding canals. I could have stayed there quite happily. How often in the years of travel that followed was I drawn to certain places where we stayed for a short time or just passed through. Sometimes it was a small village in the French Provence, sometimes a landscape in Italy or a special ancient town that called to me. There were places I wanted to stay, and they remained in my thoughts for a very long time.

We continued to Lille, stayed overnight in Cambrai, continued via St. Dizier, Langres and Belford to Basle and Zurich, where my fate for the coming years was going to be sealed. Mother had heard about a girl's boarding school in a village above the town of St. Gallen in Switzerland. I was to be enrolled at the end of May, one month hence, an idea that did not please me at all.

We left Zurich on April 27, driving south through Bern and Lausanne to France, to Nantua, Vienne and Orange where we saw the colossal roman theatre. Wherever one could view a theatre building, be it an imposing ancient edifice or a little country stage in a village meeting-house, my father had to see it, make notes and research it further later on. We went to Avignon, Aix-en-Provence and finally landed at the Mediterranean coast in Juan-les-Pin. There the Hotel Mimosa provided us with a foothold for three weeks while we went on daytrips exploring up and down the coast looking for a place to eventually settle.

"It is time," my mother announced one day, "Time for you to get to school and for us to return to Hannover, pack up and sell the house." Back into the car we piled.

"We should get a gypsy wagon and live in it," I grumbled under my breath.

We took another route this time. We drove west, passed Van Gogh's Arles, on to Marseille then to Montpellier, Narbonne and Carcasonne's forbidding walls. From there the route took us north. Father and I climbed the endless corkscrew stairs up the unbelievably high tower of the cathedral in Albi, marveling at the glorious view that spread below like a vista toward a new life. There was a strong wind. I held onto the iron railing at the top, my hair whipping across my face. Birds were circling overhead, floating in the strong breeze with outstretched wings and rarely a flutter. I stretched and breathed deeply. Why can't I just go on like this, I thought, traveling around and seeing the world? I did not want to go to a strange school and be cooped up again.

On we drove via Le Puy to Lyon and Geneva, then relentlessly east to St. Gallen and up into the mountains until we reached the village of Teufen.

CHAPTER FOUR

School in Switzerland

"The child will be very happy with us," declared the tall and fulsome gentleman in a tone that left absolutely no room for my feelings or inclinations: I was going to be happy and that was that. His black beard nodded in affirmation and his blonde wife smiled angelically.

They were Herr Professor and Frau Professor Buser, owners and operators of a girls' school, Buser's Girls' Institute in Teufen, a small village above the Swiss city of St. Gallen. My parents enrolled me at the institute, and I was supposed to remain there for two years until my graduation. I recall bright spots, some fun and excitement while I was there, but always pain and pervasive depression smoldered underneath.

I wrote another letter to Ursula. It did not say too much, but it was safe.

May 21, 1933

Dear Ursel,

You probably missed me in school, and I want to let you know where I am. I am sitting at the window of my room in a boarding school in Switzerland in the foothills of high mountains above a little village. The sun is shining; the meadows are green and full of wildflowers. Narrow, rocky paths run into the main driveway that leads up to the big house where our classrooms are, the dining and social rooms, and also, I believe, some of the teachers' lodgings. Several other buildings are clustered about. One is the director's home, one is for the smaller girls, and one is for the thirteen to eighteen year olds, and that is where I am.

I have a roommate and her name is Blanche. She is French, but speaks several languages, including ours. She is very lively and elegant and can't understand when I want to be quiet and just stay in bed and feel like never getting up again.

I don't know how many students the school has, certainly more than a hundred. There are fifteen girls from Germany who are here for the same reason that I am, most of them fourteen to sixteen years old. The teachers are all very nice and the classes interesting. Will I ever see you again?

I miss you!
Fe

"Now the kitchen is closed," said Blanche, coming back from breakfast. "Mon Dieu, you are not even dressed. Aren't you hungry? Here, I snitched this for you." She tossed a buttered bun on my bed, followed by an apple that almost landed on my nose. "Latin in fifteen minutes: Dr. Keel will be looking for you. Ooh, la la!" Her ringing laughter ran with her down the corridor and out of the house. I secretly admired young Dr. Keel, and she knew it. The study of Latin was new to me and my progress was remarkable. No other subject could have gotten me out of my covers that morning.

That afternoon about ten of us had gathered on the broad front balcony that ran along the whole length of the main building. The air was crisp and bright, a light wind blew cold from the high snowy mountain slopes that looked deceptively close to us, as we sat, sheltered by a glass wall, warmed by the penetrating rays of the alpine sun that caused many a girl's nose and arms to blister and peel.

This was to be a needlework and sewing class, but since little old Miss Nufer, Nufi the Mouse, as we called her, had left us to our labors for awhile, nothing much was accomplished.

Blanche was sitting next to me, her feet up on the railing; the sleeve she had been pretending to baste onto a shirt that now lay on the floor was draped over her knee. Her short black hair glistened in the sun and with quick, experienced fingers she extracted a smuggled cigarette from her pocket. The mountain air would blow the smoke away, avoiding detection, and she delighted in our admiring glances. "*Zut alors!*" she said.

Blanche's mother, busy in the fashion industry, was known to us as the lady who sent perfume and chocolates from Paris or Geneva, but rarely a letter for her daughter, so Blanche said, "*Zut alors!*" almost more often than necessary and generously shared the contents of her packages with us, not keeping much for herself.

Hertha sat next to her, short, slightly plump, her frizzy brown hair parted in the middle and clamped down with bobby pins behind the ears without much success. Hertha was gentle and kind. Her coarse features were dominated by large, melancholy eyes under heavy lids. She never talked about her parents, and we all sensed that we should not ask. She came from Munich, and she hoped to study medicine, sometime, somewhere, after graduation. That was all we knew. But we also knew that she idolized Frau Director, as we called Mrs. Buser. When Frau Director was present, Hertha was nearby, her mournful gaze following the figure of the tall, blonde, robust woman with the ever-sunny smile.

We represented a United Nations in miniature, we, the girls of Buser's Institute. There were French and English and Middle Eastern girls. There was Sonia, Cuca, from South America, and a girl from Egypt.

There was Lore Elkan from Berlin and twelve or fifteen other girls like me sent out of Hitler's Germany. But somehow there was a silent understanding among us: We did not talk about what had happened and what our experiences had been. We had drawn a curtain. That part of our lives was locked up in each of us. The unspoken agreement was Don't Touch.

Little Alice who came from Bavaria tenaciously wore her short, Bavarian boy's leather pants and embroidered suspenders whenever she could get away with it, in spite of the disapproving clucking of some of the lady teachers. And I do not think that I was the only one who secretly slept at night with a favorite doll or teddy bear, smuggled from home and hidden under the bed during the day.

Ellen got permission to have a little birthday party for six girls in her room one evening, but it had to end at ten o'clock. The cook had provided a cake, but the little cake could not go very far. A celebration? The news went from room to room, and here they all came, ten, twenty, thirty girls. Each brought whatever she could lay her hands on. There were cookies, a can of sardines, one of tuna fish, bits of cheese and crackers, candy, some apples, a salami sausage, and cough drops. Even two bottles of chianti wine appeared, probably snitched from the teacher's pantry.

Someone had a small portable record player, turned to its lowest volume. The room would not hold us, so the hallway turned into a cramped dance floor. Every step of the stairway that did not serve as buffet for all the snacks, gourmet or otherwise, was occupied by giggling, whispering girls, shushing each other, squeezing together, skinny and fat, pajama-clad and bare-footed. We danced together or giddily alone. The chianti made the rounds in shared bathroom glasses, and only the Italian girls, who were used to wine, did not acquire rosy cheeks and noses.

It got to be midnight. The front door opened and Hertha almost swooned, for there was Frau Director, preceded by her spaniels, her almost constant companions. There she stood, hands on hips, not saying a word. Someone grabbed the needle on the phonograph and a loud scratch scrawled clear across the record. The spaniels, tails wagging wildly, offered their love from one to the other, happy to see us all and delighted to discover the goodies on the staircase.

Quickly we picked up the plates, the wrappings, the tuna cans, the cracker crumbs, the orange peels and empty bottles. One by one, we slunk away to our rooms, trying to be invisible, muttering "I am sorry," and glancing over our shoulders at the imposing figure standing in our midst, silent, glowering with narrowed eyes, immovable, pronouncing Judgment Day without making a sound.

The next morning there was no breakfast. "We thought you had enough to eat last night, girls." Bedtime and lights out were advanced to 7 P.M., right after the evening meal, for that day and the rest of the week.

In Fraulein Welti's English Literature class writing was dissected and analyzed until no pupil had escaped voicing an opinion. Then Fraulein Welti had her chance to argue against them. She just *had* to be right every time.

So we prepared ourselves for endless discussions to follow when we were bused down to the little town of St. Gallen to attend a guest performance of Shakespeare's *Hamlet* one Saturday night. It was to be given by an Austrian theater company. Alexander Moissi was the name of the star, and he was very famous on the German-speaking stage, well known to my father, who had worked with him many times. I had never met him, but knew of Father's admiration for him.

Sitting in a real theater again, being, so to speak, almost on my home turf, seeing the audience stream in, hearing the undertone of conversation, seats audibly reacting to more or less hefty weights of bodies being applied to them, ushers politely responding to questions, skirts swishing, program pages rustling, feeling the undercurrent of excitement, and being aware of the inimitable smells of insect sprays, polish and carpet cleaners, people's garments and bodies, perfumes, breath mints, and occasionally cigar smoke clinging to some gentleman's overcoat filled me with a mixture of excitement and sorrow. It was like looking at a thing loved and irrevocably lost.

Slowly the lights lowered, and out of habit I discovered myself turning in my seat to check whether we had a good audience turnout.

I glanced at the program in my hand.

Hamlet . . . Alexander Moissi.

Polonius . . . Kurt Valentin.

I knew of him, too. But here, one man was playing three parts: Ghost, First Actor, and Fortinbras . . . Raoul de Lange.

"Oh, no!" I almost jumped out of my seat.

"Shush!" hissed Fraulein Welti, and Frau Director, sitting in front of me, turned around wide-eyed and put her finger across her lips.

"I know this man," I whispered excitedly. "He is my father's friend."

"Later, later," she waved me down.

Raoul, an impressive-looking man over six feet tall, with black, long hair, an olive complexion, and large, black eyes with long eyelashes, was of South American extraction, born in Germany, I think. Often, he worked under my father's direction; I remember him in Goethe's *Egmont* and as the lovelorn Duke Orsino in Shakespeare's *Twelfth Night*. He visited our home frequently with his diminutive wife, whose head did not reach his shoulder, even were she to stand on tiptoes.

We sat rather far from the stage. As I wrote to my parents later:

Your direction in Hanover was ten times better, Dad. Moissi was off-and-on wonderful, when he permitted himself to get caught up in the action. But otherwise I had the impression that he was tired or depressed. His voice was marvelous, and his eyes fantastic. Almost the whole time I watched through binoculars until I got seasick.

The lights went on for intermission.

"Frau Director, I have to say hello to Mr. De Lange."

"See if someone can call him to the stage door," she said. "But . . ."

But by this time I heard no more. Grabbing Blanche's arm I ran, jostling people on the way out.

"Well, Shakespeare too much for you, eh?" growled an old gentleman, barely saving the wine in his cup from our onslaught.

Out we raced through the front entrance, around the building and unerringly to the back, where the stage door was. The guard was nodding behind his newspaper. Blanche was still flabbergasted.

"What's up?"

"Just come!" I said, and we went up the narrow, dusty stairs. "Mr. De Lange's dressing room, please?"

The armored youth took his helmet off and wiped his sweaty face, eyeing Blanche with puzzled admiration. "Number six," he said, and pointed with his sword. And there came Raoul down the steps, on his way back to the stage.

"Don't you know me anymore, Herr Lange?"

Gazing down at me were his large, black, penetrating eyes. "I know that little face," came his deep, melodious voice, and his hand fell on my shoulder.

I wrote to my parents:

I knew quite well he had no idea who I was. But when I told him that I was Dad's daughter, he was dumbfounded. He was honestly pleased. He took me by the hand to see Moissi, and they both asked about you. Then Raoul took me to the stage when the play started again and I stayed behind the scenery until the end, so I had a great view of the action.

There the letter ended, but not my adventure.

"Come," Raoul said, and took me by the hand. "You don't want to see the rest of the play with your binoculars; you'll watch it from the scenery."

We stood, his arm around my shoulders, the drawn-back, heavy curtain bunched up next to me, ropes hanging down, hidden in the dark by the backs of plywood castle walls. A spotlight on the stage shone on Hamlet and I was lifted off my feet, wrapped in strong, velvet-covered arms, and kissed fervently. "There is my cue," Raoul whispered, and strode out onto the stage.

My first kiss by semi-dark stage lighting and Shakespeare! Unforgettable, and so romantic. The rest is somewhat hazy, except that I found Blanche at the stage door after the play, arm in arm with the young knight we had asked for directions when we arrived. "Meet Horatio," she giggled.

Frau Director was upset. "Where have you been so long? I worried throughout the rest of the play. You left so fast, I was going to send Fraulein Welti along with you. Really, girls.

"Oh, but we saw the play from the stage, Frau Director. We saw it ever so much better."

The long bus drive home through the dark night enforced the sense of unreality I felt. People were tired, some dozed. Even Fraulein Welti refrained from prodding us to voice our impressions of the performance and make comparisons between Hamlet and King Lear. Thank God.

I felt like a new part of my life had begun, a vista to another landscape as yet unknown. I had been recognized as a person, a sense of self had been born.

There was movement on the staircase one night, hushed voices, a door or two opened or closed. A half-suppressed shout of "No—!" was heard, more in horror than in refusal. Sleepy-faced, we peered down over the banister. There was the doctor, drying his hands and talking to Herr and Frau Director. "She'll make it now, I think," he said. "Better call the ambulance." A door stood open behind him. It was Hertha's door.

"Go back to your rooms, girls! Everything is alright. Go back to sleep."

What is alright, I thought. Everything? Nothing is alright.

Dazed and shaken, we huddled on our beds together, whispering, worrying. The warm night air brought a faint flower scent through the open windows. It was still summer. Leaning back against walls and pillows, we became quiet and quieter. Someone yawned, a few deep sighs were heard and finally everyone crept back to their own rooms.

I stayed awake. I squatted on the windowsill with drawn-up knees, slowly drawing on one of Blanche's cigarettes, blowing the telltale smoke into the night. A faint veil of light from the moon lay on my friend's dark hair on her pillow. The curtain moved from a soft breath of air, almost tentatively, as if trying not to disturb.

I was filled with a sense of sadness, of wonder and of yearning. Thinking back to that night, I see fireflies glimmering around the bushes in the little garden below me, but I am not sure that they were there.

The sun shone bright on our breakfast table the next morning, but none of us had any appetite. There was much sighing and hanging of heads. Not much talk, a few questions. How? Seconal, a whole bottle. Why, for heaven's sake? Much hemming and hawing, uncomprehending.

"I think love." Cuca's Spanish accent did not sound melodious for once.

Love? Love for whom? Silence, heads were shaken in disbelief. Blanche leaned over and whispered in my ear, "For Frau Director."

But it was more than that: it was the cry of a lost child for her mother.

The only small hotel in the village of Teufen was The Linde, The Linden Tree. There my grandmother, Oma Marta, took residence after a few months. I do not know whether she was supposed to keep an eye on me or was told to wait there for my parent's return, until the family had finalized its plans for the future.

Adjacent to the hotel stood a little restaurant, the Patisserie Spoerri, and when Blanche and I entered Frau Gertrude Spoerri looked even more exasperated than usual. The six tables in the sun-streaked room had little vases of delicate blue flowers that had been freshly picked in the mountains that morning. Near the window, looking out to the village street, sat my grandmother, her still very black eyebrows drawn together and her lower lip protruding in utter annoyance.

"Twice I had to send my coffee back! She just can't serve it hot enough, and I don't think the cream puff was made today." This cheerful greeting accomplished, she beckoned to Frau Gertrude with a queenly wave of her hand to take our orders.

"Have you heard from your son, Grandma?" I asked to get a conversation rolling.

"My son, dear, happens to be your papa," she grumbled. But then, taking note of Blanche's barely suppressed smile of amusement she decided that maybe a more pleasant attitude was called for. After all, these young things did not visit her very often as it was.

She was lonely. The only other guests at The Linde came for a day or two, passing through on their way to somewhere else.

So she had her breakfast served in her room after a usually restless night, read her paper, took a brief walk, sat brooding on a bench in the forest, had lunch, napped, read a book, and wrote letters to her son, complaining about everything plausible and implausible.

"Your father wrote," she said. "Your parents are in Hanover, packing their belongings. I can't believe it. I just can't believe it! They are planning to have his whole library, thousands and thousands of books, shipped to France."

"But Oma Marta, you know that Father's library is tremendously important to him, his life's blood, so to speak. It is a library of great value. Also, his art objects, his paintings, his ethnic theater masks—how could he bear leaving those behind?"

"How much money is all that supposed to cost?" she sniffed. "And your mother, taking her porcelains, her carpets. All that foolishness. Sell it all, lock, stock, and barrel. Take the money and leave, I say!" (She had obviously forgotten that taking money out of the country was not allowed. So Mother was wise to ship at least some of her possessions out and pay for the transport in Germany.) "Your mother never used her head."

With that last pronouncement she hit the table, of course not with her fist, but lightly with the flat of her hand, a ladylike punctuation mark.

"And your brother in Berlin! Still working on his doctoral dissertation, delaying and delaying. No discipline, no organization. He'll never get anywhere this way. Should have gone into banking, like his grandfather. No ambition."

This made me mad. The brother, whom I loved dearly, was not to be put down. "You know perfectly well under what ghastly conditions he is working," I said. "Anyway, he did finish his dissertation. And now the medical board has to approve it and give him the date for his oral examination. *They* are dragging their feet, not he."

She muttered something like "Seeing is believing," or some such wise remark, and, choosing not to hear it, I concentrated on my chocolate éclair.

She now turned her attention to Blanche, whose elegance and sophistication always appealed to her, and Blanche knew how to make herself agreeable to the old lady.

"I am sure you write to your grandmother often, don't you, Blanche? Your girlfriend here never does, when I am away. You look so nice today. I like your shoes."

She examined Blanche's high-heeled pumps and glared at my well-worn tennis shoes. "My granddaughter does not care to look neat." She pulled her head back a little, regarding me with narrowed eyes, as if looking at something from a distance. "Look at Blanche. Couldn't you have your hair done like hers? Yours looks disreputable."

The éclair was not quite finished, but I pushed the plate aside and looked at my watch.

"We've got to be back in 30 minutes. It's a long way up the hill." I placed a quick peck on my grandmother's cool and powdered cheek.

Holding the door open for us, Frau Gertrude Spoerri smiled with a knowing wink. "A short visit, young ladies!"

Out we went, not to return for almost two weeks. I felt angry for the rest of the day. My grandmother's disparaging comments about my brother Ralph kept coming back and prodded my carefully suppressed feelings of depression and homesickness back to the surface.

On the occasion of my father's birthday I sent him this letter.

June 15, 1933

Dear Pappi,

I wish you everything that is best and good for your birthday! We know how much we hope and live for each other, it does not really need any long speeches. We must not lose courage, no matter how disgusting things are. Let us try to make things easier for each other. Don't permit Germany to depress you again, but be aware of your own personality and stand above the nastiness. Don't make it more difficult for Mother by being fussy and complaining. Help her and realize that it is as hard for her as it is for you.
I am counting the days until we are together again.

Big kiss,
Fe

At this time my mother spent a few days in Zurich, Switzerland, again to consult with her bank adviser and mailed the following letter to Dr. Robert Benson in the United States. Dr. Benson was a professor at a university in Portland, Oregon and the husband of Father's cousin Hazel. Mother was asking him for help in getting Ralph into the medical school in Portland to enable him to complete his degree upon arriving in the U. S.

September 19, 1933

Dear Robert Benson,

This is the first time that I write to you. Ralph gave me this letter to you, written from Germany in invisible ink. I developed it here in Zurich, Switzerland. This will tell you much about the goings on in Germany, where nobody dares to mention anything about these happenings. Because of the persecution of the Jews, my husband has lost his job and it is doubtful that we will get much of our money out of the country. So we are very depressed.

No educated person agrees with this regime and if no help arrives from the allies, through the disarmaments commission, Germany will sink into Bolshevism.

In your reply to this letter, please write carefully. Do not say anything about Germany because they might drag us off to a concentration camp. Destroy these letters, so nobody else can get them into their hands. There are spies everywhere. In one hour I will return to Germany. I enrolled my daughter here in a boarding school. At home no Jewish child should have to go to school. In one girls' school the teacher asked the children: "Would your parents allow you to sit next to a Jewish child?" Such humiliations abound.

Greetings to Aunt Eugenia and your wife. I wonder whether we will ever meet. Do not mention the contents of this letter in your answer. It is too dangerous. Help Ralph so at least one of us has the means to exist.

Your Alice Altman

Ralph's letter:

My Dear Robert,

It took me so long to answer you because the terrible conditions here seem to monopolize all one's thoughts. It feels as if one is not able to breath anymore. People who were having a conversation stick their heads together in fear that a neighbor might be spying on them. You don't see many laughing faces. Everybody lives under awful pressure in this prison atmosphere. Many people have been sent to concentration camps. Nobody knows why. This is what happens in these camps:

At 3 a.m. they have to get up. Then they have to do fifty knee bends and if they are too old and weak they get beaten with rubber hoses. In a camp for women, in order to satisfy their sadistic desires, two guards would hold an unfortunate woman and a third would beat their naked behind with a wooden board.

The Nazis wreaked havoc in the Berlin Ghetto where the poorest Jews live. They were beaten, stomped, their beards were torn out and they had swastikas carved into their scalps. God only knows how many died of that. Similar things happen all over. Four people that I have known casually have been killed: Mr. and Mrs. Alfred Rotter, Professor Theodor Lessing and the clairvoyant, Hanussen.

That Hitler's troops are thoroughly armed is obvious. I know that they practice shooting every night, sometimes in large basements, sometimes in bowling alleys, and so on. That is as open a secret as the famous Reichtags Brandt (the burning of the Reichtags building).

Quite a bit went on in the medical profession. Nazi professors arrested their Jewish colleagues. This is typical for the general loss of character and integrity. Women are being mistreated. In many cities Jewish families don't dare to go out after dark for fear of being accosted and hurt, since that has become a daily occurrence. Many people are committing suicide. Many are, according to the newspapers, "Shot while escaping."

Even if not a single atrocity were committed, alone the fact that every means of earning a livelihood is being taken from the Jews is preposterous. If a stranger walks through the streets of Berlin, he will not notice anything wrong. Nothing unusual seems to go on, except for the constant parades with flags and marching bands. Otherwise there is not much traffic and one sees many unhappy faces. The atrocities go on behind the scenes.

*We really do not know the full extent of all the things that happen
here, all the murders and horrors, but will surely learn of them
one day. Nobody dares to say anything. Even the emigrants do
not talk for fear that their families and friends that are left in
Germany will be harmed. The few typical scenes that I described
have been witnessed partially by me, or by friends of mine.*

*It seems to me that the general enthusiasm for Hitler, this
insane, perverse fanatic, is waning somewhat. People need bread,
not only circuses. The dissatisfied ones are getting already a
little more audible. The former German-Nationalists are as
horrified as the Socialists. In Berlin alone there are 100,000
Communists active in secret.*

*Deepest, inhumane barbarism reigns here. To call the
conditions medieval is an insult to the Middle Ages. Everything
is so unimaginably disgusting. The sadism of the brutal masses!
The megalomania, the arrogance! The trumped up pathos that
aims to divert the attention from the sick and perverse aspect of
the "Revolution of the Neuropaths".*

*On the other side there is the disgusting cowardice of those
who did not dare to protest. I have learned a lot in the chapter:
"Judging human nature." It does not matter what else will happen.
That all of this was once possible in Germany, I will never forget!*

*When Sacco and Vanzetti were executed the U. S. A. the
whole world was horrified. In view of the Unspeakable occurring
here, unpunished, the world is quiet.*

I DO NOT UNDERSTAND IT!

Here the letter ended. The last few lines were either
torn or cut off for some reason.

The summer passed. A melancholy autumn began.
Letters I wrote to my parents in Germany, where they
were working on the dissolution of their household and
other affairs, letters that I found many years later,
carefully preserved by my father in cardboard boxes, tell

a story of turmoil, depression, feelings of uncertainty and rootlessness.

Nevertheless, a desire for joy and a persistent sense of humor are evident. My admiration for the Latin teacher Dr. Keel, and consequently the fervor of my devotion to the study of that language kept my spirits up.

At the beginning of October I wrote:

October 4, 1933

Dear Mutti and Pappi,

Every morning when I get up I am so glad that another day has gone by and you will be here soon. I am very curious as to what your further plans are going to be and I would not at all object if you would take me along. How is my four-footed girl, Bella? I can see her already, sniffing around near the Amsterdam canals, at the London Bridge or the Bois de Boulogne in Paris. Dear people, you can say what you want; these are interesting times! In spite of the nasty weather, today I am looking quite hopefully into the future.

Kisses from your homesick
Daughter

On October 11, 1933 my parents, having finally completed their arrangements for the big move, left Hanover and went to Berlin to visit my brother once more before leaving Germany.

At this time I received a Letter from Oma Marta, who had since joined my parents as they visited my brother in Berlin. She wrote:

I was happy to receive your nice letter. I do not know when your parents are ready to leave, but it cannot be much longer. I am sad that I cannot join you in Teufen again. Too bad that Blanche has left. She managed to make you a little bit more vain. That was good for you. The hotel in Berlin was all right and reasonable.

Your dog Bella was very sweet. She always insisted on riding in the elevator and the food in the hotel agreed with her. She did not have an upset stomach once.

As far as Ralph's girl is concerned, she is nice, has a bad posture and is completely unsuited for Ralph. He has to go to America with a clear head. He can't choose a wife until he has a job and can relieve his parents from their money obligations to him. Unfortunately he does not consider that. He is lacking a sense of honor. He should marry into an American family in order to be able to really settle down in that country. With a German wife they will both remain outsiders. Well, everybody has to arrange his own life. A difficult task!

When you are at the coffee shop Spoerri, think of me. I would like to be there with you.

Your loving Grandmother

Again those nasty remarks about Ralph! I was furious and laughed at the same time.

At the end of October I again wrote to my parents:

We are now in the middle of winter here. Yesterday we went on an outing. For once there was no snow. Over hills, meadows and creeks, through forest and morass, groaning up the mountain, huffing and puffing, galloping down the mountain with dizzying speed, stealing the farmer's last apples and rolling squeaking in the hay under the roof of a barn. So passed Saturday afternoon.

When are you finally done with your packing? You said you'd come for the holiday. Can't you come earlier?

Pappi, I have a job for you. You must direct us for the holiday performance that will celebrate the Twenty-Fifth Anniversary of the school and the Christmas season, a grand affair! The Boys' Institute from St. Gallen will come, plus eighty invited guests.

My friend Erika and I are supposed to pick the play. We were told that it couldn't be too sad, not too funny, not too heavy, not too light. It has to be festive and of value poetically and from a literature standpoint. Quite an assignment, eh? So we drove the librarian and several bookstores crazy, worked our way through "Natalie" by Racine (too heavy), some East-Indian plays (too complicated), Love's *Labors* Lost *by Shakespeare (not dignified enough), Goethe's* Faust *(too difficult) and finally we picked* Hannele's Himmelfahrt *by Gerhardt Hauptmann.*

Can you picture me as a poor little beggar girl in rags on her way to heaven? Which is to say, I'll have the lead part. So, you just have to be here to witness my embarrassment.

Kisses,
Your Daughter

Embarrassment? I flash back to an earlier time, at age thirteen. Father directed Schiller's *Wilhelm Tell*, the story of the fifteenth century Swiss freedom fighter who was forced to shoot an apple off his young son's head with a crossbow and arrow. The son, Walter, was to be played by a boy, who got the measles at the last minute and, lo and behold, Dad heeded my pleas and gave me the part.

I learned my few lines fast and well. I lorded it over little Elizabeth, a child actress portraying my younger brother. She was a squeaky little thing, prancing about with professional cuteness. Whereas I, in hindsight and judging from photographs of the performance taken at the time, was a sturdier, slightly plumpish teenager in boy's leather pants and brown mountain-air makeup. My dark hair was greased and smoothed behind my ears and I looked stern and terribly serious.

As Walter, I was placed far away from Tell when he shot the apple off my head; so far into the proscenium, as a matter of fact, that the audience could not see me. Conveniently, they were told that the goal had been reached successfully when I came rushing onto the stage, triumphantly presenting the pierced apple to the tyrannical General who had ordered the torturous proceeding.

To show his tremendous relief at seeing his child unhurt, Wilhelm Tell, a big powerful actor, hauled out and gave me a resounding cuff on the side of my cheek and then crushed me against his armored chest in a mighty bear hug. I saw stars in front of my eyes every night of the performance, but was too proud and embarrassed to complain.

My father must have thought Tell's action was simulated. Two years later we learned that this actor was the first Nazi and longtime anti-Semite of the theater, and it probably gave him great pleasure to let his secret feelings of hate out on his Jewish director's child.

So I was going to be on the stage again. I was going to have the lead, if only for a single performance. The play, rather dark, very poetic and dreamlike, suited my churning adolescence perfectly. It opens in a poorhouse when the village teacher carries an orphan girl, Hannele, onto the stage, having rescued her from the icy river where she had thrown herself to escape a mean and drunken stepfather. She gets put into a bed that is resentfully surrendered by one of the ragged denizens milling around. She hovers between consciousness and a feverish dream in which appear her dead mother, the stepfather, angels, and even a Christ-like figure in the form of the teacher. The play ends with her ascent to heaven, carried triumphantly by beautiful angels.

I know this does not sound like a festive Christmas play, but the poetry that is woven throughout the dreams of

Hannele is truly very beautiful. It is a sentimental fairy tale, but born out of the deplorable conditions of the lower classes before World War One, when it was written.

My parents arrived three days before the big event. Two more rehearsals took place on the raised stage that stood at one end of the large dining hall, this time under my father's guidance, and he committed himself to the task with sincerity and devotion.

The damp smell of winter clothing brought in by excited girls dashing in and out from their various houses, not wanting to miss any of the festive preparations, mingled with the aroma of Christmas baking from the nearby kitchen and the woodsy scent of the huge pine tree that had been brought down from the mountains, waiting to be decorated.

"Ladies!" My father rose from his director's chair and strode to the middle of the room, raising his right arm, book in hand, commanding attention.

"Ladies!" he called, "All visitors are to be seated quietly while rehearsals are going on. Otherwise, I will request them to leave the room. My actors are hardworking artists and need your support." The voice sounded stern, but there was a twinkle in his eyes. Even the eight-year-olds stopped running, and Alma the cook looked around the kitchen door, drying her hands.

The rehearsal continued and tall Erika carried me precariously onto the stage. She was the village schoolteacher, having rescued poor Hannele from the icy river. "Stop giggling," she whispered, huffing under my weight in her arms.

"Miss Erika, your burden and your step will be lighter if you believe in your part." my father admonished. He took us very seriously and we responded.

Three weeks before Christmas Eve the big festival took place. The next day many of the girls would go home for the holidays, except of course for the ones that did not have a home anymore. Some parents had been able to come to the school for a short visit from who knows where and disappeared again after a few days. And some girls only had each other.

The dining hall was festively decorated. The drapes were tightly drawn over the tall windows, shutting out the light of the late winter afternoon to let the many candles play and shine the more brightly on the silver strands and colored glass ornaments now decorating the enormous tree. Plates of Alma's cookies were liberally interspersed with pine branches and red ribbons on the white cloths of the long tables.

There was happy chatting and laughter, busy milling around, greetings, and hugs. Three of the older girls had dressed up as Renaissance pages and passed among the crowd playing carols on their recorders as wandering minstrels. In the little space behind the stage we actors clustered, waiting for our big moment, for the curtain to be opened.

The signal came.

Herr Professor Buser in person stepped up and rang a big cowbell with great vigor, stunning one and all into immediate silence and attention. The ceiling lights were extinguished, some of the candles blown out, and the audience settled down.

The curtain slid back and Erika, that is, the schoolmaster, carried his burden onto the stage without a hitch and laid her on the rag-covered bed of the poorhouse, whose occupants objected with great fervor indeed.

The audience disappeared for me. The play took over. This was not rehearsal. It became a dream. It carried me beyond myself into another's life. I was Hannele, the waif, tortured with doubt and fear and finally, released, floating to heaven, dissolved in poetry that sang of a city called eternity, where peace and joy are never-ending, where the houses are made of marble, their rooftops of gold. Red wine spouts from fountains of silver and flowers are strewn on white, white roads.

And then it was over. It had been ecstasy, and the return felt unreal. I dodged the well wishers and extricated myself from my mother's smothering embrace of approval. "You *are* an actress!" she said. Everyone applauded enthusiastically and toasted with cups of hot cider. I slipped outside into the waning light.

The snow glistened on the fields and roads, the hills and mountains. A bell sang from the village church, and from the open door of the inn down below, a light shot out into the icy air. The ebb and flow of song and laughter bubbled out from within, celebrating the Christmas season.

And celebrate they did. Three noisy men, bottles in hand, came tumbling out and greeted a sleepy-looking cow with hugs and kisses. They decided that she too should join the fun and, propping up her muzzle, poured what seemed a goodly slug of booze down her throat.

The inn's door closed and little lights from the shuttered windows blinked out into the darkening air. I moved away, further up the hill. Where have I been, I thought, where am I now? A sudden wave of fear, a sense of panic had driven me from the festive hall at school, away from admiring friends, proud father, even from my mother's approving and, for once, not sarcastic smile at the end of the play.

The singing, the bells, the village were left behind. Only the snow crunched under my feet. My eyes and nose stung from the cold. Stars had come up in the sky and the whiteness around me glowed in the moonlight.

I was afraid. If I become an actress, would it be like that, I thought. Would I dissolve into someone else from play to play? Would I lose myself? Who would I be? Who am I?

"NO," I said out loud, and I saw it floating with my breath into the wintry air. "No, I will not lose myself. I will be me."

My own small Gethsemane.

Or was it prophetic of my actress mother's quiet wonderment on her deathbed, some thirty years later, when she confided in me: "You know, I never knew who I was."

Many years later, when my parents were no longer with us, I found this rare note in my Father's diary:

Today we surprised our Daughter Felicitas, who stayed at an Institute near St. Gallen in Teufen.

"Good that you are here," she said on the telephone. "You have rehearsal tomorrow morning."

At first I thought this was a joke and asked: "What am I supposed to direct?"

"Hannele's Himmelfahrt."

"How do I deserve this honor?"

"Because I am going to play Hannele," came the answer.

Now this was getting to be serious. More than twenty years ago, my wife had performed this part on my stage and now it was to be my daughter.

We worked hard and diligently and Father and Daughter were very pleased when the Critic of the Neue Zuericher Zeitung called the performance "Masterful." I must not forget to mention that, to my amazement, the first person to present us with congratulations was the German Consul.

After much cajoling and promises of good behavior and early return home, Blanche, Alice, and I were given permission to travel down to the city of St. Gallen. We were what we called, "On furlough."

The ancient little train moved slowly down the curving tracks, rocking gently down the mountain, hugged by white pillows of snow on either side of the road. Had it not been for the occasional tinkling of its warning bell and the joyous anticipation of our Christmas shopping trip, we could have easily been lulled to sleep.

"What if people who go on furlough simply don't return?" It was said in jest, but there was also a note of serious contemplation.

Alice looked at us, her lips pursed, and her big eyes wide with the discovery of a very appealing idea. She could not wear her customary Bavarian lederhosen and suspenders in winter, so her long green Loden coat from home was now her constant companion. I sometimes wondered whether those garments from home, held on to so tightly, would follow her throughout her life.

"Dreamer." Blanche took another puff from a cigarette, her symbol of independence. She extended her elegant legs to the seat across the aisle. "And where else would you go, please? Back to Germany?"

I said nothing and rubbed the misty windowpane with my woolen gloves to look at the snow-laden trees, rocks, and occasional farmhouses passing by in the pale winter sun.

We skirted a cliff, piercing the air high above the train and fleetingly my own narrow face appeared in the reflection of the shaded glass before me. I gazed into my own eyes for just an instant, and then I was gone, as if part of me had drifted off into the landscape.

"Go where?" I heard the question again coming from behind me.

Prowling around the holiday-festooned streets of the town we were happy again. Light snow settled on our caps and shoulders. We felt like small children gazing at the animated displays in shop windows, the nodding, bouncy Santa Clauses, elves and reindeer, the toy trains and decorated trees. We feasted on sweets at the famous Konditorei, the best pastry shop in town. We bought presents for families and friends and finally, getting tired, ducked into a little bar off the main boulevard for coffee and the inevitable forbidden cigarettes. First, of course, we looked carefully around to be sure no teacher or acquaintance from the village was in sight. It was indeed a daring enterprise.

We sat tightly squeezed in a dingy leather booth, bundles at our feet and on our laps. Elbows almost touching, we drank coffee, black, of course, since cream and sugar did not seem grown-up enough, and we smoked, trying hard to look nonchalant.

"Next year this time I'll have graduated," said Blanche. "I'll probably live in some big fancy hotel in Paris with my mother. That is, if she's ever around."

"What will you do?" we asked. She shrugged, "Go into some business or to college or go find a guy." She laughed and then stopped abruptly. "Maybe I'll have my own family some day. Might be kind of nice."

Almost embarrassed, she looked at us sideways and brushed her snow-damp hair back from her face.

Years later I thought of Blanche. What happened to her when the Germans entered France? Being Jewish, did she escape, was she deported? Did her bravado last? *"Zut alors!"* Her favorite expression.

Through the narrow window of the bar we saw twilight descending.

Alice murmured, "Do we really have to . . . ?" We did not even answer her.

Slowly, we sauntered through the darkening streets, watched the lamp lights go on and munched on hot chestnuts out of huge paper cones.

Long after dark when the train delivered us back up the mountain, we were the only ones descending to the empty platform of the little village station into the moon-drenched whiteness of the night.

Like ice-cold hands, the air laid itself on our foreheads, eyes and ears. We hunched our shoulders and started to climb up the steep narrow road towards school. The remnants of a tiny brook still drained meekly along the path and made the only discernible sound to be heard, except for the crunching of our boots. But even that seemed muffled.

Dark majestic trees towered above us, straining to reach the full moon above with the topmost branches in their crowns and running their shadows like outstretched fingers over the ground. A small brown creature paddled through the snow without making a sound. Only his furry back and pointy ears could be seen. We stood still for a while, not speaking. I think the others felt as I did. We were intruders in a quiet, peaceful world.

Battling to keep slipping packages from escaping our mittened hands and entangling scarves, we trudged on.

"What did you buy? Let's see!" Curious girls came from the other rooms in pajamas, curlers in their hair, acne cream on their noses. The lights were carefully kept low so as not to attract the authorities. Peeling wet clothes and shoes off and leaving them trailing on the floor, we dumped our purchases on the beds.

"Boy, that's neat!"

"Oh, how cute!"

"What is that supposed to be?"

"For whom is this?" Everyone was excited and we were happy.

"This book is for my brother," I said, "And this one is for me."

Blanche had picked a Swiss cuckoo clock for her sister, and Alice held up a bright-colored man's sweater. "For my dad!" she said proudly.

"Where does he live?" someone asked.

Alice stood still. She gazed at the sweater held in her outstretched arms and slowly let it sink back to the bed. "He may not live anymore," she whispered.

We all crept back to bed.

Furlough . . . was there really such a thing for us?

The lights went out.

It was Chanukah and two weeks before Christmas.

Christmas vacation! I had moved in with my parents who had rented rooms at a small pension, the "Chalet Hoehenblick" (Mountain-View) near my school for the duration.

What a glorious feeling it was, waking up under a big puffy down comforter on a wintry morning. Half raised, leaning back on my elbows, I squinted at the snowflakes coming down outside my window, floating slowly and peacefully.

I stretched and snuggled back down under the covers. It was so quiet. No slamming doors, no yelling girls' voices, no running water noise, no calls for borrowed toothpaste or hairbrushes. No one burst into the door screaming, "Can't you ever get up on time?" Quiet. Heavenly quiet.

I lay there for a long time and then remembered: my brother Ralph was there from Berlin, just for a few days. Those few days were to be relished, not to be wasted in sleep.

In my robe and slippers I stepped out onto the covered balcony in front of my room and stretched over the railing, just long enough for a snowdrop to land on my nose and to take a quick, ecstatic sniff of the fresh cold air.

Peaceful and happy, I padded to my parents' room. Halfway down the corridor sounds of angry quarreling drifted from behind their closed door, raising in pitch and suddenly stopping abruptly. Rushing into their room, my worried face fell in utter amazement. My parents sat in their twin beds that had been pushed close together. The big breakfast tray the hostess had provided was placed between them. This constituted their usual morning routine. But the hair-raising sight was of both my parents sitting stock still, open mouthed, both splattered over face, hair and bedding by the dripping yellow contents of their soft-boiled eggs. My father looked at me. "Your mother threw them on the tray," he whispered.

They looked at each other and broke out in hilarious laughter, reaching out and hugging each other across the mess.

I loved them very much.

For a few short days we all huddled close together, trying to be calm and peaceful. Even Mother was sweet and did her utmost to spread an atmosphere of warmth and relaxation. She bought a little tree and set it up in our rented room. We went on walks in the snow, preceded by Bella in her red knitted sweater. When evening fell our hostess brought soup and sandwiches to our rooms.

The candles on the small tree tried to talk, not of religion, but of family and love and being together, like the ones on the large tree we used to have at home every year at Christmas Eve. Valiantly we tried to keep nostalgia in check.

"Well," said Father, "Next year at this time we'll have a big celebration. We'll be settled then."

He was forever the optimist. A BIG CELEBRATION was almost a mantra he evoked on every possible occasion. Every time something really good happened, particularly on the occasion of a birthday, he insisted on A BIG CELEBRATION. I believe this stemmed from the emotional neglect he suffered in his youth. His cold and stern mother reigned over a rich, opulent household that was run by servants.

There was not much intimacy or love. He told us often, "When I turned ten, I hid under a stairwell and cried. Nobody had remembered my birthday."

The love and care denied him in his childhood he gave amply to his own family, and his desire for enjoyment and his ability to relish the good things life had to offer was truly infectious. He could also rant and rave at adversity, but if there were no way out, he would make the best of it with dignity.

It had been a special week for all of us, but now Ralph had to leave, and I was to go back to school. I felt horrible and tried not to show it, apparently without success.

"There you go again, Little Chicken." Ralph put his arm around my shoulder. "Will you quit worrying?"

I was still the small sister to him, the one that had to be protected from further upset and adversity. He did not want to talk of his own anxieties and apprehensions. He had to go back to Germany after those few days of holiday respite, back to wrestling with his doctoral dissertation amid the atmosphere of hate and upheaval surrounding him there. I knew full well how he felt.

After years of studying medicine he was so close to getting his degree . . . It seemed unthinkable for him to quit just before reaching his goal. Technically, he was able to continue his study at the University in Berlin due to his American citizenship. Going to America later as a certified doctor would make it easier to obtain his license for the practice of medicine in the United States.

I saw his restlessness, his endless smoking, one cigarette after another. In these few days we had together I did not burden him further with my own depression, although I think he was aware of it. We were always very close, in spite of the span of eight years between us.

He had arrived at Christmas and left at the first of the year. I missed him so much. I clung to my parents more than ever. I refused to go back to school. Whether or not my parents realized the depths of my unhappiness I do not know. They gave in to my insistence on leaving with them. Today, in hindsight, I wish they had not permitted me to cut my education short. I would probably have adjusted. It ended my formal schooling.

CHAPTER FIVE

Searching for a Home

In the first week of January, 1934 we left Teufen and drove south over the St. Gotthard Pass toward a new life. Frozen waterfalls gleamed on either side of the road. Heavy gray clouds drifted low above rocks and snowy slopes, brushing the whiteness with their shadows.

Nine months of travel followed. We lived in hotels, ate in restaurants and debated about where to settle.

Father loved France and spoke the language well, so we thought that we might settle on the French Riviera.

It took us ten days driving from Switzerland through Italy to reach the Cote d'Azure. Father, inseparable from his beloved travel-guide, the German Baedeker and later from the French Michelin, insisted on having us visit every cathedral, every museum, every memorable landscape, and every "Sight of Historical Interest." I think it was his way of making up for what he lost, by enriching his life with new experiences and discoveries. He was tireless, as on all our travels before and in the future.

I vaguely remember staying in Lugano and at the lake in Como for several nights, but the pinkish-gray dusty room at the Ambrosiana in Milan with Leonardo's *Last Supper* remains clear in my mind. I see myself standing there and looking at the fresco through Father's eyes. Theater for him was life and here was a stage reenacting life through legend and poetry. You could hear the apostles debating and murmuring through the haze of deteriorating paint and crumbling walls.

An entry to my diary at this time states, *"The Duomo of Milano is one of the greatest and most beautiful impressions of my life. A sublime, holy symphony!"*

The battle for independence from the constant domination of my parents, who were both strong personalities, started to be quite pronounced at this time. In museums, from Father on one side and Mother on the other, I was told what to like and what to dislike. I still remember standing in front of a painting showing an ascending Christ rising in a wide, spacious landscape in luminous sun-drenched air against a bright blue sky. I think it was by Bellini. I was overwhelmed. I felt myself floating into that landscape and being filled with an exhilarating sense of unearthly light and beauty.

"Oh, you *must* see this," said my mother, pulling me away to a painting of a group of robust looking cherubs playing with puppy dogs and dangling bunches of grapes above each other's pouting lips. "Look at these grapes," she said. "Don't they look real?" The spell was broken and I boiled with impotent rage.

For two months we stayed in a hotel in Cap d'Ail at the French Riviera while being driven all along the coast by real estate agents looking for a suitable house to rent. We saw palatial homes perched high above the ocean in this magnificent landscape, with swimming pools hacked into the steep rocks. We saw rambling mansions at the waterfront with their own anchored yachts or sailboats. There was no small or medium house that fit our needs, mostly because of the lack of wall space for shelves to hold Father's library. We were constantly on the go, even on our own without the realtors, restless, exploring, always looking for distractions.

We saw a lot of films, which advanced our language skills. We went to the Casino Municipal in Nice to attend a concert by a famous Italian tenor Lauri Volpi. I wrote in my diary: *"It was magnificent! In front of me sat a hysterical old spinster who went into ecstasy and next to me a half idiot. That should bring me luck."* A feeble attempt at humor.

Mother loved opera. Father had no ear for music, except when it occurred as a by-product in ethnic performances. About opera he asked, "Why ruin a good play with music?" He also questioned the wisdom of paying as much for a ticket to a chamber-music performance as for a whole symphony. "Just for four players?" he would say. I suspected he was only half joking.

So Mother and I saw Carmen and on another occasion Offenbach's "La Belle Helene" at the opulent, gold and red Opera House in Monte Carlo without him.

From my diary:

"It was delightful. But Helena had legs like a dachshund and Paris' ears stuck out." No doubt I echoed my ever-malevolently critical Mama.

"It was a gala performance," I wrote. *"The audience was exceedingly elegant. It was teeming with Monsieur le Conte's, Baronesses So and So, Ladies and Lords, etc. The King of Sweden stalked through the foyer on his endlessly long and skinny legs with his courtiers two steps behind him."*

The large outdoor area of the Café de Paris in Monte Carlo, with its sea of light blue umbrellas shielding the tables, was a welcome haven for melancholic travelers and tired feet. The ritual of coffee and pastry in the afternoon had a soothing effect even on my cantankerous grandmother, who had recently joined us from Switzerland and was now sitting with us at one of the round tables, tightening the fur collar of her coat. It was still a little cool.

The skirts of the umbrellas flapped lightly in the breeze, but the sun shone and the sky was bright. Very few tables were unoccupied and white-jacketed waiters scurried about with trays of salads and sandwiches and, of course, patisseries.

People came from all over the world in all manner of dress, all colors of skin, speaking innumerable languages. They were fittingly entertained by a ten-piece Gypsy orchestra with its romantic, sensuously wailing or joyously frantic music. The leader of the band was a broad, stocky, brown-skinned man with long, straight black hair and a large golden earring: And did he make that fiddle weep!

My adolescent heart responded.

"Look," Mother said, "Isn't that Dr. Adler?" Yes indeed, it was Dr. Adler, the same Dr. Adler we had encountered in Switzerland, Rome, Venice and Paris. Wherever we went there was Dr. Adler. It was uncanny. Maybe he was an international spy, I thought.

He was a slight, colorless man, pale-faced with mousy hair. His suit was always light beige, and so was his hat. A skinny mustache on his upper lip and light blue, watery eyes completed this picture of someone who seemed destined to fade from one's memory. I only recall him because of his prophetic words when he joined us at the table that day.

"My God," he said, "You want to settle in France? Get out of Europe! The most horrible wars are coming." He knew.

I saw Father's hands tighten to fists where they lay on the table. His eyes narrowed to a determined scowl, "France is safe. We need a home."

He needed his library, I said to myself.

Two elderly ladies approached our table. My parents had made their acquaintance in the hotel lobby. They were Frau Eisner and Frau Heidenreich, prime examples of a certain type of German Jewish upper-middle-class womanhood. Hair was tightly pulled to buns in back of their heads. Skirts made of good solid material, dark green or brown herringbone, long mannish jackets painfully cinched at the waist, trying to attenuate the masses within and buttoned firmly, holding ample bosoms in check. High up around the neck some fluffy embroidery showed, secured with a round brooch that looked like a medal of valor. One of the ladies wore a narrow-brimmed Bavarian hat with a little feather in its band and it sat straight on top of her head, as if to say: That is how things should be, straight and exact.

Emigration had not taught them much humility. Complaints about French people and their culture were one of their favorite subjects. And how did the superior Germans treat them? I was tempted to ask.

Escaping their company, Mother and I went for a walk and strolled through the park of the Monte Carlo Casino that bordered the oceanfront. Flowers. Blue sky. Peace. Wide terraces led down to the water.

Shots rang out, dull popping sounds. Instinctively I grabbed for Mother's arm and she for mine. Then we saw birds fluttering in the air over the ocean and birds tumbling down into the water.

"What is happening here?" we asked an old man next to us. "*Les Riches!*" he said, tipping his black beret further over one eye, spitting on the ground. "They pay to shoot pigeons, pay plenty."

From the lowest terrace live pigeons were successively released from cages and from a higher point men in elegantly relaxed attire shot them down. This was called a sport. It was revolting.

Is there a need to kill? I thought. Animals now, humans later?

Another afternoon, a rainy one. My parents took me to a fancy hotel. "Thé Dansant" was announced. The beginning attraction was a stage show, *The New York Midnight Follies,* consisting of elaborately costumed American showgirls tap dancing and wiggling their barely covered bosoms. The tea hour followed. People foxtrotted and tangoed on the dance floor, surrounded by gold-framed mirrors and crystal chandeliers. Gloved waiters scurried about in ceremonious servility.

Here I sat with Mama and Papa and Oma Marta, plus the inevitable ladies Eisner and Heidenreich, who had wheedled their way into our company. Father had given me a meaningful wink beforehand, "I bet there will be an admirer who'll ask you to dance." He had a knack of saying the wrong thing. I shriveled.

From my diary:

"The Follies were excellent, very professional and good looking. I, of course, did not get to dance one time. A girl with parents and a bunch of old ladies at the table is not going to be asked by anybody. Girls are supposed to bring

*their own partners. Where am I supposed to get one? The
King of Siam was also there and actually danced once with
one of his court ladies."*

A time of great longing for solitude, I recall. We visited
the small village of St. Paul high up on a hill above Nice. I
climbed on rocky steps up its steep, winding streets. I sat
on the low stone wall of one of the small squares that opened
just where you did not expect it, like a landing at the end of
a crooked pier. My parents must have been off somewhere
by themselves.

It was hot. I remember the humming of bees, a smell of
herbs. I saw the ocean far below. On a short pole over the
door of one of the ancient houses hung a thin metal sign on
chains. It had a silhouette cut into it that looked like a loaf
of bread. An old woman climbed up the street from below
with a basket on her arm. *"Bon Jour, Mademoiselle,"* she
called, *"Comment cá vás?"* She waved cheerfully and
disappeared down the steps at the other end of the square,
without waiting for an answer.

I felt at peace. I felt at home. Oh how I wanted to stay
just there, quietly, by myself, listening to the bees and looking
down at the landscape, the cypresses, olive groves, endless
hills and the ocean beyond.

Comment cá vás? Trés bien, Madam, *mérci.*

At the end of March we left the Riviera again, our search
for a house having been unsuccessful. We traveled north
through Grenoble, Aix-Les-Bains and Geneva to Zurich,
where we stayed for two months until the end of May.
During that time, my poor father had to travel back to
Germany twice, battling with consulates, banks, and the
German authorities for the release of his mother's
possessions, Hungarian papers, and matters of passport,

etc., things that I did not try to understand. I only knew that the worry and anxiety Father experienced on top of our other recent upheavals was taking a toll on his health, and I justifiably feared for his well being. It was later discovered that high blood pressure and diabetes were his inheritance from the tensions of the time.

For me the days spent at the hotel in Zurich during April and May, sitting in restaurants, going to movies, spending time in the company of elderly acquaintances of my parents, passed in aimless succession. I sat through afternoon visits with my parents and their friends, who debated endlessly about what had happened and why, and what *would* happen and where. With pastries, coffee, and cigarettes they tried to ameliorate their worries and lessen their tension by sharing their anxieties. There were many refugees in Zurich coffee houses, drifting from table to table, finding old friends unexpectedly or making new alliances. A few were well off, some just got by, and some were destitute, looking for help, writing promissory notes to friends who contributed to their sustenance. That these notes were generally useless everybody knew, but they supplied an aura of dignity to the transactions.

Sometimes we met interesting writers, artists, and actors, but I was usually happiest when I could retire to our hotel where I had taken possession of a heavy table that stood against one of the darkest walls in my room. I promptly relieved it of the lace doilies, the ashtray, the phonebook, and the travel brochures spread out on its top, pushed it laboriously across the carpet, and placed it under the window in perfect light. My books, writing utensils, diary, and watercolor box were spread out upon it, and I declared it my territory. Here I could sit and write, read, and brood undisturbed, hoping that Mama and Papa would forget about me for a little while. There was only one hitch: Every morning when I went down for breakfast the maid summoned the houseboy, and together they transported my table back to its assigned spot along the wall. At least they left the papers intact. It took a week to convince them that I really wanted it left where it was, the place to which I promptly returned it every morning after breakfast.

Finally, Mother's negotiations with the bank and Father's efforts to unravel the last German document difficulties came to an end. On the first of June, we took off again on a drive through Italy.

"I still want to see as much of Europe as I can before we go to the United States," Pappi declared.

For three weeks we stayed in Florence at a little private boarding house, the Villa Elsa, at 3 Via San Felice a Ema. On hot nights, fireflies in the cypress garden of the villa battled with the stars overhead. A wide view way down to the glimmering water of the Arno and its bridges lay before us. A sea of ancient houses and narrow streets flowed between the looming palaces and cathedrals and campaniles, folding and weaving together into one giant tapestry.

There was one night, a special night, the fifteenth of June. It was Father's birthday. A celebration was in full swing at the villa. All the guests took part. There was laughter and music, good food and wine. I was tired. A strenuous day of running around and sightseeing had exhausted me, and I escaped down to the sunken garden. There a gnarled wooden bench had become my favorite resting place for many an evening. There I had peace. The city lights blinked from far below the cypress trees. I could still hear the sounds from above. Someone was playing a guitar. I turned to look back up to the house, and there I saw my father standing at the railing of the balcony. He looked so alone. The party was still going strong inside. He too had fled. He was smoking a cigar.

Earlier that day I had heard someone say, "The man is only fifty, already well known and was at the height of his profession." Is that what he is thinking about, I wondered. He had lost his job, the chance to create, to be involved with the work he was so passionate about. Poor father. I got up and joined him. I hooked my arm through his, and we stood quietly together watching the fireflies.

We took unforgettable side trips to Sienna and San Gimignano. Ten days in Venice followed. We traveled on Via Vizenza, Milano, and Varenna back to Switzerland, and finally to Father's beloved St. Moritz.

CHAPTER SIX

And Always St. Moritz

Slowly the narrow-gauged electric train strained its way up the winding, steep mountain tracks. At every turn there was a new vista, towering trees, waterfalls plunging down deep ravines, stretches of farmland way down below, with toy-sized cows grazing. Then again we groaned into a gorge of rock walls flanking the train on both sides, coming so close to our window that we could see the smallest ferns and flowers painfully struggling out of stone crevices. Climbing out of the cliffs' restricting arms that dimmed the light, bright sun and breathtaking views of surrounding snow-topped mountains greeted us. It was the eighth of July in 1934, and I was seventeen years old.

I sat forward on my seat, folded arms resting on the sill of the open window, and sniffed the clear, thin air of the high altitude, so familiar after traveling the same route each summer for so many years. It felt like coming home.

As a small boy my father spent all of his summers in St. Moritz and, inveterate traditionalist that he was, he found it natural, even inevitable to continue this custom with his wife and children for, he hoped, the rest of his life. So from my earliest childhood, during every summer vacation, from the end of June to the middle of August this was indeed our second home.

I remember clearly being small, maybe six or seven or eight years old, and the train squealing to a halt at the St. Moritz station, spilling its load of vacationing folk, my family among them, onto the small platform. We were five people then, for Seusa, my nanny, was indispensable. A horse-drawn open carriage awaited us. After we, with our extensive luggage, and one or two other potential hotel guests had piled in, I was allowed to climb high up onto the seat next to the top-hatted driver, if my brother agreed magnanimously to take the back seat. There I sat enthroned, high above the world, shaken back and forth on the hard, cracked leather seat. Mother's frequent admonishments from below to hold on tight were really quite unnecessary. I held on all right. Bouncing up and down above her, I felt completely out of her reach.

The warm, pungent smell of the two horse's shiny-brushed swaying behinds wafted up to me. Their ribbon-decorated tails swished green-black flies into the air, causing me also to shake my long hair in not only sympathetic, but also needful response. I pretended that I held the reigns and traveled all on my own under the bright sun, in crystal clear air, in view of the glorious, immense, high mountains.

We stayed then at the Engadiner Hof, that had spacious public rooms on the ground floor, a paradise for children to roam about in. Each summer I found some old friends from last year's vacation, and little by little a few new boys and girls of recently arrived families would join our little group.

Some of the grownups congregated in the large, elegant front entrance hall, forming small conversation circles around the many round tables and deep upholstered chairs. Some were sitting in solitude, comfortably smoking and reading the international newspapers and periodicals that were provided. For some it was of great interest to watch the comings and goings along the length of the broad, flowery carpet runner that extended from the big outside entrance door all the way back to the elevators, bisecting the entire hall right down the middle. Nobody could arrive or leave without being duly noted.

There were also two dining rooms, a library, a writing room, a billiard room, and a room for the bridge players, a whole if somewhat small world in which to roam, as far as we children were concerned.

The very best room was the huge ballroom that was only open for special occasions. It was most exciting, of course, to sneak into this forbidden realm on rainy days and stealthily close the door behind us. The room was almost dark, even in the middle of the day. A little outside light escaped the heavy drapes covering the windows and filtered in through the narrow space between the curtain rods and the high ceiling. It managed to glance feebly down the crystal chandeliers, only to drown in the darkness below. Sheets covered bulky furniture that cowered, animal-like, throughout the vastness of the room.

We played hide and seek, crouching under the sheets, huddling behind the drapes, whispering, tip-toeing and getting scared, seeing our own shadowy silhouettes sliding across the tall mirrors that lined the walls. Passing footsteps on the outside would send us scurrying through a small exit door into a narrow corridor and out one of the ground floor windows, jumping into the wet garden, chasing each other, laughing and pretending to have escaped from some great danger.

When the sun shone and the snow capped mountains shimmered in the clear air around us we could be found on the large municipal playground with its swings, parallel bars, and sandbox. The greatest attraction was the magnificent serpentine slide that started its long run high up on the hill and careened down to the grassy field of the playground. One was only permitted to travel its swooping course on cloth covered straw mats which were piled up on the top of the run and later had to be dragged laboriously back up the hill, a long climb.

Every evening at sundown a heavy chain was installed across the bottom of the slide to prevent its use after dark and the mats were locked up. Nevertheless, one summer's night an enterprising youth from the village decided to have a little fun in the dark and went down the slide in his slick worn pants at top speed. The chain cut his throat from ear to ear. Of course this horror was hushed up, especially kept from us children. Yet we learned of it anyway.

I was never allowed out on the playground without my Seusa, who watched from one of the wooden benches like the proverbial mother hen. "Stop running," she would call, "You will get too hot! Come here, let's read a story." There she sat, having lugged a host of paraphernalia along, a blanket, an extra coat, a sandwich, milk, sunburn lotion, cough syrup, and books, all on orders from Frau Doctor. My ever-worried mother was convinced of her delicate daughter's frail health and delighted in dragging her from physician to physician throughout her childhood.

My mother adored doctors. I am sure I was perfectly healthy. Sometimes I wonder how I developed a sense of self and security. Certainly not by hanging by my head in a leather orthopedic basket for interminable minutes every second day at a special clinic to improve my posture. I was also told that, because of my weak constitution, I had to take the beneficial mud baths at the Spa in St. Moritz. With my long hair wrapped tightly into a bathing cap, I lay submerged up to my chin in a tub full of warm, disgusting black mud. Seusa sat on a chair reading one of my favorite books to me, *Tommy Foxterrier*, while the slimy stuff oozed between my toes. I kept my legs closed tightly, always worrying whether it would go in where my pee came out.

St. Moritz was famous for its mineral springs. Well dressed ladies and gentlemen paraded in front of babbling fountains in a large glassed-in, tile-floored building, filling their glasses with the horrible tasting water, feeling health conscious, virtuous, and entirely up-to-date. Drinks in hand, they proceeded out of doors where benches and folding chairs were set up. Here they strolled, chatted, or listened to the orchestra that performed from the bandstand.

Unusually good, mostly classical concerts were conducted by a well know Italian maestro, whose name was something like Sabatini or Salvatore. I think it was Sabatini. He was a very small man with bushy black hair and large black eyes and a strong, expressive face. When I was about twelve or thirteen I was greatly impressed by this fiery conductor and rarely missed a performance. Rummaging around at the local bookshop, I discovered a book of poems he had written and at the end of one of his concerts held it out to him shyly for his signature. *"A la Bella Signorina,"* he wrote, and I bathed in his luminous smile from head to toe. I was ecstatic.

We took hiking trips in the mountains that I remember with great fondness. Narrow trails lead upwards in deep shadow under dense trees. We crossed small brooks that wriggled across paths, alive and shimmering when flickers of sunlight zigzagged suddenly across them, then bubbled down into twilight again. Pine needles were soft under our feet and little rocks made us slip and hold on tight to our walking sticks.

Sometimes we came to a clearing, a strip of meadow and an overwhelming view of the majestic mountains around us. Way below, surrounded by forest, the lake spread its sheet of water, calm and unperturbed by the village of St. Moritz, with its large hotels nibbling at one edge of it, unable to reduce its great size.

Nowhere was Father as enthusiastic a walker as in this high altitude. There was usually a special place that he led us to, be it a famous lookout spot, an ancient little chapel that sat way high up on a craggy ledge, or to a hut deep in the forest that sold postcards and refreshments, most welcome after a strenuous two or three hour hike. We would even venture as far as one of the neighboring villages, Celerina or Pontresina, that could turn into an all day trip. The hotel provided us with neatly wrapped sandwiches and other goodies to carry along.

We wore small backpacks and sturdy shoes and carried walking canes that we purchased in local stores. These canes came in a great variety of shapes and sizes, from a small child's version to big, hefty ones for accomplished mountaineers. Some had expertly carved handles in the forms of animal heads, of bears, and chamois, the agile, small antelope of the mountains. It was important that you picked just the right size and the most beautiful, knowing that it would be well used as you scrambled over rough terrain or balanced on stones traversing the brooks that ran across your path.

I rested on the sun-warmed hardness of many a rock during our hikes, cracking a hardboiled egg, my favorite picnic food, and brushing an ant or two off my bare legs.

The sudden jerking of the train brought me back to reality. "Why are you shaking your head? What are you thinking about?" The train was not very crowded, so my mother had been able to stretch out on the seat across from mine.

"I am thinking about all the years we've been coming here. I am thinking about being seventeen. I am thinking about why we could not come last year and how everything has changed."

"Yes," she said, and for once she had no rebuttal.

The terrain leveled out little by little until the train slid onto the platform, squealing its customary greeting, the same every year. But some things had changed.

A small black and yellow bus awaited us at the station instead of my wonderful horses. The name of the smaller, more modest Hotel Metropole was printed in shiny letters on the doors that opened to receive us. This time there were only three of us. Ralph was trying to finish his studies in Berlin and our Seusa, who had to stay behind when we left Germany, was keeping house for an acquaintance of my mother's in Hanover, unhappy and missing us as much as we missed her.

The Hotel Metropole sat right next to the Engadiner Hof that had housed us in years gone by. It was considerably smaller, but comfortable. Again there was the combination entrance hall and social room, where one read the newspaper, greeted each other, and chatted before dinner. There was no gauntlet down the flowery carpet. The atmosphere was friendly and relaxed. Herr and Frau Schmidt were the hosts and owners, jovial, concerned, and very efficient.

St. Moritz had always been a place of refuge from stress and care. But soon we felt that even there the air of peace and calm had developed disquieting undercurrents. As always during summer vacations many of the same guests stayed at our hotel or at places nearby, people we had gotten to know well through the years, and we greeted them again this time. They seemed the same, but they were not. There were happy smiles, there were handshakes, coffee hours, false joviality, and then the nagging worries that could not be contained by pleasant chitchat and that spilled out relentlessly.

An early, drizzly afternoon. Reading and brooding, I sat in the small, glass-enclosed veranda that opened from one of the social rooms and was rarely visited.

I looked out at the sky. The clouds were moving, and a little bit of blue peeked out here and there. A much-mistreated piano stood in the corner of one of the adjoining rooms. It was used to being pounded inexpertly with tunes like "Tea For Two" or, heaven help me, the "Beer Barrel Polka." Only now it seemed someone else had discovered its existence, someone who touched it gently, expertly, with a few tentative notes at first, getting acquainted.

Then slowly the music rose, the music of Chopin, beautifully and lovingly played, reaching out to me, flowing into my aimless brooding. I closed my eyes and drank the music in. It cared for me, it hugged me. I wish I had known who the pianist was but I never found out.

"Hello! What a surprise," I heard from the direction of the front hall. There was a cacophony of chattering, shrieking voices.

"Hello, hello!"

"I can't believe it!"

"How nice."

"How are you?" Endless exclamations.

The hotel bus had arrived from the station.

"Come, the Bechers are here." My mother, unfortunately, discovered me in my hideout.

Herr Becher had been my parents' lawyer and was an old friend from Berlin. He was a square, squat man with a round, flat face and a short, hooked nose that gave him a slightly owlish look. He wore a tight little mustache over a tight little mouth that belied the impression of fierceness created by two nasty long scars that ran from one of his cheek bones down to his chin, bearing glorious witness to his very German university student days, beer guzzling, and saber dueling. Only later, reluctantly, he had to admit to being a Jew. His wife I remembered as being a lively person, outgoing, and eager to laugh. The one special thing I recall about her was the advice she gave to everybody who would listen, and she was perfectly sincere about it, that one should eat as many cherries in summer as possible, including the pits. Nothing could be more beneficial for one's health. I always predicted that she would die of a burst appendix. A silly thing to remember a person by, Frau Becher and cherry pits.

So there they sat in the hotel lobby, chatting with my parents and berating them for being too hasty in leaving Germany.

"It can't last," Herr Becher said. "The German people won't let it happen. We are staying." I looked at Frau Becher, who was unusually quiet, and I noticed she had acquired a tick on one side of her face, twitching from under one eye across her cheekbone.

I left them all to their arguing and went outside.

The blue sky had won and the sun shone brightly. Slowly I went along the covered walkway that ran in front of a group of stores, a candy shop and my favorite bookshop, among others. The book people's name was also Schmidt. So there were the Hotel Schmidts and the Book Schmidts, as we called them. I had bought quite a few of my favorite books there: Rilke, Herrmann Hesse, the poems of Hoelderlin.

On this day I did not stop. I walked past the small house that was the domain of Herr Fahr, the Friseur, as the sign over his door announced. He was the local hairdresser, approved by my mother and appointed every year when I was younger to subject me to a fancy haircut in the latest style, after which I felt like hiding in the nearest corner. Later, of course, I would not submit to such indignities.

Herr Fahr was leaning against his open door, squinting at the sky. He saw me, put the most winning Cheshire-Cat smile on his crinkled face and inquired about my health. I quickened my step.

I walked towards the lake. For me it was the center of St. Moritz, the heart and soul of it. The unpaved road that ran right next to the water's edge around the shore would take me, in less then an hour's walk, from St. Moritz Bad, or Spa, where our hotel was located, to the edge of deep forest on one side of the water, to St. Moritz Dorf, or Village, on the opposite side. There, imposing luxury hotels were enthroned surrounding the homes of the local inhabitants, whose dwellings seemed to want to escape by climbing up the increasingly steep terrain that rose from the shore.

The original main street of the village, narrow and cobble-stoned, was dominated now, aside from the post office and a laundry, by elegant, tourist-oriented stores. One could buy Balli shoes, French and Italian designer clothes, and fine luggage. Famous Swiss watches could be found at Scherbel's jewelry store. One of my mother's passions was looking at watches and Frau Scherbel was able to supply her with quite a few of them.

Wega's bookstore was the place Father and I gravitated toward and the tall, blond manager, always courteous and accommodating, loved us. When we went to St. Moritz for the last time, in nineteen thirty-seven, he was gone. It was rumored that he had been a Nazi spy.

Where the road encircling the shore turned onto the backward track there was a hilly meadow leading upward toward a large farmhouse and dairy called the Meierei, a favorite destination for an afternoon stroll. There they served coffee, sandwiches, and lemonade under umbrellas in the courtyard, but their specialty was Dicke Milch, thickened milk. This was raw milk that had been allowed to sour for days to a heavy yogurt-like consistency. It was served in individual soup bowls and had a heavy skin of cream on top. When I was a child it was a special delight to sprinkle a good dose of sugar and sometimes cinnamon on it to start with, slowly peeling and eating, the thick yellow skin off the top and then relishing the rest, cool, snow-white and sour.

A wooden dance floor had been laid in the middle of the courtyard and on some sunny afternoons a little three-man band would play waltzes and foxtrots. Everybody danced, from grandparents to little tykes. Young people's summer flirtations blossomed there, and that was where my big brother shone. Being a good brother, though, he even danced with me from time to time.

Looking at the lake, I thought of him. Oh, how I missed him. The letters he wrote from Berlin were so full of stress and anxiety.

The forest climbed and rose away from the level paths and the lake where I slowly walked along the water's edge. There was bright sun, deep blue sky and the air was crisp and clear, as only the high altitude, the enormous snow-capped mountains and the green meadows could produce. The forest seemed to be alive. A light wind played among the trees. It felt like they were breathing.

Not far from shore an old man in a clumsy wooden rowboat toiled along, and I listened to his oars slapping the water and creaking, as if in protest in their iron rings. Splash, creek, splash, creek—a steady rhythm.

I stood a long time, following his slow progress with my eyes. It was as if the boat were sending a message to

me, calming and steady, moving with assurance in its own
kind of beauty.

I veered off and climbed up a narrow forest trail,
winding deeper into the scent of pines and the dance of
light and shadow among the trees. Here and there, almost
hidden in the undergrowth, tiny wild strawberries could
be seen. Gingerly I held them in the palm of my hand,
breathing in their pungent smell before I let them slowly
dissolve in my mouth. No garden or farm grown
strawberries that I have savored since compare to the aroma
of these small forest dwellers.

There was the rough-hewn wooden bench I came to
often with my books and my thoughts. I extracted letters
from my pocket, letters from my brother, rereading them
for the third time. All of his letters, I knew, were strictly
censored, resulting in veiled allusions and obviously
avoiding any mention of facts that could bring harm to
anyone.

July 1934

Dear family,

*Yesterday I sat down to write to you but did not send the
letter since nothing that I really wanted to say was expressed in
it. Today is about the same. I can only tell you there is shit all
around and it is very depressing.*

*Does Pappi have any expectations from the theater congress,
or does he just sit and listen? Has he thought of America? Raoul
L. has plans to go to Spain.*

*Right now I have vacation. I was very happy that Mia's
mother invited me to come to G. for the holidays. It was
interesting to me to see a smaller city. When it gets dark there
one does not leave the house these days. To make up for that we
drank a wonderful old Tokai wine.*

I do not have to assure you that I study much! Too bad that one cannot go swimming in this heat (no Jews allowed). You write so sparingly short, probably for the same reason that I do. There is not much to tell!

All my love!

Another of his letters had arrived that very morning.

Yesterday I saw my former friend Peter, who now sits in the National Socialist Organization of the Charite (large hospital). *In that faculty, like everywhere else, big changes are taking place, conforming to the demands of National Socialist science. So a Gynecologist, Dr. Liepman, was taken to a lengthy prison stay for "protection," as I was told. The Surgeon Sauerbruch will also leave, supposedly. Haber has left.*

I was together with one of my compatriots, who agrees with me that Germany treats its foreign students as hospitably as always and does not make any difficulties for them, as far as examinations are concerned. Any other opinions are irresponsible lies. (Heavy sarcasm on his part.)

Concerning business (sale of our house in Dahlem), *everything is much more difficult. Have you news from the man?* (Concerning his letter for help to Dr. Benson in Portland.) *Karli* (boyhood friend) *thinks of London. I talked to his parents* (Ludwig Fulda, the writer). *His father has thoughts of suicide, except he thinks of his wife and Karli. He also told me of the rotten actions of some of his colleagues, which reminded me of my erstwhile friend Peter. The atmosphere in the laboratory where I work is disgusting, because always the same theme* (probably the glories of the new regime) *is being discussed and it obtrudes into every thought in your brain.*

The Academy of the Arts in the meantime has been put through a strainer. Many new writers have been accepted and many old ones have been eliminated: Franz Werfel, Thomas Mann, Fulda, Renee Schickele, Bruno Frank, Kaiser, etc.

Today is a big German holiday. Everywhere flags, flowers, placards advertising The Nobility Of The Future and Hail to the German Socialism, or something like that. Berlin really looks beautiful. I have not yet been outside today! (Not safe). *Just now the Zeppelin flew over our house. Supposedly one million people are on Tempelhof field. Fantastic!*

I am working a lot. Surgery.

> Love,
> Ralph.

P.S. I continue to research our family tree. What do you think about our Out-of-Wedlock ancestor? Oma Marta will deny it! Please ask her right away what she knows about her grandparents Heilborn. She should at least know their first names. The family tree of the Sterns (another branch of the clan) *is just as large. The three sons of Jakob Samuel took three different last names. The Sterns still live in Niederstetten, supposedly in our original ancestors' house. Please prod Oma Marta energetically to remember about her mother Adolphine's family Heilborn. I am almost certain their names used to be Hirsch.*

The day before yesterday, I got a phone call at eight thirty in the morning: Max Stern from Niederstetten! (a relative Ralph discovered during his research). *He is here on a trip. I met him at five at a café. A delightful, dear old gentleman who looks a bit like Uncle Theodor. Old? Not yet sixty, but has suffered already terribly. He is of the generation of your father, Pappi. One son is studying medicine in another country, another is in the restaurant of a large department store in New York, a third studies law in Paris. He himself owns a small store in Niederstetten, population 1700. I was amazed not to discover a trace of small town life in him. He is a very educated, modern man, nevertheless still strictly orthodox. He is circumciser for his community, reads a lot, and studies the Talmud daily.*

He showed me photos of his old frame house, were Jakob

Samuel lived (around 1780). *It was full of beautiful old furniture, a showcase crammed full of old things of tin, copper, and ceramic. Of course there were many diverse cult objects, all old, family owned or collected. Something else will interest you: his great, great Uncle was the famous Jakob Stern, who was a good friend of Spinoza's and the first man to translate his writings. I also have to announce to you, and this will amuse you, that you are related to the boxer Max Baer, whose father comes from Mergentheim and is related to Max Stern's wife. I am curious what else the family research will come up with!*

I am delighted with this new uncle. He invited me to come to Niederstetten. The astonishing thing is how a person can be so intellectually versatile and interested, living in such a small town. I could imagine the Jews in Renaissance ghettos being like that, in the outside world little shopkeepers, at home learned men.

Why don't I hear from Fe?

P.P.S. Strangely enough, I still have a certain reserve of optimism.

Ralph

I put the letters down and sat for a long time. The book I had brought remained unread.

Heavy clouds hung over the mountains the next morning. It threatened to rain again. After breakfast I sat in the lobby at one of the little two-sided desks at the window and tried to write to Ralph, without too much success. What could I tell him? He did not need descriptions of boredom and sadness.

Looking up, I discovered somebody new sitting in one of the lounge chairs across the room, a young girl, maybe somewhat older than I. She was leafing half-heartedly through one of the magazines and looked about as bored as I was. She must have felt that I was studying her. She looked up in my direction. Very blond hair, blue eyes, German looking. Oh God, a Nazi for sure, I thought. She put the magazine back on the table and came over.

"Are you German?" she asked.

"Yes and no." I was not very communicative.

"Well, I am Jewish," she stated with an air that could have been the prologue to her turning her back on me and stomping off, had I reacted negatively.

This was how I met my friend Ruth.

She was my age, but much more worldly, grown up. My days became brighter. We walked, we talked, and we made excursions to the village with inevitable stops at the Konditorei Hanselmann, a famous pastry shop and coffeehouse. We feasted on meringue glacé and strawberry tarts crowned with gobs of whipped cream, on éclairs, and my most favorite of all, an almost assured cure for depression, the Mohrenkopf, or moor's head—a round, apple-shaped pastry, that was filled with custard and had a thick chocolate icing on top.

Hanselmann was renowned for its coffee and cake and its international clientele. Especially on rainy days in summer, around four or five in the afternoon, it was packed with the rich and famous, the ordinary folks like us, and the gawkers. The observers and the observed alike pushed their way through to the counter that displayed the wonders of Hanselmann, vying for the chance to select and order their most favorite indulgences and then squeeze around little tables where lively conversations often developed among total strangers. Ruth and I adored being in the thick of it. A few times some young men tried to pick us two girls up, and I think Ruth was not disinclined towards a little adventure, but my cold-nosed huffiness in such instances spoiled it for her. My parents preferred to go during off hours and meet with their friends to talk, reminisce, and keep each other company.

As usual during summer vacations, the meeting ground for old friends and new was the hotel lobby. From there one went on walks, out to dinner, to dances or, as we did on one special evening, for leisurely conversation on sofas and in armchairs around one of several coffee table arrangements. It was the 25th of July in 1934. Aside from my parents and myself, there were Ruth with her mother, the lawyer Becher and his wife, a Herr and Frau Strauss, and several other people who had gathered for a peaceful chat.

Father was about to light his last cigar of the evening when Herr Schmidt, the "Hotel" Schmidt, rushed out of his office, hands raised in the air. "Ladies and Gentlemen, I have bad news from the radio. Hitler had Chancellor Dollfuss of Austria murdered!"

Stunned silence followed.

"Oh my God!" Herr Strauss turned white and his wife clapped her hands to her head, digging her fingers into her hair.

"Our son, our son is in Vienna. What if the Nazis take over? We've got to pack. We'll leave tomorrow. Who knows what will happen now?" In a panic they dashed to the elevator.

Other people left.

Our little group remained, shocked, almost unable to move. If only Ralph were with us, I thought. What would come next?

The atmosphere during the days that followed was one of suspense and uncertainty. The people who had proclaimed that it would pass did not seem to be so sure anymore, and the ones who had actually gone back on that presumption were probably convinced of its fallacy by now.

During the following weeks of early August, several of our acquaintances arrived in St. Moritz, people we had not expected, people who came out of anxiety. Some had arranged to meet their children there. The Becher's son Uli, who later became a well-known writer, came with his wife.

Oswald Freund, an old admirer of my mother's when she was young and on the stage, gathered his three sons around him. One of them was Ernst, my brother's good friend, the next was Willy, and the last was Peter, the youngest, at fourteen already an accomplished concert violinist, a wunderkind. They all finally went back. Some years later Peter's hands where crushed by the Nazis and he died in a concentration camp, along with his parents. Willy and Ernst survived. I met Ernst again in France and many years later in New York.

A week after the devastating news from Vienna, a small woman, alighting from the hotel bus with a group of new arrivals, dashed up to my father, squealing with surprise and excitement.

"Dr. Altman, I can't believe it! No, I can't believe it. Snookums, Baby Pet, look who is here!" She dragged a man even smaller than herself to the forefront by his lapels. Her name was Grete Ilm, an actress from Berlin and Vienna. Almost out of breath with excitement, she dropped into the nearest chair, supporting the sling-held cast on one of her arms with the other hand. Only then was it possible to get a closer look at her and the signs of stress and fatigue were obvious. Her round and slightly puffy face was topped by short, curly hair, like a black powder puff. There were shadows under her eyes, and the always carefully applied actress' makeup was missing.

Her husband, little Dr. Meier, wiped his pale, tired face and eyed the two suitcases the bellboy brought in from the bus. Sadly, he shook his head. "That's all we took along in our haste."

"What will my patients say when they come for their appointments tomorrow, and I am not there?" He looked at us as if we had an answer.

Grete's hand dismissed that worry and waved it off. "Putzelchen, they'll go to a Nazi Doctor, that's all."

She turned to us "We were told that he was going to be arrested for communist activities and we ran." She snorted. "Ha! The last thing my Snookums has ever been interested in is politics."

"At the station she fell and broke her arm," he added. "I dragged her along, and we just made it." He shuddered and finally sat down. "Our daughter . . . she left also, but we don't know where she went."

"Oh, my little baby girl. Where are you?" The tragedienne's tears threatened.

"Grete, for heaven's sake! She got over the border somewhere. She is quite capable. She is almost thirty." Fueled by stress, his irritation was palpable.

But we forgave his flustered wife.

We took a long hike to Pontresina one day to visit the writer Stefan Zweig, who resided there for a time with his secretary Lotte Altmann. I admired him and his writing. Also present were Erich Ebermeier, a German writer who was not Jewish, but was strongly opposed to the Nazis, and his young friend Max Baedecker.

It struck me how Lotte silently served us coffee out of doors on their terrace without joining us and then retired to type Zweig's writings, returning only from time to time to ask him for clarification on certain words or meanings in his work. There was an air of devoted servitude about her.

Years later I learned that he had married her in London, shortly before they committed suicide together in Brazil, because Zweig was in deep despair, witnessing the destruction of the world he had known and of the culture in which he grew up.

That afternoon on the terrace in Switzerland the sun had been shining and the immense mountains surrounded us, like a bulwark against all evil.

In August Ralph joined us in St. Moritz for a month during his summer vacation. He arrived exhausted.

On the night table next to his bed I made an installation around a little Chinese Quan Yin figure that I had bought for him as a post-birthday present. I surrounded it with moss that I had gathered in the forest, and I built an arbor of dry twigs to encircle it.

His presence drew other young people to us and some nice days followed. As usual, when he was there I was much happier.

The last days of August. Cold autumn weather set in early at this high altitude, and we began the trip back to the south of France via Milan, where I spent a few days with Ruth, who'd lived there with her parents since they'd left Germany.

Before consuming numerous cups of espresso in the famous glass-roofed Galleria shopping mall, going window shopping and strolling about, Ruth instructed me on how to walk by the various groups of Italian men who were always standing about, smoking, chatting among themselves, and leering at every female that walked by.

"You just have to keep your nose in the air and don't ever look at any of those men, if you do not want to be accosted or get pinched on the butt," she said. "No Italian girl of good breeding would be seen walking about without a man or a chaperone, so they think that we must be either loose women or foreigners."

Ignoring the whistles and teasing calls of, "BELLA, BELLA," we put on our most dignified airs, trying not to giggle and enjoyed ourselves in spite of it.

We were back in Nice on the fifth of September, house hunting again.

CHAPTER SEVEN

Settling in Nice

Standing on the Promenade des Anglais in Nice, I looked down at the beach below. Rows of striped cabanas were lined up to provide shelter for bathers drying their bodies and changing their clothes. In deck chairs shaded by colorful umbrellas, older humankind sipped lemonade, read the *Figaro* or the *Paris Soire*. They surveyed the younger generation, parading by in all its unrestrained, sun-browned near nakedness or roasting on the mats and towels that protected them from the heavy layer of pebbles that covered the oceanfront along the total length of the bay.

It was the end of May in 1935, soon the end of the tourist season. The ocean waves glittered, and the sun nearly blinded me. Shielding my eyes, I turned and faced endless rows of palatial hotels and luxury apartment buildings across the wide street. Windows were shuttered, awnings drawn low. A few chauffeur-driven cars passed by. A doorman leaned against the decorated portal of the hotel Negresco, listless and hot in his gold-braided uniform.

Shifting the straps of my camera from the shoulder to hang around my neck, I wandered east towards the end of the promenade to the Quai des Anges. Here the Esterelles hills that embraced Nice in a half circle reached down towards the ocean and the old part of the city crept up the mountainous terrain until it almost reached the top of the hill.

I loved roaming the narrow, cobble-stoned streets that climbed laboriously upwards, dropped off sharply and rose again, winding their way between tight rows of ancient houses four and five stories high. From the grillwork of tiny balconies, washing was strung up to dry and windows were shielded by wooden shutters. Old women dressed in black, with kerchiefs tied around their heads, sat on the steps of open doorways, knitting and squinting into the occasional ray of sun that managed to reach down into the shadows of the tall buildings.

I took pictures of the women, of a street corner, and of a cat snoozing, cuddled up to a vacuum cleaner in the window of a small store.

A cramped square was home to a flower stall, a vegetable stand, and to a small bar, where a group of men congregated with their dark caps, heavy boots, pipes, and a penchant for good debate. I aimed my Leica at the scene and particularly at one wildly gesticulating gent in the midst of a seemingly rapt audience. I snapped a few pictures. Pleased with myself and by the fact that I had not been noticed, I left the streets behind. I climbed farther up where a fortress once stood, hundreds of years ago, until it was destroyed early in the eighteenth century.

I could see the bay and the mountains backing the city below, the real city, the working city, spreading away from the collar of wealth and leisure that was wrapped around the curving neck of the oceanfront. The air was clear, the view open and wide. Across the harbor and beyond the ships I could see Monaco to the east, Cap d'Antibes to the west. I knew Italy was not far away. Marseilles and Spain lay in the other direction. So beautiful, I thought. Here I'll live for a while.

Then the question came: did I belong here? I was an outsider, an onlooker. I feared I would remain an onlooker for the rest of my life—an interested and appreciative one, not belonging to any one country or culture. My family, the people I loved, that was home, and that was my identity.

I always enjoyed riding the bus through the tree-shaded streets of the city, watching people and traffic go by, passing shop windows that advertised their wares. There were no supermarkets in 1935. You went to the open market or to the various stores specializing in your different needs. One butcher prominently displayed his sign: *AUX COCHON SANS RANCUNE* (to the Pig without Rancor).

When I got off at the end of the line, leaving the city behind, I had quite a lengthy walk into the hills. It was tiring, especially in the heat of early summer. The winding road remained paved for a while, flanked by rocky terrain, cypresses, and native bushes. I first passed some comfortable looking homes and also some that were quite stately. Then came small, low-slung houses of stone, hugging the slopes here and there, their tiny windows and narrow wooden doors tightly drawn and closed. Sometimes a goat or a few chickens rummaged about within their low, encircling walls of piled rocks.

Just where the paving came to an end a gravel path veered off to the right, letting the main, now earthen road continue its climb into the mountains. This path, just wide enough to permit one car to travel on it, was marked by a rusty sign nailed to a tree: *Avenue Gravier*, it proclaimed proudly, the Avenue of Gravel. Snaking ever upward, with high trees and bushes on either side, it passed an olive grove on the left and on the right a shed, serving as a one-car garage. From there a broad driveway ascended to a white two-storied house with balconies and a red tile roof. That was our house, the Villa la Baraque.

The garden was wild and untended. Rock-lined paths ran aimlessly between persimmon and fig trees and agaves and various other unwatered plants, struggling for survival. A big, fat old palm tree spread its huge crown.

There was a wooden pergola, overgrown with vines. There my father would sit on hot days in its cooling shade. He wore a sleeveless shirt, gabardine shorts that barely held his belly, city-white legs and leather sandals on his feet, absorbed in his book and, as always, the inevitable cigar in his mouth. Except for shooing away a pestering fly with his handkerchief from time to time he was oblivious to the world around him.

A wild gray cat had adopted us along with the dish of milk we put daily at the kitchen door for her. She had brought her new litter of five kittens out from somewhere under the house. Josephine, our one-eyed cook and housekeeper, looked down at them with a rather dubious scowl. I consoled her: "They'll keep the rats in check."

When Josephine stuck her hands into her apron pockets, the lid of her one blind eye half closed, so only the white of it showed. She would turn her good eye in your direction, her head cocked slightly sideways. This gave her a questioning, suspicious look, a look that said, "I am not sure I believe you."

Josephine and her husband Franz were a middle-aged Austrian couple the French agency had sent us. Franz was a slim, prim-looking man, bespectacled, and slightly balding. He switched from chauffeur's cap to gardener's apron, as the occasion warranted. Josephine kept house and delighted us with great Austrian dishes. They lived with us for the three years we stayed in France. We were sorry to say goodbye to them when we left, but the closeness of our relationship with Seusa, Martha, and Luise, who worked for many years in my parents' home in Germany, could not be equaled.

When the remaining possessions of our large household arrived from Germany, it would have been terribly difficult for us to unpack and resettle in our new home without Josephine and Franz. The furniture Mother had decided to bring along was that which was most dear to her. There was the antique Biedermeier room, all of it. The big Renaissance chest came, as did the round oak table with its blue, glazed-tile inlay. Her chaise lounge and her heavy, ornate Louis Fourteenth chest of drawers came, and Father's desk chair, with its red leather seat that had been especially crafted for him by a designer in Berlin. What, I asked once impertinently, would happen if he gained even more weight? Would he still fit in it?

His library steps were there, his reading stand and lamp, the ethnic masks and the theater collection, and most importantly his huge library. Only then could he relax and feel at home.

Mother cried over broken dishes. Her beloved antique porcelain collection was intact, but most of the crystal glasses, some of the K.P.M. (the King's Porcelain Manufacture) dinnerware, and all of the matching cups were smashed. It looked as if the crates that had FRAGILE stencils had been purposely thrown and dropped by the Germans out of spite.

Did we realize at that time how unbelievably lucky we were? I do not think that the extent of the horror that was to affect thousands of other people had fully registered with us as yet. We were saved by our American citizenship, but our roots had really been in Germany. We were displaced and deeply shaken, but without a doubt, lucky.

Where to live, rather than, where to work

136 Empty lives. No purpose. *Felicia Altman Gilbert*

No help to others either   No educat—

Sad

Lonely

In the three years that we lived in France we made no friends among the French people of Nice. They were polite, but distant. We talked to service people, waiters, and market vendors. A few nice words were exchanged here and there with occupants of a nearby table at a restaurant or with fellow bathers at the beach. Sometimes we would strike up a conversation with someone sitting on a bench at the promenade along the oceanfront, enjoying the ever-changing flow of humanity passing by.

Rich vacationers from Paris were there, even richer Americans, Moroccans, Japanese, and English nannies with primly dressed children. Sunburned young people from all corners of the world, half-naked, strolled with beach balls under their arms and towels over their shoulders. Sari-clad Indian ladies gathered in groups. Many of them were young and beautiful. A few of the older ones were fat and waddled laboriously under their sumptuous silks and gold ornaments, while others walked tall and queenlike, still handsome in old age.

The Indian gentlemen invariably preceded their flock of women, looking stern, reserved, and prosperous, trusting their glittering flock to follow. The young men could be extremely good-looking, a fact not lost on my observant eye, whereas some of the older ones had puffy bags under their large, black eyes, marring their beauty, and their bellies swelled mightily under well-tailored jackets that were buttoned high up to their throats.

Young local girls in costumes of the region, carrying huge armfuls of carnations, circulated among the crowds, selling their aromatic wares and trying to dodge the various big and small poodles, great danes and pekinese who, in spite of being leashed, tried to bark, snap or just sniff at their swinging skirts and bare legs.

I often sat on a bench by myself, watching and dreaming and watching again, wondering about my life and about those other lives parading before me.

Sometimes a middle-aged couple would walk slowly by, aimlessly, without joy, arms linked, subdued, unfashionably dressed, gray in all that swirling color—a misplaced word of reality in the midst of a poem. I felt I knew all about them.

A young man stood at the railing of the low wall separating the wide promenade from the beach below, his hands dug deep into his pockets. There was nothing festive about him, nothing noteworthy, just a lonely, lost-looking man, gazing out to the ocean. I knew about him, too.

I knew about the nervous grandmother holding two little girls tightly by their hands, children with serious, sober faces, as if laughter had been forgotten. Among the people of many lands, these were not vacationers; these were outsiders, displaced ones, refugees. Was it the way they were conventionally dressed, not of the latest fashion? Was it the gait, the gesture that gave them away? No, there was nothing specific one could point to that gave away their origin and status. There was just an aura, a certain atmosphere about them that was unmistakable.

A family of four came to sit next to me, parents and two boys of about six and eight years of age. After a polite nod and a quick, sidelong glance, the parents proceeded to exchange just a few remarks to each other in very halting French. The smaller boy threw a little ball from one of his hands to the other, missed it, and it landed in my lap.

"Ah, *Mon Dieu!*" His mother was horrified.

"*Das macht doch nichts,*" (never mind.) I said.

An amiable exchange followed and the man introduced himself: "Herrmann Joske."

His wife bristled: "*Du bist Rechtsanwalt* Dr. Herrmann Joske!" (You are Lawyer Dr. Herrmann Joske!)

"Lottchen, that was once upon a time. Now I am Joske, who sells eggs. You'll have to get used to it."

Gently he brushed a strand of blond hair from her forehead that had slipped out of the tight bun at the back of her neck.

"We are raising chickens now," he turned to me again, "and we deliver eggs to people's houses. My wife sews and does alterations. You know, we are not allowed to have jobs, of course. The boys are happy. They are doing well in school. In fact, they refuse to speak German with us. They teach us French!" he chuckled. This is not a man who gets beaten down so easily, I thought.

Soon he and his wife became part of a little circle of friends around my parents. They were all refugees, mostly people who had managed to get out in time with a little backlog of funds to maintain themselves modestly for awhile. Some of them were writers who still received royalties from translations of their books, or, if they were lucky, from advance payments for works in progress. A few formerly prominent German actors had managed to get small parts in French or English films here and there, but how they got around the *no work* law I do not know. Mostly people had nothing but free time, time without a goal, time in limbo, unless they managed secretly to have some little business of their own, were artists, wrote books, or were engaged in some kind of research.

Social life consisted to some degree of meeting at coffeehouses towards the end of the day or after dinner, either by design or by chance. One knew that at a certain hour one was bound to find an acquaintance, either at Monnot's or at the Massena, having café aux lait or noir and a croissant from the basket *the gárcon* had placed on the table. When it came time to pay your bill, the waiter would count the remaining croissants in the basket and charge you for the missing ones.

People like us who had houses or apartments would extend lunch, afternoon-tea, or after-dinner invitations. Real dinner invitations were rarely made. Some of our acquaintances lived in lodgings that either embarrassed them or that were just too small to hold any more bodies than their own.

There was the apartment of the Abelmanns. Old Dr. Abelmann was a Russian physician who maintained that he treated the Tsar, Lenin, Stalin, and Trotsky. His greatest and most glorious story though, often and willingly recounted, was that Tchaikovsky had died in his arms!

We sat in his small living room, filled by a huge, round, wooden table with chairs wedged tightly around it. If people had managed to squeeze into their seats, and someone opposite the door had to get to the bathroom or go home, practically everyone had to rise and leave the room to allow that person to slide towards the exit.

And that was where voluminous Madam Abelmann sat, queenly and substantial, with heroic melancholy inscribed on her brow. Her favorite music was not that of Tchaikovsky, but of Borodin and *The Volga Boatman*. But did she bake cookies! A great gleaming samovar gurgled away next to her. It added to the companionable atmosphere among the guests, who were squeezed together shoulder to shoulder in intimate coziness.

There was lively conversation. An essay on a topical or philosophical theme was frequently discussed, and invariably someone recited a poem of, preferably, soul-wrenching impact. Sonia, the middle-aged Abelmann daughter who lived with her parents, had inherited her mother's height and volume, but not her strength. She wept regularly.

Another after-dinner gathering took place at the small but well-appointed apartment of the Wolff family. Theodor Wolff had been the owner and Chief Editor of the *Berliner Tageblatt*, the biggest newspaper in Berlin that was, of course, immediately taken over by the Nazis.

So there he was, lucky to have escaped, but minus his life's work, the paper he had built. His lavish home, his art-collection, and his library were gone, but his wife and two sons were with him. I don't know how old he was at that time—older than my father, I think. He was a man of above-average height, with a large protruding lower lip, white, wispy hair, and glasses that were sometimes pushed up onto his forehead.

Once I encountered him on the promenade during one of my lonely walks. He invited me to accompany him and for a while we strolled along silently.

"I read your poem," he said, stopping for a moment, facing me. With great trepidation, I had sent him one of my literary attempts of the previous week.

He nodded down to me. "Gifted," he said, "Very gifted." And then he shook his head. "You ought to be spanked," he muttered. It sounded so tired and melancholic.

What he meant, I presumed, was that a young person like me had no business writing such sad poems, but, after all, what could one expect? It was a sign of the times.

He proceeded to walk, pushed his glasses high up on his forehead as was his habit, raised his chin slightly and looked ahead, and you knew his thoughts were elsewhere.

Mrs. Wolff seemed to be the one keeping the household going, quietly overshadowed by her three tall men, her husband and two sons, Richard and Rudolph, both in their early twenties. At a gathering in their home one evening, she busied herself with coffee cups, offering plates of cold cuts and home-baked Napfkuchen. My parents and I were among the guests. I sat at one side of the room next to Richard, who tried his clumsy best to make conversation with me. I nibbled unhappily on a cracker loaded with cucumber and mayonnaise that someone had stuck into my hand, and, as usual was unable to say anything even halfway sociable.

Mother sat across the room, watching me with eagle eyes, mouthing silently: "Say something," in my direction, followed by sign language: "Powder your nose." None of this proved to be encouraging.

From my diary:

April 27, 1936

Rudolph Wolff asked me to go to the beach with him. We took the bus to Cap Ferrat. Believe it or not, I actually talked and had a good time We sat on the rocks at the tip of the cape, the ocean below us, and the sun was shining. We had a nice conversation and I felt so good. Then Rudolph said: "I like you so much right now, can I give you a kiss?" Of course I said no and he turned blood red. The seagulls screeched as if they were laughing at me. I think it was very decent of him that he asked and did not bother me further. Soon after, we returned home and had coffee at Monnot's. My tongue was stuck again. I am such a fool.

Ten years later I met Rudolph Wolff accidentally in New York and he said, "You know, I wanted to get to know you. I was attracted to you, but you seemed so mature and unapproachable." Had he only known what a scared cat I had been.

At about this time Ralph wrote us from Berlin:

July 29, 1936

Dear family,

Here I am, sitting at the Schloss-Konditorei without money, waiting for cousin Bruno of Niederstaetten to rescue me.
The passport business is all straightened out again.

My esteemed professor deigned to inform me that he is satisfied with my thesis. However, he suggested two slight changes and the inclusion of references to two scientific papers, some of his own, of course. All of my colleagues were astonished that he did not have anything else to criticize. It is more usual that the work is returned two or three times before it is accepted.

The unbelievable Olympics traffic roars in front of the coffeehouse where I am sitting. You cannot imagine the masses of humanity that have descended on the city, neither would you recognize the street, the Unter-den-Linden. All the way along the middle of the road giant Swastika flags are flying and along the sidewalks banners and coats of arms of all of the major cities of Germany are posted. A lovely sight indeed! What wonderful colors, what grandeur!

Wandering up and down the street, cousin Bruno and I looked in vain for a flag for our peaceful little Niederstetten, but I spied one for Pyritz, where our Oma Marta Simon was born. I don't think, though, that that was the exact reason for displaying that special banner.

At the Pariser-Platz the flags of all nations were displayed. House fronts as well as the Brandenburger-Tor are decorated with flowers and flags and the front of the Opera House is festooned in red silk.

Incredibly imposing is the Lustgarten. The beautiful façade of the New Museum is facing the expanse of it on one side and the front of the castle looks down on it from the other end. The two remaining sides are built up with huge grandstands, backed by towering swastikas. In the very center of the place a high altar is erected where the Olympic Flame burns day and night.

Everywhere, throughout the city, amplified loudspeakers give running reports on the progress of the competitions, interspersed with various musical outbursts. The cops are dressed in dazzling white uniforms and you cannot imagine the degree of politeness on their part without exception. When police, streetcar conductors, and the man in the street observe the little American flag in my buttonhole, they are absolutely enchanted.

On Saturday the games were officially opened. Visiting with friends, I was able to view the procession on the way to the stadium from the second story window of their apartment. Lo and behold, there were Hitler, Goering, Hess and Von Neurath passing right in front of our window. I'll never forget that day.

Soon I will go and visit Theodor (Father's mentally ill uncle) *at the hospital. I don't think that there can be any change for him.* (The Nazis killed him and other patients a short time later.)

Today I celebrated the Olympics in my own way, by going to the museum. Even here things have been rearranged, according to the times, in all departments. To my amazement, the dedication to Uncle James is still there (for contributing much art and money to the museum). *I marveled at the Gruenewald Crucifixion, on loan from Harlem.*

Are there any new cases of Polio in the Engadin and St. Moritz? At this time of year they happen everywhere. There is no news of an epidemic here.

Love to all!
Ralph

"Mademoiselle est si triste!" The waiter, setting the café au lait in front of me, scanned my face quizzically over the barricade of his voluminous moustache.

"Mais non, mais non, je suis seulement fatigué." He seemed reassured, flicked some crumbs off a neighboring table with his napkin and retreated, but not without glancing back at me over his shoulder.

I was not tired. I was annoyed, disgusted, lonely, and sad. Yes, damn it, *I was* sad. I had fled our house up on the hill for the day. I had fled the tyrannical reign of my paternal grandmother, who brought nothing but daily strife and discord to the life of our household in the absence of my mother, who in turn kept watch over my brother in Berlin for a month or two. There she meant to assure his relentless dedication to the completion of his medical degree and to keep distracting females from his door.

I sat at one of the sidewalk tables at the Café Monnot, looking out at the broad Place Massena as twilight began to fall and the lights came on over the city. I pulled a letter out of my purse and laid it on the table. I looked at what I had written. It was to my girlfriend in Germany.

August 18, 1936

Dear Ursel,

My writing is not progressing today, which upsets me even more, since yesterday I was so full of hope and joy about it. Today I was not able to form the simplest sentence and felt that I had nothing to say. My brain was nailed shut and everything in my soul was dead and empty. Maybe I am too lonely, maybe not alone enough in order to concentrate on my work. Sometimes I long to talk to another young person, to exchange ideas.

I sit up here in our house for days, even weeks, without seeing anybody else except my parents, my grandmother, and the servants. It is my own doing. Often I could drive downtown with them. But what should I do there? One can't always go to a movie or go to a coffeehouse with acquaintances that are mostly old people.

I know a very nice twenty-year-old boy, but first of all he has very little time and a lot of studying to do, and secondly, like an idiot, he seems to have fallen in love with me. Of course our being together is therefore complicated. I've let him know, as nicely as possible, that there is nothing to be expected from me, no necking, etc. I have to weigh every word I say in order not to encourage him, so that is not an ideal friendship, as you can imagine. I like him, but avoid him, if possible. So then, I am lonely.

I am not as lazy as you seem to think. I do NOT play with our dog Bella the whole day and spend the rest of the time totally

with reading. I get up at seven thirty or eight and dig around in
the garden, making the worms fly all about.

Here the letter ended. What else could I add?

"Sans blague, c'est toi, ma cherie?" (By God, is that you,
darling?)

There he was, Hans, my sadly rejected friend, coattails
flying, hair tousled, in a hurry to get somewhere as usual,
books under his arm.

"Surprised to see you," he said and plopped himself
down on the chair next to me. *"Pour une petite minute,"* he
reassured me. I was pleased.

"Comment ça vas?" Hans had been brought up in the
Alsace-Lorraine. When that country was divided between
Germany and France, his father, the writer René Schickele,
opted to become a French citizen, so Hans was quite fluent
in French.

Anyway, a few little French phrases here and there
seemed to assist the flow of conversation between us and
to point towards an effort to assimilate into the new culture.
It was also the conventionality of these set phrases that
somehow served as a tool for avoiding more intimate
speech. We stayed on a casual, friendly, bantering level,
Hans and I. At that time, in my mind, love was to be the
big, important, romantic happening with sexual union only
at the height of it. Casual flirtation was not for me, I
thought—the result of years of careful indoctrination by
my dear mother. In addition, I saw myself as unattractive
and awkward, thanks to Mother's constant criticism.

So there, Hans, who was to be a good friend in later
years in San Francisco, sat next to me, snitched a few quick
sips of my café au lait, and grinned at me affectionately.

Searching for words to describe the personality of
Hans, I can only come up with a picture akin to a pointy-

faced, eager animal peering out of forest undergrowth to see what went on in the world, sniffing the air, ready to explore everything within its reach with gusto. There was an intensity shining out of his light, piercing eyes and in everything he did. The idea of resting did not occur to him very often, unless an occasional asthma attack laid him low, or a bout with allergic eczema made him miserable.

"I've finally decided," he said, "I'll become an architect." With his forearms on the little table, he showed me how many months and years his varying studies would take, by counting them out on his fingers. I was pleased that he shared his plans with me and I listened intently.

My friend the waiter smiled with obvious approval as he passed us with a tray.

"By the way," Hans cocked his head and looked at me quizzically, "Why are you sitting here all be yourself?"

"I like it," I said, trying to sound convincing.

"Ah, ça va bien alors," that's alright then. He gave me a quick peck on the cheek. *"A tout à l'heure,"* see you soon.

He dashed off and the waiter looked disappointed.

It started to get dark. The lights came on around the square. Now I felt lonelier than before. I got up and looked across toward the Café de France. Maybe I would find a familiar face there, I thought.

Much time was spent in those days wandering from one coffeehouse to another, looking for and finding friends and compatriots to share news, concerns, and ideas for possibilities of settling down or for getting work. Memories of the life and culture left behind were also exchanged. There was the Café de Paris, the Monnot, the Massena, and the Café de France. Having coffee or a small meal, like a Croque Monsieur, a baked white-bread sandwich with ham and melted cheese, or just the inevitable croissant, you would most likely soon be joined by one, two, three, or more acquaintances. Nobody was ever surprised at meeting each other during the day or the warm summer nights around the little tables on the sidewalk, or in winter or cool evenings inside the red-brown smokiness of one of those restaurants with their unceasing sound of gossip and clatter.

A lively crowd of people pushed me through the door of the Café de France into the smoky room. A hand grabbed my shoulder and an arm went around my waist.

"Well, hello there! Haven't seen you for some time!"

I remember his eyes, inviting and slightly teasing, forever appraising all womanhood, especially of the young kind. His name was Valeriu Marcu, a writer and historian from Rumania, who looked like a French painter and should have been sitting at the Deux Magots Café in Paris with his black beret and pipe. He was intelligent and interesting, but I did not trust him. Nevertheless, I felt flattered by his attention in spite of it. (Years later I heard that he had been able to escape the Nazis in France by fleeing over the Pyrenees to Spain.)

Then I saw Father with his newspaper and cigar in discussion with Theodor Wolff, who sat next to him and had a cigarette hanging glued to one side of his large lower lip, his eyes squinting slightly to avoid the drifting smoke. Sholem Asch was there, a well-known Polish writer who wrote novels in Yiddish. He was invariably preoccupied with his work and scribbled quick ideas or just single words on the tablemats or napkins while a conversation was going on. He tended to be silent in company. He was always very nice to me. I slid along the bench behind the table and sat next to him. Soon I was flanked by René Schickele, who entered after me, wheezing with asthma. His small, piercing eyes glittered with intelligence that even the heavy lenses of his glasses could not hide. Like his son Hans, he suffered from frequent bouts with eczema on his hands and face that turned his skin into a veritable minefield. I liked him and his writing, especially his latest book, *The Widow Bosca*. The lawyer Joske waved to me from a nearby table.

I sat quietly and looked around me at all of these erudite men. Each one was accomplished, each one stranded in his own way. Who would publish books in German or Yiddish that were written by expatriates? Where could Father find occupation in the theater again? Herrman Joske would continue selling eggs instead of arguing law in court.

I somehow had the feeling that while they were sitting there talking, smoking, and having their coffee or aperitif, they were waiting for something. Waiting for what?

One hot, early afternoon I was passing the Café de France. There sat Sholom Asch in the shade of the awning, piles of paper in front of him.

"Come sit with me," he said.

Then he started to talk to me about his latest book, *The Nazarene*, a novel about Jesus that was published in 1933. I did not tell him that I had already read it and had been fascinated by it, for fear that he would ask me to comment on it. Me, express my opinion? Verbally? He had heard that I was writing and asked me about it. (Oh, Pappi, I thought, you spread the word again! How could you?)

I stammered and stuttered around, so he kindly patted my hand and talked about the sequel to *The Nazarene* that was to be *The Apostle*, the second book of a planned trilogy. I felt overawed. Here was someone who pulled me from the sidelines and treated me as an adult.

I sat in the kitchen with Josephine, trying to make a drawing of her. She was rolling and pulling thin sheets of dough for her famous apple strudel, occasionally swatting at an errant fly that had found its way to her table in spite of the wooden bead curtain rattling in the breeze over the open kitchen door leading to the garden. Outside, the kittens were playing and tumbling all over each other, chasing lizards among the rocks.

"Madam Grandmama is again not happy with me," Josephine scowled, pointing her good eye in my direction,.

"Mother will be back soon." I tried to soothe her obviously hurt feelings.

At that time Oma Marta had free reign again in our house, and she gloried in her unchallenged power. Mother had gone back to Berlin for a month to check on Ralph and to *"Straighten him out,"* a pronouncement she had made with fierce determination upon receiving the following letter. She had handed it to Pappi and me to read with one hand, raising the other to high heaven in horror, as if the world were coming to an end.

August 23, 1936

Dear Parents,

Whether you believe it or not, following our last telephone conversation I was simply not able to write to you and sound sensible, because I was so upset and filled with desperation, especially because of the harsh manner in which Mutti talked to me. I do not expect to be treated with kid gloves and realize that some reproach is warranted. You do not realize how much tremendous blame I put upon myself. You don't know how utterly crushed I feel when I hear the disappointment and worry in your voices. Please understand me, Mutti, I do not complain. I do know how good you are to me. You do not realize how much I love you and Fe, how unimportant any private interests, any hopes and longings are in relation to my feelings for all of you. Unfortunately you are not able to recognize the extent of my desire to give you pleasure with my existence and by accomplishing something concrete in my life. It upsets me terribly. Believe me. That much more catastrophic is it when I hear the justification in your voices over the telephone for my abysmal sense of shame and failure. I am fighting constantly with my Goddamned instability and the feeling of being torn apart within myself. At the same time, I believe I see and know myself quite clearly. There are energies and drives in me, but so many that I am torn in all directions. I am capable of knuckling down. I have proven that to myself while working on my thesis and I am satisfied with the result. Don't tell me that I am trying to have everything the easy way and that I am lazy. Believe me, I do not play with your good will and love. I am trying hard and fight with myself constantly. I want to mean so much to you and am unhappy that I cannot convince you how much I struggle to succeed.

Physically, I feel well again. The tooth business was nasty, but is done with. I do not look bad; I eat well and with good appetite. Those concerns are not necessary, but I live under the pressure of your expectations and hopes.

I embrace you all!
Ralph

My poor brother. He surely needed help, but not from Mutti. He was floundering in a morass of conflict, between a mother's manipulative tyranny, implemented by the weapons of love and unrelenting possessiveness, and the horrendous upheaval of the world he was forced to live in.

The decision to study medicine had been made for him at an early age, and indeed it had caught his interest. He was also drawn to other sciences, to art, to the study of animals, the study of other cultures. He had an eager and open mind. But the loving and still pliable young son that he was did not really get the chance to search and make his own choice of profession. He was destined to become a physician, and he was made to believe that. His studies, his medical exams throughout the years, became excruciating struggles. Too many other interests and concerns were in the way, and when finally Lottle, the girl he loved and had lived with for nearly six years, decided to marry someone else, he nearly broke down.

A letter Mother wrote to my father during her residence with Ralph in Berlin.

September 1936

Dear George,

You know that I always have to have a clear mind before I write to you. I was incredibly upset that Ralph has muddled his head with marriage plans again. He is encountering energetic opposition from my part, because this young woman is really way below our class. It all comes because of his terrible fear of going to America all by himself and nothing else. My only hope to get him out of these conflicts and to seriously save him from foolish decisions is to get him together with Nadia. (My girlfriend in Nice, whose elegance and sophistication mother admired.) *I told him about her and he asked immediately whether Fe would also approve. He is willing to meet Nadia during Christmas vacation. Tell Fe to take good care of her friendship with Nadia, so when Christmas comes it will not look obvious when we introduce the two to each other. Also Fe shall try to obtain a sample of Nadia's handwriting. You know how much Ralph believes in Graphology. Maybe Fe can send a postcard to Ralph when she and Nadia visit at Café Monnot and ask Nadia to include a few words.*

I cannot see any other way than to see Ralph married. Lottle would have tormented him constantly. Mia would be harmonious and motherly to him. She seems to be quite nice, not dumb, but I think calculating, from what I can understand, after all. He assured me, thank God, that he would not do anything without our consent. I asked him how he would feel if Fe proposed to get married to a man of a lower class. He answered that he had not thought about that. I just think that if he likes Nadia, the problem would be over. He absolutely has to have someone to be with otherwise, he cannot cope. So, this is my great worry.

Ralph is working intensely to hand in his current work so he can return with me in December for Christmas. He looks very thin, so I spend more money than I planned on food.

I like Berlin again very much. The restaurants are well attended. Ask our fur dealer immediately how much a dyed ermine coat would cost in the United States. Darling, how are you all doing? I am longing to see you. How is little Bella? Does Fe go to bed on time? I want to find her well and alert. Greetings to Mama, kiss Fe. Keep loving me! Now I will go to try some corsets on. Write to me immediately.

Mutti was a good woman, generous, and never intentionally mean. She was child-like in her resentment that the drama of life around her was not always played out the way she wished it to be. She fought relentlessly to rewrite the scenario, sometimes with success, but more often not. After her great triumphs and the adulation she received as an actress in her youth and early married life, she suffered many disappointments. She looked up to the medical profession as if it were practiced by wise and holy men to be revered, and that was where she wanted Ralph to be, the handsome son she loved so fiercely. She wanted to be proud of him.

When finally, in later years, he followed his childhood interests and became a recognized expert in the field of cultural anthropology and art, I believe she was still not satisfied.

Mother and
daughter,
1930

The house in Krahenwinkel

My retreat by the pond

On stage as Walter, in Schiller's Wilhelm Tell, 1931

Ursel, the only true friend, 1934

Still friends but not for long, 1932

St. Moritz Village and Spa

Off to the playground
with Seusa, 1925

Excursion in St. Mortiz, 1923

They love to walk, 1929

Hotel balcony with Ralph
and Bella, 1932

Clowning with Christel, 1931

The last goodbye with the Hotel-Schmidts and
hairdresser Fahr, 1937

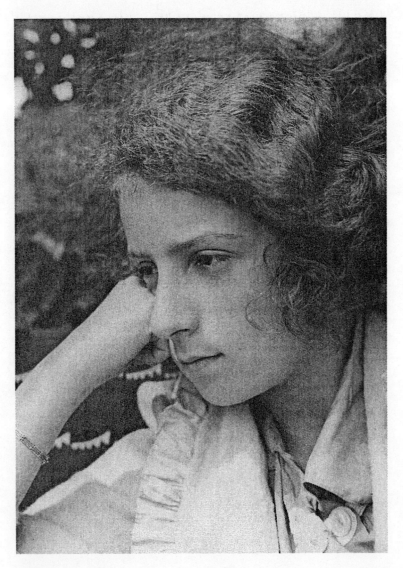

Melancholy, 1933

The campus of my school in Teufen, 1933

Christmas in Teufen, 1933

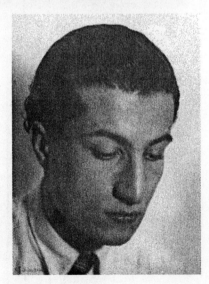

Ralph, 1933

The student of photography, 1935

Our house from 1934 to 1937,
the Villa La Baraque

Promenade Des Anglais in Nice

Sholom Asch and
his son Johnny

Hans Schickele

My friend Ruth, 1936

The Café Monnot.
From left: Mrs. Marcu,
my father, Mrs. Schickle,
my mother, Theodor
Wolff, René Schickele
and Valeriu Marcu

CHAPTER EIGHT

Adventures in London

It was October of 1936. My friend Ruth had moved to England with her family. When the invitation came to spend time with them in London I was overjoyed. It was the first time that I would venture out on my own without Mama and Papa.

Mother stocked my suitcases with clothes and paraphernalia for all imaginable climates and occasions, an effort that I quickly sabotaged just before leaving the house by reducing the load considerably and piling it all up on the bed in my room. I was to be gone until Christmas, a little over two months, but looking at my parent's faces one would think I was departing forever.

"Be sure to keep warm," Mother still admonished at the train station.

"Write us every day," my Father said.

So after waving goodbye to them from the train window, trying not to look too deliriously happy, I sank back into the seat of my sleeping compartment, conscious of the typical smell that I knew from many of the trains on which I had traveled with my parents in the past, a musty smell of stale smoke and leather. It had been a part of our wanderings in years past, but now it belonged to me alone.

I pulled off the fashionable little hat that Mother had insisted I wear and tossed it on the rack above. I made a pillow out of my heavy coat, leaned against it in the corner near the window and put my legs up. Unwrapping a sandwich and a bunch of grapes I had brought from home, I felt very smug and satisfied.

My first letter home, saved as usual by the Family Archivist, my dear father:

Oct. 18, 1936, 1 Sydenham Hill, near London, 7 A.M.

Dear People,

Arrived in fantastic shape last Friday. Thank God I had a compartment all to myself on the train. It could have been very uncomfortable with another person. Of course, I had to get my period and on top of it the train shook considerably. Hurrah for Dr. Jacoby's pills! Luckily I had saved some bread from the evening meal, because the dining car got detached during the night and no food was available until eleven thirty the next day. The transfer to the boat in Bologna and the channel crossing went very well. The water was not furious, but still rather angry. Following your council, I went to sit in the middle of the ship, where you said the rocking would not be as strong. I did not realize that it was first class, so I got booted out as a second-class passenger and directed to the back, the fanny of the ship. Instead, I descended to the ladies room, where it was possible to stretch out beautifully on broad, soft, upholstered benches. Under each seat a friendly invitation was issued by an accommodatingly huge pot, but I was not even inclined for a minute to accept the nice offer.

The customs procedure in Folkeston was very thorough. When and where did I buy my dresses and the hats, they asked, especially the hats were of great interest to them. I had to state the purchase price of each one. When they checked my passport on board ship I got a lengthy interrogation: where was I going, for how long and, anyway, what for? They were not friendly at all, quite unpleasant. I was glad I had Ruth's invitation letter with me.

They stamped my passport: I am not allowed to do any kind of work, not even without pay. Now it does not make any sense that I call your friend?

(Father had given me a letter to a well-known German Jewish theater director who worked in London. I had so hoped to get some kind of apprentice job through him, working on scenery or getting into costume design. I was very disappointed.)

At Victoria Station Ruth and her mother hugged and kissed me and remarked immediately and approvingly on my hat and hairstyle.

It is quite a stretch from the city to their house, but transportation is excellent. They have a nice, comfortable little home. My room is not much smaller than my own at home. Thank God it has a large electric heater and is beautifully warm. Bed is good, light is good, food is good, everything is good except, well, except the relationships in this family. They are most peculiar.

The meals are served according to English custom. Large breakfast, small noon meal, high tea with cold cuts and cheese, lots of toast and cake and then follows a large hot evening meal, quite late.

So around nine o'clock on the night of my arrival we were sitting around the table having dinner. There was Ruth's father, a pale, paunchy man with a petulant and brooding expression on his face. Her mother, Rose, had been a self-assured, very nicely dressed woman when we knew her in St. Moritz. She could easily laugh and sit with us teenagers at Hanselmann's, drinking coffee and chatting.

You would not believe the change in her! She is very nice to me, but otherwise she goes around in an old housedress, with a face that looks so listless and dispirited that one would like to pat her on the back and say, there, there old girl, buck up already!

The only lively family member at the table was Ruth's younger brother Steppi, a strapping thirteen year old, bragging about sports events in school.

Rose dished the food out and served her husband first. He looked up and scowled at her.

"There is no more meat than that?"

She shook her head.

"Then why the devil didn't you buy more?"

"I thought it was enough," she said.

"What did you do with the extra money I gave you?" The growl of his voice changed to rolling thunder.

Steppi's breaking tenor chimed in: "Bought herself a new hat, probably."

A shadow of anger flashed across her tired face: "You are talking nonsense, Steppi."

"Oh yea?" he squeaked, "Don't tell me what to say, you old goat."

I looked at the father, expecting him to jump up and beat the dickens out of the boy, but lo and behold, that darling Papa just sat and smiled his approval. Can you believe that? Poor Rose stood there with the plate in her hand and turned white. Then the tears came and she ran out. Father and son kept eating. "Come on," Ruth said, and we, too, left the table.

I was tired from the trip and it was late, but the scene at dinner had been quite upsetting and neither of us could sleep.

"Father has never been very warm and loving, but he was good to us, never mean or nasty before he lost his job." We both huddled on Ruth's bed, wrapped in our blankets.

"He was an engineer in Germany, very busy, not home much, not very concerned with his family, but he loved us in his own way, I think. His secretary was more important to him. You remember, Mom and I always came to St. Moritz by ourselves. When the Nazis took over and everything crashed down around us, Mother and I thought for a while we were losing my father

*as well. He did not sleep. He did not want to eat. He stopped
talking. Finally we were able to come to London with the help of
his business connections in England. Now Father is a
maintenance man, in his eyes not much better than a janitor. He
is so bitter now, completely changed. He hates the whole world,
including us, except Steppi, of course."*

"Can't you get away?" I asked.

"And leave my Mom?" she replied.

*I am so sorry for Ruth. We'll just get out of the house as
much as possible. We have fun when we are together.*

*Ruth goes to the French Academy of Dressmaking for two
and a half hours every day, so I'll have time to take English
lessons. I am reading* You Never Can Tell *by G. B. Shaw with
the help of my dictionary. Quite an effort!*

*They are calling me for breakfast now. We'll go shopping
afterwards.*

Lots of love!
Fe

The day after I wrote this letter we were invited to a
party at the house of one of Ruth's friends. It was a long
trip by train and bus, and we were to stay overnight.
Hearing the din of voices coming from inside the small
suburban row house when we ascended the front steps
made me squeamish right away. Would I appear as dull
and stupid as usual in company? I felt like turning back,
but knew that there was no escape.

It was midday, cool, and damp. The October sun shone
through the moving clouds off and on, just enough to send
quick shafts of light through the windows of the crowded
living room, creating the effect of stage lights skimming
sporadically across the scene. Ruth was immediately
monopolized by a group of young people, and I stood alone

for a few minutes. Everyone spoke German. There were no tea and crumpets, but coffee and apple cake with lots of whipped cream.

"Hello, I am Anneliese." A nice looking dark-eyed girl stretched her hand out in greeting. "Where are you from?"

"And when did you get here?" Another girl inched her way out from behind the first one. "Might as well get you pegged immediately," she laughed, "And if you feel like practicing your English, there is only one chance. Hey, Mr. America, come join us."

She waved to a grave-looking young man who stood at the other end of the room.

He came and greeted me politely. "Is Miriam making fun of me again?" he asked in perfect English.

"I was just going to tell her that your mother tongue is German and you refuse to speak it, Jakob."

"I was born by American parents in Germany, was brought up there, and my first language was German," he said. "I loved everything about the country—its inhabitants, its culture, and its language—and it rejected me. Why should I speak the language of people who hate me?"

"I am an American, too." I was launched, and from there on we had a lot to talk about. He even abandoned his principles for a little while and reverted to the hated German, to make it easier for me, since my English vocabulary was still rather limited. He came from Leipzig and was going back to the United States at the beginning of the year.

"You'll just love it there. The best country in the world," he said.

In the guestroom that night, Ruth and I moved our beds in front of the fireplace that tentatively touched the nearest walls with a flicker of its light, but gave little comfort to the rest of the room. The blankets were thin and we slept in our clothes. I lay hugging my pillow. I stared into the sputtering little flames, and I thought about Jakob's description of America. Soon I'll be there, I thought. It was exciting and not quite as worrisome as before.

October 24, 1936

Dearest Parents,

I feel like I am in some sort of recovery here, not so much from any bodily ills, but from a sick spirit and mood. It is so stimulating here, sometimes almost a little too much. After my first exhausting trip to town, walking the streets for hours and marveling at it all, Ruth dragged me into a coffee shop, and I only recovered after gulping a cup of excellent coffee and savoring several hot crumpets. The first days were really strenuous. In town, I did not let go of Ruth's arm. But now, when she is doing her dressmaking I travel alone in town with stoic calm, relish the rolling staircase at the underground train station, master all kinds of transfer traps on innumerable buses and stroll around Oxford, Regent or Bond streets as if I were on the sedate Avenue Victoire in Nice.

Dear Mutti, when we stroll through the streets window shopping and especially when we stop in front of a jewelry store, groaning with admiration, I always think how nice it would be to have you here. Frankly, I was glad to get away by myself, but now I miss you already.

Pappi, you should see the cigar stores on Regent Street. They are not simply cigar stores; oh no, they are rather luxury lounges for company presidents with deep leather chairs and Persian carpets.

The art dealers' establishments are like something out of a fairy tale, in spite of the fact that one can't see much of them from the outside. Through a medium-sized display window, where a single painting seems to brood all alone like an old English gentleman sunk into his club chair after dinner in stupefied dignity, one can, although with some difficulty, discern a large room behind it, in whose depth the subdued lighting mysteriously gets lost toward the back. There, I presume, an elegant staircase will lead up to a gallery where the paintings are shown. One senses soft, deep carpets and thinks of the novels of John Galsworthy and his Forsyte Saga:

"Soames, deep in thought, his hands folded behind his back, strolls slowly through the gallery, stopping from time to time in front of one of his favorite paintings. He nods to it, like to an old friend, and his squinting eyes hide a gentle smile," etc., etc. I bet you don't know Galsworthy.

The big department stores are quite opulent, but the clothes here cannot be compared to those of Venice and Milan, although they are mostly of good quality. The Italian chic is just not there, not remotely. Evening dresses especially celebrate orgies of tastelessness. It glitters and swishes around, pink, light blue, lollipop colors, feathers, bows, gauze; it glimmers and rustles with much tradition and lack of elegance.

By the way, I now understand "English Puritanism." Nowhere have I seen couples kissing in the movie theaters with as much uninhibited fervor as here in London. Right'o, don't you know? I am starting to sound very British, eh what?

On Wednesday the whole Kremnitzer family went out to the Cumberland Hotel in my honor. We had an incredible meal: Sole au Vin Blanc with shrimp and for desert vanilla ice cream with chocolate sauce.

Even father and son were relatively nice to me. The pleasure of the meal was quickly erased though. It happened on the way home, just before boarding the train. I still don't know what brought this on.

Steppi yelled at his mother, "I am glad that not all women are like you! I would love to give you a solid kick." At the same time he raised his foot in her direction.

Papa chuckled!

I would have never thought that such depth of raw hate

could exist within a family. How can these people live under the same roof?

On Monday I am going to visit a language school. It is supposed to be excellent and the cheapest, three pounds per month, every morning for three hours.

Love you,
Fe

November 1, 1936

Dear Ones,

The language school is very large. I am together with six people in my class, all different nationalities. Next to me sits a very nice, eternally smiling Japanese man. He is fantastically polite, a real gentleman. Across from me sits a young Dutch reverend, who looks like our chauffeur Albert. Then there are two German Jews, a Belgian, and a French Girl, all young people. For the first time I find that the study of grammar can be enjoyable, because it is not only taught as a scaffolding for sentences, but as a means toward obtaining the most effective expression for what one wants to communicate. The main text we use is the newspaper that I have to buy every morning. We read from it, get dictation, explanations, and then have discussions. A good way to learn.

I am really sorry that I have to ask for more money already. I seem to need about one pound per week. Believe me, I think about every penny I spend and save as much as possible. I borrow cigarettes and check every piece of cake from all sides before I decide whether it is really necessary that it should be acquired. I only go to museums on free entrance days. The worst expenses are the train and bus fares. That cannot be avoided.

The Kremnitzers would be terribly offended if I moved to the city. I would have liked to live independently somewhere by myself. Instead I have to go and visit their relatives, sit in the living room in the evening, making conversation and listening to the radio. Ruth and I leave the house as much as possible. By ourselves, we are quite happy and have fun. I get up at seven-thirty and at nine-thirty I am in school. Ruth's tailoring starts at ten and we both meet at Oxford Circus afterwards. Either we go for a combined noon meal and coffee time to Lyons, or to a pub for about one shilling and then to a movie (half price before one o'clock), or we eat and then throw ourselves into sightseeing.

On Saturday we went to a big ball. Father Kremnitzer sent us for the sake of his reputation! It cost him fifty shillings, and he made sure we understood this and marveled at his generosity. It was a fundraising affair for women and children in Palestine. All three of us had our hair done and we looked really nice. It started with dancing, and then came a four-course dinner. It was good, but not exceptional.

We sat with a large group of people, all friends of Ruth's. The boys treated us to champagne. That was delicious. We had already had some cocktails before dinner. People, I will become a drunkard! It's great to be tipsy! I danced quite a bit and learned from my compatriot, the American boy from Leipzig, the American way to dance. It is a completely different rhythm, not easy. At two o'clock "God Save the King" was played and that was the end. Rose had already gone home by herself.

We still went to the house of one of the girls and had whiskey. I found the entrance steps there to be very uneven afterwards. Badly built, of course. I was barely able to get into the car when we left. Very funny! We stayed again in the home of the girl whose house we visited two weeks ago. We arrived there at five in the morning. At two o'clock they woke us and we got a beautiful breakfast with scampi sandwiches. It is an especially nice family. The father is a little bit the type of Herr Friedlaender, maybe not quite as grand, but still, the generous gentleman who emerged *from a previous age, a carnation in his buttonhole and wearing spats. It was a wonderful morning!*

On Friday we went to the French exhibit. You cannot imagine how crowded it was. One had to literally box one's way through to see the paintings. But it was well worth it. About twenty Renoirs, many Van Goghs, Gauguin, Manet, Monet, Courbet. Pissarro was sent from Moscow. There were Corot, Sisley, Ingres, Delacroix, and two of the most beautiful Daumiers: Les Curieus Devont L'Etalage and Le Pardon. *There was Degas, Cezanne, six unbelievable Toulouse Lautrecs and Seurat. Grand, just grand!!*

Go see the films Louis Pasteur *with Paul Muni,* My Man Godfrey, Romeo and Juliette, *and today the film* Rembrandt, *with Charles Laughton, is coming out. Should be wonderful!*

Love,
Fe

November 14, 1936

Dearest Mutti and Pappi:

Thanks for the check! A few days ago I took it to the bank and was not really very astonished that, in order to celebrate this historic moment, the whole city was in turmoil, just where the Credit Lyonais and I were situated. They dedicated marching bands and whole regiments of horses and riders in historic costumes with long trumpets, flags, and flowers to me. I was really moved by this and was just about to greet everybody with a condescending but friendly wave of my hand, when everybody's attention turned towards a large ceremonious parade of soldiers in garb of past centuries, accompanied by a group of dignified gentlemen in white peruques. In the middle of the hullabaloo a magnificent coach, it's sides beautifully painted and gold encrusted, rolled along. Inside sat a tremendous Alonge-peruque who took care of nodding to the crowd for me. They told me that the Lord Mayor sat under that thing, the new Mayor of London, who made his traditional entrance into the city. Did you know that by an old law the King is not allowed to enter the city without the permission of the Lord Mayor?

All right, I obeyed! I went to see your Dr. Plesch. (He was a famous Hungarian society physician who practiced in Berlin before Hitler, and had established himself in London. My mother adored him as she adored many doctors, but this one had a special place in her heart.)

Boy, oh boy, I bet he is a triple millionaire. He lives and practices in an apartment house in Park Lane, THE most expensive place to live. It is like a house from a movie set: there is a uniformed valet on every floor, one elevator next to another, their walls covered with brocade. There are columns and thick, soft carpets everywhere. The whole business is so elegant; they do not even have nameplates on the doors. A valet conducts you to where you want to go. Your good Plesch sports genuine copper engraving on fine paper for his prescriptions and appointment cards. God, if only Ralph could be in his shoes, only he would never go for all of this ostentation. There was a Miss Butt, or something like that, who sends you greetings. From HIMSELF: a hand-kiss! Ever the gracious gentleman! Even from afar!

The first thing he said was, "This is a real acne. There is nothing we can do about it." Then, after this encouraging verdict, he started to squeeze around on my face. I was just in full bloom. Otherwise he did not check me at all. He gave me a prescription. I shall smear the stuff all over my face and hair every night and wash it off in the morning. After that, he said, I'll look terrible. I am to do that for months. Aside from that, I am to eat like a horse, eat everything indigestible, raw, roughage. Fruit, fruit, fruit with skin and seeds, particularly raw pineapple and grapefruit, also sauerkraut. Oatmeal in the morning. Otherwise I'll need patience, patience, patience.

I was very depressed. I had hoped he would give me some kind of immediate cure and I would be done with it. Right now I am looking terrible, worse than ever. My face is full of bumps. It is to despair! Even if Otto Brahm were here I would not show myself. That awful salve I will not use until I get home, if ever!

Mutti, the money you sent to the Kremnitzers for my upkeep was really ridiculous. You want me to live here so you can feel that I am well taken care of. For me it is just very disappointing. I so wanted to be independent and to be living alone. Can't you understand this? They are all nice to me here, but the atmosphere in this house is terrible. The Father accuses his wife, in my presence, of not having had enough of a dowry and of not spending enough money on food for the family because she wants it for herself. Isn't that pretty? If they do not get divorced Rose will kill herself, as her own Mother did. Ruth is very scared about that.

Ruth and I just went to the National Gallery after meeting at Oxford Circle at twelve thirty after our classes. We ate our sack lunches on a bench at the park and then feasted on art: Brouwer, Teniers, Pieter de Hooch, Frans Hals and above all else, Rembrandt!!! "The Rabbi," "The Jewish Businessman," "The Bather," and the "Philosopher." OH! All so wonderful!

We usually go home for tea, otherwise we get too tired. Often we roam the streets though. The other day we stood in front of Buckingham Palace in pouring rain and laughed at the ridiculous tromping around of the Royal guards under their bearskin caps. Such monkey business!

One week ago there were big communist parades, very calm and well behaved. Also, a parade of Jews in honor of fallen Jewish soldiers was very well accepted by the public.

Is Pappi's new article, "Side-Trip to Asolo," published yet? (He wrote about a visit to the grave of Eleanore Duse, a famous actress, in Italy.) *I can't sleep for excitement until I get it. What an unspeakable delight awaits me!*

Franz and Josephine sent me a very nice card. Give them my very best greetings. Greetings to all of our friends.

Love,
Fe

P.S. Pimples are horrible!

November 22, 1936

Dear Mutti,

The days are flying away, one after another. Five weeks have passed already since I left home. Unbelievable! Today is Sunday. This afternoon I was at the British Museum for the first time.

Oh, dear Mutti, if only you could be here to see it with me. The sculptures from the Parthenon in Athens! Overpowering! Only what a pity they are so terribly ruined. How fantastic they must have been. Just fragments are left. The other Greek and Roman sculptures left me cold, except for a few very pretty boys and women's heads. The ones we saw in Rome were much more beautiful. The Egyptian collection would be paradise for your son. I do not profit as much as I should, since I do not know enough about Egypt. For me, most of these objects have more historical value than artistic significance. There are exceptions, of course. Oh, I almost forgot, four wonderful statues from a temple at Lykien would have enraptured you. They were incredibly graceful.

Next Thursday my English classes will be over. I will not sign up again. I have learned a lot as far as grammar, special expressions, and a sense of the language is concerned. Now I need to just speak, something I did not get to do too much as yet. There was little conversation in class. The teacher spoke. That was a good way to get the ear acquainted with the language, but the brain and the ear did not get trained to express quickly and clearly what they meant to communicate. I have already written little essays and translated things quite decently. Now I need someone to have conversations with me. I try to talk to people in the train, at the hairdresser's and at the restaurant, but that is not enough. I heard that there are very good and interesting free lectures on art and world and cultural history at the British Museum every day. That's where I'll go.

I visited with Lotte Altmann. She was very nice but seems to be ailing somehow. Her boss, Stefan Zweig, lives here permanently now. I walked with Lotte to his house. It is in the most expensive area, so I guess he is doing very well. Lotte thinks that Ernst Toller is on a tour in South America. That is probably why I can't reach Christel again. I am so sorry about that. I seem to miss her everywhere. Hans wrote to me from Nice, and I answered.

Do you think Pappi would be pleased with a program from the Drury Lane Theater, dated eighteen-thirty-three, announcing the performance of Antony and Cleopatra *with the players' names: Maccready and Miss Phillips? A new book came out about Mrs. Siddons. Do you have a Christmas present for him? I could get wonderful things here for Ralph, for example, a beautiful Egyptian chain, guaranteed genuine, for about thirty shillings. They also have a green carved stone figure that looks a little like the nephrite bird's-head ring that I have, only bigger, for eighteen shillings.*

Just one month till Christmas!

Miss you all!
Fe

Christmas! It already felt like Christmas.

I wandered down one of the narrow side alleys that connected two large, noisy boulevards. It was late in the afternoon, the end of a damp and gray day, just before the street lights came on. The tall, old buildings loomed dark above the little lighted shops that lined the pavement on either side of the road.

There was a tiny Indian restaurant advertising all kinds of tandoori specialties on a tripod easel on the sidewalk, and the paper lotus blossoms in the window had yellowed from fumes of curry and spice.

Next came an antiquarian bookstore, where I had seen the old theater posters for my father the other day. A large newsstand showed international publications and further on a Jewish delicatessen blinked invitingly.

Several steps took me down to a basement and Sam's Antiques. I opened the door, a little bell tinkled, and Sam, who looked more like an Omar or an Ahmed, looked momentarily up from his book, peered at me over the rim of his glasses, nodded, and returned to his reading.

"I'd just like to look around. Do you mind?" My question elicited no more than an absentminded wave of his hand. His book must have been riveting. So much the better. I loved to wander slowly from shelf to shelf, stacked with old clocks, jars from Greece and Iran, figurines of German porcelain, ancient daggers, and Indian bronzes. A heavy piece of Kilim carpet was carelessly thrown over two Chippendale chairs and, turning around, I almost fell over a large African basket. The slightly open doors of an ornate and imposing French armoire yielded to my attempt at closer inspection, but creaked so pitifully that Omar-Sam finally abandoned his book to see what I was up to.

"Belonged to a princess," he took an Indian silken Sari from the rod and then a Chinese mandarin coat. I shook my head and reached for something that lay on the bottom, underneath the shawls and garments above, among a wild selection of spiky-heeled shoes, Eskimo boots and Moroccan slippers. It was a little female figure with a sweet, expressive head that could have been part of the décor in an old Italian church, except that it was about twelve inches tall, dressed in a blue velvet gown with gold braid around neck and hem. The soft body underneath was covered in cloth, while head, hands, and lower legs were firm and solidly sculpted. What was it? A puppet? There were no movable joints or strings.

Omar became positively loquacious. All of a sudden I had become worthy of notice. "Ah!" he said, "You like? I have two more!" He rushed to the back of the store and emerged with another figure in each hand, waving them triumphantly above his head.

"Set up for Christmas in church," he said. "Very, very old." It dawned on me: they were creche figures, an angel and two of the wise kings, a white and a black one, Nepomuck, as far as I remembered his name from studying the Bible in school. Their clothes, in silks and brocades, clearly meant to be sumptuous once upon a time, were tattered and threadbare and some fingers were missing on their delicate hands.

Father's Christmas present! Here it was. Ritual, drama, performance, it was all theater for him. Clearly, these little figures had to go into his collection.

Now it came time to bargain. "They look so ragged," I handled them gingerly.

"Oh, made long ago, Miss. Old, very old," he repeated, wagging his head and pressing his hands to his chest.

"Look at those clothes and the missing fingers." I felt very grown up and efficient. I looked at his worn and pleading face and started to feel ashamed of myself. I relented and the deal was done.

Now it was dark outside. The streetlights were turned on. I cradled my precious find, wrapped in last week's *London Times,* carefully in my arms, mindful of each step on the damp and slippery pavement.

November 23, 1936

Dear Parents,

Oh, if I could buy all of London out! Don't get scared; until now I have not spent one penny unnecessarily. Today I went to the British Museum again: old books, miniatures, manuscripts, etc. Wonderful!

Couldn't you come here for Christmas? I do not deserve it all by myself. It is not even as expensive as it seemed to me at first. Now I know better the ins and outs. Do you think it would be possible for me to come back here again after the holiday? Here I feel like a completely different person. On top of it, there is a special school for photography and a school for journalism, and I discovered a university where I would be allowed to take classes. Wouldn't it be possible for you to give Nice up already and come to London? It would be ideal.

Dear Mutti, how crazy it is for us to hide away from the world. I only now realize how dull and stupefying our existence in Nice is. Or maybe you'd like Paris better? Please, please think about it. It is such a terrible thought to come back to Nice and to go to sleep again. It is just as awful to contemplate being away from you all any longer than Christmas. It seems I am always torn from one end to the other. Think it over with Pappi; he HAS to be sensible. I am young and cannot suffocate my hunger and desire for learning. I do not relish spending my life in the darkroom of Edith Zistig and with the endless groaning and moaning of old people on the Promenade Des Anglais. But of course I also want to be together with you. There is nobody here who gives me even the smallest kiss. I am simply homesick. The only solution is: you come here. What do you say?

By the way, if you think Ruth's mother could spank Steppi, as you suggest, he would just hit her back. Well, enough of that.

It is very cold here now and foggy. All of London is in a state of excitement, first of all because of the coronation and

Mrs. Simpson, the mysterious Mrs. King, and also because of Christmas. The displays in the department stores are incredible. Ruth and I delight in the toy departments. I swim in all this like a fish in water.

The other day I stayed home, went to the neighborhood, and bought a watercolor box, chestnuts, and chocolate. Then at home I painted a little watercolor to illustrate my short story: "The Old Man at the Lake."

I finish now. It is late.
Fe

November 27, 1936

Dear Pappi,

You too shall get your own personal letter. I was very pleased to receive your article about "The Trip to Asolo" that you had promised to send me quite some time ago.

It is good, but you have made it too easy upon yourself. To be honest, you did not put very much effort into it. Other pieces you have written were more intense, thoroughly researched, and colorful. This one seems to be casually tossed off when you had some time on your hands. For somebody who had not previously indulged in the tremendous pleasure of reading some of the other productions of your creative brain, this would be a good piece of writing. But since I have had the invaluable fortune to be able to relish earlier masterworks by my esteemed Father, I do not consider this latest output as fully realized as it deserves to be.

There, I have spoken!

The beginning is very good, also when you observe Eleanor Duse on the stage, but in between it brushes quickly past important details that should serve to bind the various strands of the story into a whole. The ending is very good. In spite of it,

I had the feeling that there should have been more about the beauty of the place. Asolo is mentioned only casually. There seems to be no reason why Eleanore Duse was so attracted to it.

You should have told more about the atmosphere and the magic of the landscape than this one sentence: "Here her thoughts could roam as far and wide as the sky." This one sentence insinuates and does not tell the whole story.

So much about the idiocy of any critic! Of course, you wrote about what interested YOU, but the reader would like to learn more about what was mentioned. When a musician strikes a few notes of a melody, a short motif he just thinks of, the few tones will not have any meaning for the listener, unless he hears the whole song.

Of course, I received my carte d'identité. *I'll take care of getting my visa tomorrow. How come you think there is a danger of war breaking out? Did not the dear, sweet boy in Germany just sign an anti-Soviet pact? The Japanese situation is quite worrisome, but the Polish one, by contrast, reassuring. Here nobody thinks of anything except Royal court gossip.*

Will the King marry Mrs. Simpson? Supposedly he said, "If you do not let me do what I want, you can celebrate your Coronation without me." Furious, the Queen has moved out of Buckingham Palace.

Have you heard the newest joke about German laws?

Learn to Shit without Eating!

Beautiful!!!

Yesterday Ruth, another girl, and I really went on the town. First we saw a movie, Dodsworth, *with Walter Huston and Mary Astor, from the novel by Sinclair Lewis. One of the best films I have seen. Then we went to Dobrin's restaurant, where I flirted with Ernst Deutsch (a famous actor), who sat at the table next to ours.*

After that we went window shopping with much yakking and giggling and in the evening ate smoked salmon sandwiches and stood in line for one half hour in ice cold wind at the

Queens Hall to get tickets to an all Beethoven concert. The pianist, of course unknown to you, was Moisewich with the BBC Orchestra, and George Szell conducted. Incredibly beautiful! The Coriolanus Overture, the Mozart Coronation piano concerto and the Eroica.

During intermission, past the goatee and the tie of the man in the seat in front of me, I spied Stefan Zweig way far away in one of the front rows. So, at the end of the concert, I sought him out at the exit and he was terribly nice and inquired about you with great interest. He sort of intimated that he might invite me. He asked whether Lotte Altmann had my address.

The art book you sent me is very beautiful. I was really touched that you thought of it. You're a nice man!

I really know how to get around in this town quite well now. Tomorrow I will go to the Victoria and Albert Museum. Mutti will probably have read my account of the British Museum to you. By the way, what are you going to give her for Christmas? Do you have any idea? You better think of something!

Courageously and relatively un-pimpled, I gave Brahm a call. He is in the USA and they do not know when and if he'll return. Shit! I am working furiously on my short story. Perhaps I'll show it to Stefan Zweig one day. I am so sorry that Christel is not here. I had so much hoped to get together with her again.

I did not get to go to the Book Fair. When Ruth does not feel like going somewhere she just won't go. To go out alone at night is scary. The environment here in the outskirts is lonely and dark. I will try to get a catalog for you, though.

I will not speak a perfect English yet when I come home at Christmas, the result of living at Ruth's house and the lack of getting around on my own more. But at least I learned grammar and got used to the rhythm and sound of the language. Reading goes quite well. Right now I am reading Huxley.

The book about London by Cohen-Portheim is excellent. I

am following it and visit some of the different parts of town that he talks about, in turn. On one of these discovery trips, I committed the untimely sin of stopping in at a fantastic antique store on Great Russell Street, getting a catalog, and looking at books about theater for you. I committed the further crime of giving them your address, and you will also get other catalogs from them. Be a man and resist the temptations. I apologize to your wife and declare myself guilty of seduction.

Regretfully, I shall close now and will go to take care of a bodily need. If you do not acknowledge the fact that I do employ the most refined expressions that should emanate from the mouth of a young lady, let me tell you that formally the word would have been shit. Recognize the improvement! In this sense, after ten minutes and with great relief, a big hug and a kiss.

Your very unrefined Daughter

P.S. Why do I not hear anything from Oma Marta? Is she well? Dr. Plesch said she will live to a hundred.

Mutti shall read the "Tales of Jacob" by Thomas Mann. Incredibly interesting and beautifully written. Takes great concentration!

Quite a fog is coming up here now, partly egg yellow and then again black and it stinks.

December 8, 1936

My dearest Mutti and Pappi,

It is early in the morning, and I am sitting in bed. Oh, how comfortable I am! Sorry I had to make you wait so long for a letter this time. I do not feel guilty though, because it is not my fault.

Yesterday afternoon I moved to town. The tension in Ruth's house grew and grew between the enemy family members from day to day, and it became, to put it mildly, unbearable. To live through breakfast and dinnertime became an unpleasant chore because the men were present.

Like a few times before already, I mentioned to them that I felt I was in the way at this point and should move out. The reaction I got again from both women was absolute horror. How could I leave them alone just now and how shameful it would be to have a guest ostensibly move out before the allotted time, etc. Ruth almost cried and said her Mother would be terribly hurt if I moved out. Well, in addition to all of their upset, I certainly did not want to hurt their feelings. So I stayed on, completely ignored by the two men, an unwilling witness to their nasty encounters.

Finally it came to an incredible explosion on Thursday. The father had intercepted a letter to Ruth by a man from Milan whom she had known when she lived there. It was really not a love letter, just a nice greeting. Dear Daddy went completely off his rocker. I really believe he is insane. He called Ruth a whore, the mother a procuress and thief and claimed that both of them steal his money and deceive him. The man in Milan is a pimp and makes money from Ruth. Unbelievable, isn't it? There is no other explanation than insanity.

Ruth and her mother have only one thought: divorce or separation, as soon as possible. The father says, "All right, but you won't get a penny." Neither woman has much money. I am so sorry for both of them! They are really good and dear people who are completely blameless. Mutti should write a very nice letter to Rose immediately and invite Ruth to stay with us as long as she wants. Send it to my address though: 36 Cambridge Terrace, Cumberland House, London, W 2. Could you also invite the mother? She would not be a bother to Pappi. All she needs is peace and quiet and somebody who is nice to her. She can sleep in the small room and Ruth with me. You can really do some good here!

The day before yesterday all three of us went room hunting for me. Rose climbed all the staircases and researched every rooming house we saw. She asked about the toilets, the food, and if "Nice People" lived there. She suspected a bordello madam or procuress in every good and solid bed and breakfast owner. It was terribly funny!

Finally we found a really nice room in decent surroundings with breakfast and daily bath, running warm and cold water, relative quiet, good light, clean and decent furnishings with a couch and pull-out table for 25 shillings per week. The mostly pink décor and flowery wallpaper I could easily do without, but never mind! I am satisfied. For breakfast I get so much food that I have no appetite at noon. On top of the gas heater is a little space where I can set a small pot and actually cook something. I went to Woolworth and bought some dishes. I am now a housewife! It is a lot of fun!

Now I have to quit. I have a date with Ruth and have to leave. In my next letter I will tell you about what happened the other day: the burning of the Crystal Palace. It was sensational!

When will Ralph arrive home? I want to get there at the same time, in any case not later. Is there anything I can bring you from here? Think about it. Now I have to run. Poor Ruth is probably standing in the rain.

Much love,
Fe

P.S. My God, I almost forgot: Money! After paying rent and tip for Kremnitzer's maid, I have one pound and fifteen left.

Having finished this letter, I quickly sealed it, stuffed it in my pocket and ran to meet Ruth at Tottenham Court Road. It did not just rain, it poured. Never mind.

We went to see the Gulbenkian exhibit at the British Museum. A small glass case with just a few exceptional pieces fascinated me.

I wrote in my diary:

There was an enchanting figure of a walking woman. Shoulders, arms, hands holding the gathered robe. There was a mask of pure gold. A cat with her young, made of green stone. An incredibly energetic head of a man. A fantastic carved spoon. On the first floor were wonderful Indian miniatures and paintings. Watercolors by Turner, my very special delight.

Next came the National Portrait Gallery, but by then we were rather tired. Tea at Lyons revived us and the rain let up a bit. We strolled along the Strand, Kings College, and the embankment of the Thames. We reached the Waterloo Bridge. It started to rain again. It got stormy and very dark. The water looked wonderful with its reflected lights and flickering ship lanterns. Cranes loomed upward, like they were something solid to hold onto amidst the splashing and blowing. We headed for home and stopped at a little market on the way.

Ruth carefully balanced an umbrella over our heads, holding onto it with both her hands to keep it from blowing away. With wet and freezing fingers, I clutched a paper bag of groceries to my chest, trying to keep it from dissolving completely in the downpour.

"Awful wet today, young ladies," my landlady called to us from below. The door to her apartment was always kept open. We had just reached the first landing of the stairs to my third floor room, dragging ourselves up, dripping wet and tired, in no mood for conversation. But tradition had to be upheld.

"Yes, indeed, Mrs. Swopes." We bent over the banister, nodding down to her. "Yes indeed, mighty stormy too."

"Haven't had it that bad for some time, don't you know?"

"Is that so, Mrs. Swopes." We hoped we sounded sufficiently concerned and interested.

"Last year at this time it was even worse. Blew some people over in the streets." We saw the sincere frown of concern on her pudgy face, even from our perch above and she nodded her head several times emphatically.

"You don't say," we replied dutifully.

The greeting ceremony completed to her satisfaction, Mrs. Swopes retreated. We struggled further upwards, past a couple of gentlemen in bathrobes, towels over their arms, hairy legs, with very disgruntled faces, waiting on the second floor to avail themselves of the communal bathroom. Whoever was inside seemed to take their time.

On the landing in front of my door we stripped off our soggy shoes and shook the water from coats and umbrella. The room was cold, but the coins dropped into the slot of the little stove popped the gas to life. Soon we almost purred with satisfaction, having donned dry socks and warmed our outstretched legs in front of the heater, whose iron shelf became hot enough to heat a can of soup.

Peeling the wet paper sack off the groceries, we surveyed our purchases: bread, cheese, a can of tuna, a couple of doughnuts, cigarettes and a bottle of cheap red wine. Dinner was assured and the wobbly table set with paper plates and cups.

Rain pelted against the window glass.

"Remember when we were in Venice?" I said, "Piazza San Marco, Espresso, Spumoni." I bit into my doughnut.

"Sitting there in the sun. All those handsome men passing by our table." Ruth sighed.

"What's that?" She picked up a magazine that lay on my bed.

"A brand new American one called *Life*," I said.

We discussed movies we had seen, *You Can't Take It With You* and Chaplin's *Modern Times*. The Lindberg baby's murder was news, the occupation of the Rhineland, and our beloved Italy forming an alliance with Hitler. A book that had just come out and stood on my shelf was *Gone with the Wind* by Margaret Mitchell. There was much to talk about.

I wrote to my brother:

December 10, 1936

Dear Ralph,

Thanks for the letter that Ruth brought me yesterday. I don't live there anymore. Since a few days I have had my own place in town. In the last weeks it came to such horrible scenes and fights between her parents that I'd had enough, despite Rose's and Ruth's entreaties and tears. After all, I am here to enjoy myself and finally decided that you can not stand by and console others endlessly and let an avalanche of nastiness invade your every day from morning to night, especially since I heard the father scream that guests of his wife should have the sense to leave HIS house.

At least that convinced Ruth and her Mother better than I could to let me go. I am awfully sorry for Ruth; she is so sweet and decent! We see each other every day, and I do my utmost to help her, but I am so happy to be by myself, at least every morning and most of the afternoon.

I had not been aware of the Egyptian exhibit, in spite of the fact that I have a prospectus of all the museum exhibits and lectures in town. Tomorrow morning I will go to investigate it. I wish you could join me. Every time I am at the British Museum I think about how much more I would enjoy it if you were with me. The Egyptian Galleries are incredible. I am sorry that I do

not know more about the history and art of that country. I can
certainly get enthused about a fine little head and a huge statue
can be most impressive. I can admire artifacts and ornaments. I
can get caught up in the total atmosphere that has something
mysterious and fairy-tale-like for me, but then again I stand
before some pieces that do not say anything to me, neither
artistically nor emotionally. I tell myself that they must have a
deeper meaning that makes them interesting if one knows their
history. You have an uneducated sister!

Incredibly beautiful are the sculptures and friezes of the
Athenian Parthenon, the Elgin Marbles, also the statues of a
Temple of Xantos in Lykia. Absolute perfection! It is a joyous,
loving, sunny art, perhaps THE real art, the most true to nature,
and still I am more drawn to the thoughtful, weightier, deeper
art of Michelangelo. The Greek creations are passionless gods
that hover, rest or gesture gracefully. They have wonderful bodies
wrought in the smallest details with great love, caressing each
line and form. It is the art of idealized, idolized Eros.

In contrast, a Michelangelo has to pull every one of his
creations out of his innermost soul, hot and passionately fighting
for their realization, elemental and inexorable. There is nothing
light or easy, there are no festive sun gods who are never attacked
and do not have to fight, who just exist like flowers or butterflies,
their beauty enough reason for them to exist. Michelangelo's
work talks of human beings that suffer, fight, love and are capable
of ecstasy, and under their perfect limbs and muscles pulses blood
and they live. You expect them to move any minute.

You ask if there is anything sensational in my life. I cannot
complain about the lack of it. Without a doubt, the Crystal Palace
fire was enough sensation to last me for a long time. You write
that it must have been in my neighborhood, which is putting it
mildly. It was practically across the street. Ralph, that was a
night that I will never forget!

It was shortly after dinner at about eight thirty. I went up to
my room to get something and just happened to look out of the

window. The house next door was bathed in red light and the neighbors were all standing on the roof, obviously excited. I dashed across the corridor to another window and just could not believe my eyes! How slowly a human brain can work sometimes!

I saw a huge mass of flames that grew from second to second, but it took me at least ten or more seconds until I realized what was happening. It was just too unbelievably horrible. I alarmed the still-relatively-peaceful family, who had heavy curtains drawn downstairs. We stood at the windows that were dripping from the heat until three o'clock at night, shaking and trembling, especially Ruth and I. It crashed and howled, flamed and raged. It was horrible! Full of fear, we tried to watch the wind. Thank God it seemed to blow the other way, otherwise we could have had smoke, sparks, embers, and even flying metal and glass shards coming down over our roof. To greatly add to our horror, we remembered that a big circus was scheduled to open at the Palace the next day. Was it already in the building? What about the animals? A ghastly thought!

Our suburban street, usually so quiet, rivaled the crowded Piccadilly Circus. It became so unbelievably congested that the fire trucks could not get through until hundreds of policemen arrived brandishing billy clubs and clearing the way. I experienced for the first time how such a mass of humanity can turn into a veritable mob, horrifying, churning like an element, even worse than that, unpredictable and senseless like an enraged animal. They cursed and spat at the police and kept pushing forward toward the burning building until the smoke and heat stopped them. The two huge towers of the Palace were very much in danger. If just one of them had fallen, hundreds of these human animals could have died.

When they decided that there was no more danger to our house, Ruth's family went to bed, unmoved and unimpressed. Such dull people! Ruth and I stayed at the window for hours, still shaking and nestling close together like a couple of scared chickens. We saw the middle of the building collapse. More and more flames blazed up to the smoky, blood-red sky and death-defying planes buzzed through the fumes and shooting pillars of fire. They looked like ghostly birds. And the fire grew and grew, surging, devouring, inexorable. It was a most frightful and terrifying night! Now I really know what fear is and the feeling of being helplessly delivered to a force of Nature. One is so small, so incredibly small! I kept thinking, "Thank God Mutti is not here!" She would have had a heart attack. In retrospect I am glad I was able to have this experience. It was overwhelming!

Later on, toward morning, the surging firestorm subsided. Remaining tongues of fire rearing up here and there licked voraciously up the iron framework that stood glowing red and sizzling white against the sky. Finally, exhausted, we stumbled to bed, but did not sleep very much.

Around noon, we went out and joined all of London that had turned the catastrophe into a giant fair in the meantime. From the East End to Whitechapel, from Soho and the inner city to Mayfair, all of London was represented. There were ordinary folk, mamas, papas, and children. There were musicians, lemonade vendors, street performers, military men, and sailors. Shoulder to shoulder, they pushed toward the smoldering ruins, dockworkers and gentlemen in top hats together, open-mouthed and feverishly excited. I kept my purse tightly clutched to my chest, but my eyes swiveling all over the place.

What a display and variety of humanity there was! One could laugh, one could cry, could be scared or disgusted, but could also feel compassion and kinship.

I give you a bunch of kisses and get up. So now you know that I am still in bed. I am terribly weak and tired here when I have my period. Maybe it is the fog or the dampness and the ice-cold climate that I am not used to. I am very lonely for you!

Love you,
Fe

Homesickness took an ever-stronger hold.

December 12, 1936

Dear sweet Mutti,

Just now the maid woke me to give me your letter. Great pleasure. A letter feels often like part of the writer's presence, don't you think? Let me tell you, a big city is something very exciting, independence is great, the museums are wonderful, but without you? That is somehow less grand. After all, I am so used to enjoying everything together with you, and now I come out of a picture gallery and no awful Mutti is there to tell her about what I saw. Strange! I miss you both very much, and you can't imagine how much I am looking forward to seeing you soon. Thanks for the money! Fifteen Pounds is much too much. I want to leave here on the twenty-second so that I can be home on the twenty-third, unless Ralph comes earlier, then I want to be there at the same time.

Ruth will not be able to come because she can't leave her mother alone. That woman is capable of committing the worst stupidities about her divorce proceedings and keeps hovering around thoughts of suicide. Ruth is terribly worried about her and looks awful.

I bought a book for Ralph that had a tremendous success here, a novel about Tibet. The further delay of his examination date is catastrophic. He must be a nervous wreck. These Nazi bastards are masters in torturing people.

It is wonderful that you agree to let me come back here again, but would it not cost too much? We can still think all of this over.

Of my experiences of the last days I can tell you more when I see you soon. Just very short: on November 30, the great Crystal Palace burned down, as you probably heard, and it stood almost across the street from us. Imagine, it was a whole complex of

*buildings, tightly set against each other, larger than the whole
Place Massena in Nice. It had cupolas and towers, mostly made
of glass. It felt like the world was coming to an end. Absolutely
horrible! I was grateful that you were not here.*

*Now about OUR KING. What do you think about that boy?
Ruth and I are delighted. He has our absolute sympathy. Rumor
has it here that Mrs. Simpson is expecting a baby. Yesterday
one saw nothing but sad faces following the abdication. The whole
country seems to have loved him and would have accepted her
as their queen, they say. Until yesterday, masses of people stood
in front of Buckingham Palace and shouted: "We want Eddy
and his missus," and, "We want the King and his wife." The
new King is very unpopular. Who knows what went on behind
the scenes?*

*Again, I went to a wonderful concert: Alexander Brailowsky,
piano. A fantastic guy! Very young, great looking and played
better than Rubinstein, as good as Rachmaninov. It was a
tremendous success. He had to play encore after encore, mainly
Chopin. Wonderful was the* Carnival *by Schumann, then came
twelve* Etudes *by Chopin, then the* Hungarian Rhapsody *by
Liszt, then Ravel, and Tchaikovsky.*

*The day before yesterday I went to the Wallace Collection.
Very worthwhile.*

*Now that I do not live with Kremnitzers anymore, I actually
get to see quite a bit more of London. I am not obliged to go
along to boring relatives and can go where and when I want.
Thank God! The short time until Christmas I will use to the
limit. Today I shall visit Soho and then go to the British Museum
to see a special Egyptian Exhibit.*

*Now I'll get up, since I am sitting in bed to save on feeding
my hungry little gas heater. Be assured, the gas shuts itself off
automatically, and it is out of the question that it could leak.
Besides, I always have the window open at night. If you want to
give me something for Christmas, let Ralph bring me some good
books from Germany. Otherwise I have no wishes. Perhaps for*

my birthday in April I would very much like to get a Photo Enlarger, if possible used, then I will not be dependent on the generosity of Edith Zistig and can be independent. That will be so much more fun and maybe I can even make some money with it. A kiss for Pappi. Next I will go to the theater.

I miss you all very much!
Fe

December 15, 1936

Dear Mutti

I am writing on my knees in great haste. If you have not bought my ticket yet, please do it immediately so that I can depart from here on Monday the twenty first, in order to be with you on the twenty forth without fail. It happened that it was so stormy yesterday that all ships were canceled. That means that I could get stranded in Folkeston. God, am I scared of the crossing! The weather here is awful. I have a ghastly cold. My nose runs and drizzles without stopping. Now it is high time that I get home. Yesterday was such a storm that I was not able to stand still in the street. The wind pushed me forward against my will. When I get home, I will have to thaw out first. Fog, rain, storm, and cold do not belong to my preferred environment. Do you have sunshine? Ah! I can't wait to see you all. Right now, I am quite lonely. People are preparing to go away for winter sport vacations and have no time for visits. When I am together with Ruth these days, the mother is also there inevitably, and they talk about nothing else except their troubles. It really gets on my nerves at this point. At least Ruth will visit us at the beginning of January. Then we will be able to distract her.

Now I give you a big kiss. Oh no, I won't! You'll get my cold. Seriously, it is just an ordinary cold, no fever, guaranteed.

It just makes me stupid. I will recuperate with you. Vacation trip to Nice. I expect a festive welcome with Mimosa blossoms strewn under my feet!

Strangely enough my skin is in fairly good condition. Could be because I ate more fruit or that the dampness here did it. Think of my ticket! Love to you and Pappi.

I can't wait to kiss you! I can't wait for Christmas! I can't wait to see Ralph!

All my love,
Fe

CHAPTER NINE

A Significant Year Begins

When I arrived home, we had received a letter from Ralph.

December 10, 1936

Dear Family,

From day to day I am hoping to be able to tell you that I have a date for the beginning of the examination. Unfortunately, they gave me new subjects to include that I had not counted on that give me extra work and trouble. Other courses are also still going on concurrently and have to be studied for. The uncertainty again puts me in a miserable mood and makes me terribly nervous. The conditions here otherwise contribute to it! A rumor goes around about American citizens having to face all kinds of obstacles now. If only they would give me a beginning date! If I could only get out of here already!

The exact arrival day for Christmas I cannot give you yet, but the earliest will be the twenty-second. I will stay until New Year for sure.

I had a nice letter from Eugenia (Our great-uncle's wife in America). On the same day came an answer from Rob Benson. He does not mention anything about exams, just assures me that he can be of help. One year of internship will be required. The future looks a little brighter.

> *Much love,*
> *Ralph*

He arrived in the morning on the twenty fourth of December, looking pale and harassed, but in the evening, when we sat down for dinner and the candles on the Christmas tree spread warmth and reassurance around us we all relaxed. We were not religious. The tree for us meant family, being together, friendship, and loving each other. We remembered past times and shared hopes for the future. Mother still used real candles. She would not have it otherwise. Only later in the United States she had to give in and use electric ones, for her an act of capitulation.

My father was in a great mood. He was always the optimist. "You'll see," he said, "We'll be fine in the States, mark my words!"

"Ein Pappi hat immer Recht!" (A daddy is always right), I said.

Everybody laughed, because this sentence we had heard from him throughout our childhood and had invariably made us rebel, especially so in adolescence. Here he sat, my Determined-to-Make-the-Best-of-it-Pappi, having eaten his favorite holiday meal, half a broiled lobster and a glass of champagne, gently puffing on his inevitable cigar, content to be surrounded by his family and pushing his worries into the background, a task at which he was an expert.

I too felt content. When Ralph was with us my world was complete. When he left he always took a part of it away with him.

"You must eat well and rest during the few days that you are here," my mother said.

But Ralph could not rest. He wanted to go out, to see people, to drive into the country, go to the beach, enjoy his freedom. He was like one on short release from jail, too tense to sleep, eager to move about, to breathe fresh air.

These first ten days of nineteen thirty seven, spent in constant activity, whether walking on the promenade at the beach, swimming in the ocean since it was quite warm, or climbing the rocky steep streets with him in mountain villages, like Eze and St. Paul, were heaven for me.

We had coffee at the Masséna with some of the older generation who interested us. We teamed up with Hans, Johnny Asch, (Sholom's son), Nadia, and sometimes with one or another of the girls we met at the beach, and went out on the town at night. Ralph liked Nadia, but her cool elegance did not capture his heart, in spite of Mother's gentle prodding behind the scenes.

Dark and grimy stairs led down to the Caveau, the Cave, literally a cellar that was a small nightclub, lit by candles only. It was a dark and quite romantic affair. We sat, drank, listened to music, talked about ourselves, the problems of the world, and again about ourselves and each other.

At the Boîte à Vitesse, another of our haunts, we elbowed our way through crowds and smoke to one of the tiny tables to listen to the current sensation from Paris, La Môme Piaf, a singer who, according to my diary, "*Was a short little whore, a poor child of the common people, with a large, red, damp mouth and black greasy hair and bangs.*" Her songs were stridently aggressive, and then again so deeply emotional and sad that I was filled with compassion.

The little platform stage was lit. The audience sat in almost complete darkness, mesmerized, and except for the occasional clinking of a glass against a carafe or marble tabletop, in total silence. I looked at my companions around the table, trying to read their faces.

Only Johnny Asch's face could I make out next to mine. I could just see a cut on his cheek where the razor had slipped again. He had confided in us once that he always covered the top of his bathroom mirror with a towel so he could only see his lower face while shaving.

"I can't look at myself. I am just too awfully ugly," he had said. Poor Johnny, I thought, and then Piaf pulled me back into her realm.

One day we visited the Asch family way high up in the hills, surrounded by wide stretches of fields and olive groves. Two one-story farmhouses that stood next to each other had been connected by an enclosed walkway, fashioning them into one spacious home. It was surrounded by a vegetable garden and fruit trees. Here we saw Johnny in his element. In sleeveless shirt and muddy pants he stood in the field, stopped his digging, grinned at us, and waved his cap in greeting when we approached. He could have been a farmer on an Israeli kibbutz, very tall, sunburned, and rugged. What he saw when he looked in the mirror was a bony face with a large nose, small eyes, a receding forehead, and big ears. The face we saw was strong, virile, and kind.

When I met the offspring of famous or very accomplished parents they often felt lacking in regard to their own abilities, and Johnny was one of those. I believe, though, that later on he made quite a name for himself in the field of agriculture and research.

I do not think that cocky Hans suffered from that same syndrome, unless one assumed that his constant search to find an anchor for his eager, restless mind in some meaningful cause or occupation had something to do with it. I know, though, that he eventually became a successful architect.

His parents, the Schickeles, lived across the road from the Asch domain. With coffee cups, cigarettes, and animated talk, surrounded by bougainvillea-covered walls on one side and the view of cypress and olive trees over grape orchards and fields down to the ocean, we sat in their garden for a long afternoon. The January sun was warming us. We talked of books, of Eugene O'Neil getting the Nobel Prize, of Dylan Thomas's poems. We shook our heads hearing about the exhibit of so-called "Degenerate Art" in Berlin, the civil war in Spain, and the Alliance of Hitler and Mussolini. Chaplin's film "Modern Times" was discussed, as was the devaluation of the franc.

There was beauty around us and worry and uncertainty in our minds, as in the rest of the world. Even from the United States came reports about strikes and unrest. "They'll stop that when we get there," my brother said, and we laughed.

On the eleventh of January, Ralph went back to Berlin for the last time, as we hoped. We received this letter from him:

January 20, 1937

Dear Ones,

You have not heard from me for so long because I did not feel very well. It must have been some sort of flu. I felt constantly weak and tired. I had been in Nice hundreds of years ago. I think it must have been somewhere on the moon. It is so difficult to work here. Most of my energies dissolve when I labor to finish my assignments. It is so very hard!

Nevertheless I am quite happy within myself. I know again who I am and where I belong, but not here, but with you, in Nice!

I sometimes feel like I am suffocating. Otherwise I am not really "crazy." On the first day of my return from Nice I told Mia not to count on marriage. She decided to go to South America. She is being extremely decent and sensible. She does not make things difficult for me.

By the way, Collin's opinion is that the stagnation I experienced towards fulfilling my work responsibilities was due

*to a very hard knock to my psyche that I carried around in my
subconscious ever since Lottel first betrayed me years ago. He
may be right. I really have never been able to forget it. Nadia
said I have a guardian angel. I only hope he will get me out of
here also.*

*I am so nervous that I could burst! Forgive my complaining,
but I have really nothing else to tell you. I feel most happy when
I can crawl into my bed. At least Nice is not so far away that I
cannot remember how young and active I could possibly be.*

A million kisses with awful homesickness!
Ralph

Two more letters we received from him:

February 17, 1937

My Dear Ones,

*My last letter was written when I had a temperature and a
depression engendered by flu. Therefore do not take it too
seriously! I did not want to write to you, because it was so hard
to get accustomed to being here again. It is worse than ever.*

*You probably read about our weather here. For years there
has not been so much snow. I am so cold and try to eat a lot and
drink grog.*

*I had to run around a lot to get my passport renewed. To
sum it all up: the consulate gave me only six months, until August
the second to go to the States. I just have to be ready by then
and will be!!!*

*I heard you too had storm and flooding. How I wish I could
see the waves splash over the Promenade des Anglais! There is
not much to tell about me otherwise. Saw a film by Rene Clair:*
The Ghost Goes West. *That is a film for Mutti. I'd like to hear
her famous laughter.*

Mia writes often. She was the first of the new immigrants in Australia to get a job. She makes hats. Climate is agreeable, surroundings wonderful. But she says none of her compatriots are happy. People's letters home to parents are mostly lies to reassure them. She is satisfied for herself though.

I have not much time for my English lessons, but read English books before going to sleep. Am pleased to make progress.

I am so anxious to get out of this milieu; it just gets me down. For God's sake, Mutti, stay away, don't come!

I don't want to write any more,
Ralph

February 23, 1937

Dear Parents,

I am so glad that the passport business is in order. Pappi admired my nerve in this affair over the phone. If I gave way to nerves in THIS kind of business . . .

What do you mean, Mutti, that I should not "take things too seriously?" What then should one take seriously? I do not attach myself to anyone so strongly anymore that I fall apart when they are not with me. I had to learn that with enough pain. That has nothing to do with Taking Things Seriously. My affair with Mia only served to fill a void, since I did not expect anything else from life anymore. Nadia showed me that I still had quite a bit to discover and experience. Therefore I did not feel dependent on her. Rather to the contrary, she gave me freedom.

In this context, free of fever and very pleased, I am looking forward to my impending degree.

Your,
Ralph

Towards the middle of January, my friend Ruth came from London and stayed with us for several weeks, and when she left I wrote in my diary:

We took Ruth to the train. It was probably the last time that we will be together for an extended visit. We will not see each other for more than a few days, I guess, from now on. When we go to America in the fall, it will probably mean loosing all of our friends forever! That is so sad!

This evening I finished my short story "The Old One." I am very happy. The first time that I completed something!

"I have made a decision," Mother announced to Pappi and me one day soon afterwards. "We cannot get the rest of our money out of Germany. We are only allowed to spend it in that country. On board a German ship we are on their home ground, aren't we? So, we will go on a long cruise around the Mediterranean Sea and at least enjoy our money by seeing some of the world instead of giving it to the Nazis. I have reserved our passage, and we'll leave on the fifth of March. Alright, George?"

I knew that father must have known about some of that plan, but maybe not of its completion. He looked at me, as he had in times past, shook his head, and chuckled a little. "YOUR MOTHER!" he said, emphasizing each word.

I was excited, but then it hit me. "We'll travel with all those Germans." I shrank from that idea.

"There might also be some nice people, you never know. Anyway, we can stick together and enjoy many wonderful sights and adventures that we would never have had the chance to experience otherwise." Mother's argument was convincing.

CHAPTER TEN

The Big Cruise

In the afternoon of March 5, 1937, Franz drove Pappi with our baggage to the harbor of Nice, to Villefranche. Later he came back and picked Mutti and me up. It was hard to say goodbye to little Bella. It was the first time that she could not travel with us. She sat without making a sound, her eyes big and scared, her tail between her legs. When I returned to the house once more to get some forgotten keys she still sat in the same position in the dusky hall on the cold stone floor.

It started to get dark, and it was cold on the drive over the winding road, the Corniche, along the hills above the ocean.

"You have never been on a sea voyage." My mother decided to prepare me for the big trip before us. "I tell you, when a storm hits and the waves spill over the deck and you get rocked and tossed about, you can get so sick you'd wish you could die."

She continued to regale me with great stories of storms, seasickness, throwing up and the special consequences thereof. At other times I would have huddled quietly, subdued in my corner, but now I sat at the edge of my seat, glued to the window, letting all of those grisly descriptions float by without responding, searching eagerly for a sign of a ship on the black ocean.

And there, after another bend in the road around an outcropping of rocks, there it was, anchored quite a way off shore, gleaming and blinking with thousands of lights, like a Christmas tree, warm and inviting.

For the next few weeks I kept my diary close at hand.

March 5, 1937

"It is as if electric currents are running all through my body, pushing me to strain with hungry readiness and great curiosity to experience the things to come. We passed a very superficial customs inspection with our trunks and then a large boat rocked us across the dark water to the brightly lit ladder rising up the ship's flank. How strange a ship smells, a sweetish mustiness. I was sorry that my cabin did not have a window.

We marveled at the many rooms of the ship: the dining room, the halls, different rooms for smoking, writing and reading, the grill, bar, and various decks. We walked around, exploring, and finally went to sleep quite exhausted from all of the frantic last minute packing and excitement.

The first night in my bunk, rocking peacefully to sleep, I thought of my children's books Bibi at Sea *and* Treasure Island. *And I am going to turn twenty soon? Oh, what a baby I am.*

March 6, 1937

In the morning we arrived in Geneva. After breakfast I left the dining room to the strains of "Deutschland, Deutschland Ueber Alles," the German National Anthem. The "Horst Wessel Lied," the Nazi's special anthem, sounds that we had not heard for quite some time and had certainly not missed, followed me down to my cabin. Its rousing strains came from the upper deck. The passengers of the cruise preceding ours where thusly celebrated and sent on their way. I retired to the reading room.

The ship was to stay anchored for the day, so Father decided to take a cab in the afternoon and we drove from Geneva over the border to Rapallo in Italy to visit Gerhardt Hauptmann, who lived there now. I was to meet the man who wrote Hannele's Himmelfahrt, the play we performed in Teufen. I knew that he was old, but I imagined him to be tall and energetic, full of poetic passion.

On this glorious sunny spring day he came towards us in the garden of his hotel. With his mane of white hair encircling his big, partially bald head, deep bags under his melancholic looking eyes and with his tall impressive stature, he was an imposing sight indeed. He was a good actor. His pose was presented so artfully that it became a natural part of his personality that said: I am famous, I am the dean of all German poets, but, as you can see, I am completely above all vanity. He could easily have been depicted as one of the regal bronze statues on top of a fountain in the middle of a marketplace in a busy eighteenth-century town. There was also an almost female softness about him, though, and sometimes a lack of concentration showed in his conversation.

He did not follow the picture I had created of him in my mind. There was no vitality, no passion. Still I admired him. I also admired his wife who, almost blind, carried herself full of energy, maybe to balance her famous husband's lack of it.

After having coffee in the garden, we all walked at the shore of Lake Geneva. It must have been a fascist holiday. It was teeming with uniformed citizens, women in festive finery, boys from Mussolini's youth groups, the Balilla, and little girls wearing funny tassel-topped caps.

There were also a lot of Germans who nudged each other and whispered when we passed by. They recognized their famous countryman and at the same time directed suspicious glances at his companions, namely us. "Don't they look like Jews?" they seemed to mutter. "Is he consorting with them?" It was uncomfortable!

How expressions on people's faces could show such vulgar, mean aggressiveness and provocative, self-aggrandizing arrogance and then, in the presence of real strength and greatness, change their demeanor to cringing submissiveness, like underlings watching their master out of the corner of their eye, hoping to discover signs of weakness and fault.

It is hard for small people to see greatness in fellow men, and when they discover only a trace of weakness in their hero, they laugh and taunt: There lies the hero, the great one. They are wrong. Only in humanity lies greatness, not in heroes.

Around six o'clock the sun started to sink and we ambled slowly back to the hotel. Hauptmann showed us the house in Rapallo where he used to live when he was a young man. It was pleasant to listen to him talk; one can't avoid thinking of the old Goethe, being so wise and mellow. Only Goethe would have been much more reserved, not so comfortable to be with.

The taxi drove us back toward Geneva to rejoin our ship. Children stood beside the road waving enormous branches of peach blossoms in the glowing light of the sinking sun. Our Italian chauffeur stopped the car and bargained for the price of two branches that he then handed to Mother and me with a very gentlemanly bow. I was impressed and pleased. What a nice beginning for the trip!

March 7, 1937

This morning the new passengers, our travel companions, came on board. I looked forward to this event with great misgiving. I knew that people of many different nationalities would join the trip, but also that the German element would dominate. I recoiled at the thought of getting together with all those party members pouring their physically and morally

*noxious vapors around the landscape. Thank God, only parts of
my fears were justified.*

Mother and I stood on deck and surveyed the diverse
humanity that climbed or stumbled up the ship's gangplank.
We were not very charitable. We leaned close together against
the railing and exchanged our opinions and impressions about
the newcomers. Mother giggled and whispered like a teenager.
She had a great time and enjoyed it all as a lark. It was a comedy
to her and she was excited and looking forward to new sights
and experiences.

I had mixed feelings. On the one hand, I wanted to be happy
and to be able to laugh and to enjoy myself; on the other hand, I
tried to fight anger and hate toward these people who, knowingly
and on purpose, or through lack of concern or stupidity, spread
so much misery and suffering around them. A feeling of terrible
disgust threatened to overcome me when I looked at some of
these approaching faces that shone so clearly with the vulgarity
and small mindedness that some Germans are capable of, but I
fought against giving in to it. So I too laughed and ridiculed. It
became a survival maneuver. There were also friendly and decent-
looking people among the ascending crowd, of course.

I nudged Mother, "Look, those are nice looking, aren't they?"
But how did we know what their ideology was, what was in
their minds? Would they turn their backs on us?

Mother had a marvelous time and engaged in her own private
studies of physiognomy and psychology. Like a bird of prey she
swooped down on her victims with an eagle eye. She pointed
out to me how different people behaved and carried themselves
when they came through the gates with their newly stamped
passports and approached the narrow ship's ramp, passing two
tall, good-looking Italian officers and started their climb upwards.
Some were obviously ill at ease and clumsy and others approached
the task with a great show of assurance and alacrity.

There was, for example, Aunt Frieda, as we christened her,
Aunt Frieda from Saxony. Her name was probably Margarete

or Elsa, but we decided that Frieda was the only fitting name for her. Augusta or Eulalia would have worked too, but no, we insisted on Frieda.

Just watch, I said, she comes from Koenigsberg, East Prussia. Hmm, said Mother, I bet on Saxony. Look at the red bangs and the snub nose and the clumsy boots with the tassels on them. This can only be Saxony.

We could not agree.

Aunt Frieda approached. Firmly planting her boots on the shaky ramp, she clawed her way up the rope, pulling her considerable load of fat, plaids, umbrellas, walking sticks, and various satchels towards us.

"Gustaf, did you see the baggage?" she screamed back over her shoulder to a sweating bald head climbing up behind her. It was pure Saxonian dialect. Mother beamed in triumph.

Then there was a little old maiden lady. Of course, we had no idea about her marital status, but just by looking at her, we agreed that "maiden-lady" was appropriate. At home she would have her coffee-klatsch sisters and she would also belong to the Ladies Society Against—whatever. We could not quite decide what she would be against, but for sure against something! Her thoughtful Papa, who had been a minor official in a small town, had thought to buy a solid life insurance for his only daughter before he went to heaven. So now she receives a monthly pension and feels secure. The good departed Papa! Twenty years ago he had ruined the marriage that was offered to his already-not-so-young daughter. But she had forgotten about that a long time ago.

Now then, slowly, carefully, step by worried step she inched her way up the plank. Her long, thin arms were spread out like the wings of a bird about ready to fly. They were held extended to each side, trying to achieve balance instead of allowing her hands in their immaculate white gloves to get dirty by holding onto the ropes. Fortunately her hat, which had slipped sideways in all of the excitement, was caught by the little knob of hair twisted up on the back of her head and was thus kept from falling. Momentarily she stopped about midway on her climb and stared down at the dirty harbor water below, probably imagining, with a delicious shudder, how it would feel if she slipped and disappeared into its depths.

"Go on!" someone yelled behind her.

"I bet," Mother whispered, "This one will ask a million questions and will never listen to the answers."

As soon as the subject of our speculations set foot on deck, she rushed up to one of the many busy stewards, releasing an avalanche of questions on his patiently inclined head. Where was the luggage, she wanted to know, how could she reserve a deckchair, at what time is dinner served, will there be a storm tonight, will the ship leave on time, and how will she get to her cabin?

The man answered calmly and politely, his last words pulled along by her departing dash along the deck. But wait, she flitted back, "Where did you say the cabins are?"

Mother cried in ecstatic delight and squeezed my arm to remind me how right she had been.

Oh my, what an array of humanity was passing by. There were women right out of Wagner's Niebelungen Opera: Brunhildes and Sieglindes with big bosoms, broad shoulders and hips, but probably not with matching voices. There were girls with long blond braids and backpacks, guitars, and knee-high woolen socks. Men with beer bellies and Knickerbocker pants studied their travel guidebooks even while climbing the ramp. Secretaries and sales ladies, dressed to the hilt, displayed their newly acquired fine luggage and furs and were proudly accompanied by their bosses. Some of these males were tall, blond and swaggering with the hero's stance, the strong, straight German man with iron fists, and blazing eyes. Some, whose stature just did not fit this picture, presented themselves as dutiful and loyal to the cause. They typically wore their hair, or what was left of it, on top of their heads, always parted in the middle, while the rest of their skulls were shaved clean. I imagined that at least that way they felt themselves related to the military. But somehow everybody seemed to sport a Germanic or at least Nordic air.

But wait, what did I see there? A small, quiet man of medium height dressed well and conservatively, his black hair slightly graying, walking quietly by himself among loud and excited Germans. His intelligent face carried a very prominent nose, like an exclamation mark. Without a doubt a despised Jew. Over there, that young couple did not look one hundred percent German either.

Suddenly I started to realize what I was doing. No sooner was I on German ground, so to speak, than I succumbed to the same insanity that flourished there, that did not judge people by their character and behavior, but by the shape of their noses and their race. I felt disgusted with myself.

Looking down to the pier we now discovered, to our great pleasure, two people we had met before and to whose expected arrival we had been alerted by Gehrhardt Hauptmann. They were Erich Ebermayer and his friend Max Baedecker, called Mac for short. We saw them pass the passport inspection, their light trench coats slung over their arms. Carrying bags of books and other small luggage, they started up the ramp. The agile, long-legged young Mac was followed by the older and heavier Ebermayer. At just that moment the ship's band started up again, trumpets blazing and drums thundering. Only the Germans could produce such a ruckus and call it music. The two on the ramp almost jumped out of their skins at this sudden assault and turned to each other in desperation as well as in amusement.

Two years ago I met these two in Switzerland. One afternoon Stefan Zweig invited us all to his hotel in the village of Pontresina. Zweig had been a very famous author and playwright in Germany before the Nazis took over and he had to flee for his life. Erich Ebermayer, still a well-known writer and playwright in Germany, was not a Jew. He was, however, a passionate opponent of the Nazi regime. He was thirty-five then, blond and stocky, while his shy young friend Mac, who was very tall, could not have been more than twenty years old and was extremely good looking.

Some people, certainly not my parents, talked about these two men and their relationship to each other in disparaging, nasty ways that disgusted me and made me absolutely furious.

How quickly they all are to criticize and condemn others, these self-righteous Philistines. Every person should pursue his or her happiness, as long as it does not injure anyone else. If these two love each other, it is well and good. Whom does it hurt? I really admire them. They do not hide the nature of their relationship to please the stupidity of their critics. Is love supposed to serve population politics exclusively or the dictum of so-called morality by the clergy? Love is like art and nature; it has its own dominion, existing for its own sake.

March 8, 1937

We arrived in Naples at noon and went ashore with Ebermayer and Mac. "The Boys," as we called our friends among ourselves, went their own way on a trip to Pozzuoli, and we ambled through the town, up and down the steep, narrow streets, trailed by hordes of little boys in black frocks, emaciated dogs and a very insistent vendor of watches. The sky was bright and whenever we looked back to the bay from the height of a hilly street there loomed Mount Vesuvius, like a complacent, benevolent uncle, so calm, as if he could never have wreaked the havoc attributed to him. While Pappi inspected bookshops, I accompanied Mutti, who was interested in dresses and shoes, as usual.

Suddenly somebody called us by name in the street. It was Mrs. Winterfeld, whom we had known in Hanover. She always had a tinge of "Woman of Doubtful Repute" in times gone by, a Marlene Dietrich type, but ample-bosomed and otherwise well endowed. Now she looked so miserably run down, thin, and aged, that I felt terribly sorry for her. Later at the coffeehouse she told us how bad things were for her, how she had managed to flee Germany and was now stranded in Naples with very little money and a sick husband. Discretely, Mother slipped some cash from her purse under the table to her. When Pappi rejoined us she left us with an assurance that one day she would surely kill herself. Poor woman! Should we feel guilty about our good luck? But, oh, if one could only help!

We were back on ship for dinnertime.

March 9, 1937

In the morning we went to the museum in Naples, and I visited my special painting, the one that I had fallen in love with when we were in Naples last year, "The Drinkers," by Velasquez, a glowing, vibrant, life-embracing picture. Out of its bluish, mystical twilight hovers drunken Pan's subdued laughter. And then there was the "Transfiguration of Christ," by Bellini, which always gave me such an intense feeling of peace, beauty, and springtime. Not much time was left to really browse around. I had to hurry past the many old Italian Birth of Maria's and Lives of the various Saints with their deep, dark colors and their innocent devotion that I love so much. I could only greet them with my eyes as friends from whom I had to part again, no sooner than we had revisited. Then I rushed to the bronzes of Pompeii, the water-carrying boys and the women whose sunny lightness and beautiful dancers' movements delighted me again.

We were on our way back to the ship, crossing a street, when all of a sudden a powerful siren howled endlessly in long, regular blasts over the whole city and a sensation of horror grabbed me. I had only one thought—run, run far away, flee! And everyone around us did flee. Everyone left work, changed direction and rushed ahead, pushing and shoving with blinding urgency toward a goal that was not known to us. It was a rehearsal for war. For many minutes the siren screamed its terrifying message and whipped the people up to ever more haste. Again I experienced the trembling fear of catastrophe closing in that had engulfed me in the winter of nineteen thirty three in Hanover, when we listened to Hitler's campaign speeches on the radio and the storm troopers marched past our house at night with their burning torches.

In the afternoon the real cruise began and the ship went out to sea. Shortly afterwards a slight rocking and weaving began that grew steadily in intensity and sent me down to my cabin during the first official Captain's Dinner and spread me moaning onto my bed.

The cabin walls, originally built in a traditional vertical direction, as expected, now showed a pronounced desire to become horizontal, like the floor. On the part of the cabin floor, there seemed to be no opposition to an exchange of positions. My coat, hanging on the hook of the door, found this game very amusing and joined in happily by swinging back and forth, keeping an orderly rhythm.

Only I, as usual the outsider, stayed unamused by all of this hilarity and wished for nothing more than to die. The captain's dinner was stuck in my throat and knocking energetically at the exit door when an angel appeared, a tall, fat male angel with blooming red cheeks, wearing a white steward's jacket. A goblet of salvation he offered me, containing a dissolved tablet bearing the heavenly name of "Vasano." No "Sakuntala" could ever after equal for me the sacred name of "Vasano."

Thusly I survived the night, partly awake, partly asleep, while we passed through the Straits of Messina and the velocity of the wind reached major proportions.

March 10, 1937

I stayed in bed until the afternoon, now cared for lovingly by Frauelein Schreiber, a little, sweet, bustling stewardess.

At five I staggered up to the dining room to listen to a talk about Egypt, given by a Professor Poertner. It was amazing how courageously and openly he talked within hearing of so many Nazi ears. Off and on he elicited such spontaneous applause after touching on a sore point that it became evident that not all ears belonged to party members. A pleasant surprise.

Following a very careful, frugal supper, I went to see a movie with Ebermayer and Mac. In the news preview a ship swayed and rocked on the open sea, and I took pains to look away.

March 11, 1937

It was windy, but beautiful. In the morning we rested in our deck chairs and observed the Teutonic populace in and around the swimming pool. It splashed, screamed, yelled, and shrieked. I love real fun and rambunctious giddiness, but what emanated from these people was manufactured gaiety, loud and vulgar. It was disgusting. I busied myself with chicken broth and sandwiches, supplied by the steward at ten, and that was definitely more enjoyable. The Boys came and sat with us, and their liveliness and cheerfulness were refreshing. The ocean was green, with crowns of white foam. The seagulls had left us long ago. The wind made me tired; I just licked my salty lips once and fell asleep.

When I awoke, my eyes were met by a sorry sight. A fat, blond man with a pink, brutal face had taken hold of the deck chair right in front of me. We had christened him "Little Goering." He wore a swastika not only on his coat lapel, but also on his swimming suit. "Little Emmi," an elegantly dressed, bleached blond lolled in the chair next to him. She was probably a former sales girl, elevated to mistress. My beautiful view was ruined.

Professor Poertner gave another lecture in the afternoon, this time about Palestine. He spoke of, among other things, the close proximity of the different religions there.

He then said, "And passengers always ask me which religion is the right one? Ladies and gentlemen, this is my answer: Read

Nathan the Wise. That religion is the right one that preaches the love of your neighbor, and this the Christian, the Jewish, and the Mohammedan religions embrace equally."

Thunderous applause followed. Are we on a Nazi ship? It must be said though that the room was almost completely dark except for the lit projection screen. Nobody could see who applauded. Had it been light, not one hand would have dared to move. Poor strangled nation.

For dinner a big Bock Beer Festival was announced and Ebermayer and Mac rushed over to us in a panic. "How can we avoid this?"

Consequently we ate in the Grill Room, where it was quiet and peaceful. I still felt the rolling of the waves a little, so did not eat too much. But the food was excellent.

Later we looked down at the garland-festooned dining room from the gallery and cringed in disgust.

Bock Beer Fest. The name alone turns my stomach. There they sat with ugly paper hats on their greasy, bald heads. The women screeched, and the smell of beer and sweat drifted upward. Oh God, Oh God! They sang drinking songs and marching songs and linked arms, weaving from side to side and probably pinching each other under the table on diverse, desirable body parts. Oh gods and goddesses of Egypt, what will you say when this pack visits your holy land?

March 12, 1937

After lunch the coast of Africa appeared and the silhouettes of the first palm trees stood graceful and delicate against the pale, shimmering mist of the sky. Narrow stretches of flat land reached out for us and took us slowly into their thin arms. We leaned against the railing and looked with pleasure and suspense toward the new continent. Unfortunately I had to go down to the cabin to check on the luggage, so I did not see the minarets and harbor cranes of Alexandria first appear from the blue haze of the flat coast. When I was finally able to resurface, our ship had just been pulled close to the pier by a group of small boats, and it took a long time until we maneuvered into position.

From the top of the deck I gazed down on the first people of Africa that the harbor allowed me to see. In the shadows of great iron stanchions and cranes they sat, huddling in small groups together on the ground, silent or chattering, in their red fezzes or snow-white turbans and long, flowing robes. Next to us an English ship was docked that was full of soldiers having noisy fun inciting three little brown boys to perform incredible acrobatic feats on the pavement of the pier. They jumped into the air like fish before the rain, to catch the coins that showered down on them from above. Their handsome young faces under great masses of hair burnt with eagerness. From time to time their drooping, ragged pants had to be pulled firmly up with both hands to prevent them from slipping down altogether.

Otherwise it was quiet on this quay. With barely concealed curiosity, a few gawkers leaned on the gate at the exit and studied our pale faces staring down at them from above.

Finally, after what seemed like a very long and tantalizing time, the voice of the head steward was heard from every loudspeaker on every deck and in all the rooms below, calling on us to disembark. One more time we dashed down to our cabins, hung our cameras around our necks, jackets and coats over our arms, then climbed down the ship's ladder, one after the other. On firm ground for the first time following three days on the rolling ocean. Firm ground? A ground that still swayed slightly under my feet. My knees felt soft as I walked past a grinning gate keeper and a row of dignified Egyptian gentlemen.

Passport and baggage control over, we passed through the exit and were suddenly and unexpectedly in a large train station, overwhelmed by a mind-boggling uproar, the strangeness of sounds and people. Running along the waiting train to find a compartment, we saw a long arm poking out of a window along the line, waving to us furiously. It was Mac, having reserved seats for us. Since we were five people, we had almost the whole compartment to ourselves, except in one corner. On the sixth

seat a young man sat quietly reading the novel "El Amin" by
John Knittel, as my snooping eye discovered immediately. He
did not look unpleasant.

We settled down and only then did we feel the heat and
smell the dust. Not a breath of fresh air could be felt. The shirt
stuck to my back. With both arms resting on the gritty sill of the
open window, I looked at all that spread itself before me, so
strange, so full of color. I could have stood like that for hours.
The stories of A Thousand and One Nights came incredibly
alive. The great monarch and the dancing girls were missing,
but the beggars from the town were all there.

There were magicians, vendors, and acrobats. There were
people of all gradations of color, from light yellow to brown, to
deepest, shiny onyx black. I saw friendly, benevolent faces and
conniving, villainous ones. There were faces full of hate and
belligerence, others were wheedling, friendly, naïve, or thoughtful
and wise. Dark eyes looked at us, eyes that were cloudy and sick
and eyes that sparkled with humor and life. They all begged,
cajoled, demanded. Every register was pulled out to reach their
goal, from the humble puppy-dog look to imploring hands lifted
in desperation, to looks boring into you, deadly earnest and
hypnotic.

I saw a few very dark, tall, and regal-looking men, dressed
all in black. One of them walked from window to window, his
hand extended, ceremoniously demanding, as a Sheik might,
collecting tribute money from his subjects. His face was
beautiful, aristocratic, threatening. Who would have dared
to cross him?

An enormous, muscular arm, festooned with necklaces and
bracelets shot out, waving and jingling its wares right in front
of my eyes. A broadly smiling face appeared above it, nodding
at me encouragingly, as if to say, "Come now, dear, don't be
shy. Go ahead, take something. I'll give it to you just because I
am so nice, out of pure friendliness. I can see how much you
want this lovely necklace, come on, have courage!"

My equally beaming face, the shaking of my head and the gesture of my hands pressed regretfully against my bosom, conveyed to him, "Look, I am really dying for that pretty necklace and that green wire snake that jumps out of it's box when you press the button, but, look, I just don't dare, I really do not dare, in spite of the fact that you are really so nice."

Still, for quite a while longer he tried to reassure me, to give me courage, and finally with a shake of his head, sending me a last look of compassion and pity, he decided to leave me to my fate. Once more he turned and looked over his shoulder, loving reproach in his eyes and I—I lowered my head in desolation and shame.

A magician established himself right opposite our compartment. He wore a fire-red turban and his shirt had very wide, long sleeves. Squatting on the ground, he proceeded to line little round bowls up in front of himself. Then suddenly his hands started to whirl about, and two small, golden-yellow balls flew through the air, and the bowls were turned upside down simultaneously. The little balls had disappeared.

Again the bowls were returned to their open position; one after the other was empty, only out of the last one walked the golden yellow balls—tiny baby chicks! Immediately the poor little things, already weak and stumbling, were thrown in the air, made to disappear, and then were conjured up over and over again from the man's ears, nose or mouth, incredibly quickly and skillfully. His fingers danced unceasingly. The man himself seemed to live solely through the fingers, only they were alive; only they could talk and jump while he himself sat completely expressionless and without movement, as if he were just a casual bystander. All of a sudden, though, he jumped up, grabbed his chicks and bowls in one fell swoop, and ran like a bad boy caught in some mischief.

We did not have to wait more than two seconds for an explanation of this strange behavior. The other artists also— and they were all artists in magic, acrobatics, begging, or

*peddling—dashed suddenly away from the windows, and several
Arab policemen in khaki uniforms and fezzes on their shaved
heads came dashing onto the scene, lashing out at the crowd
with whips and long sticks, yelling, "Ulla, Ulla!"*

*They could have tried to disperse an army of ants with as
much success. In front of and behind them the swarm pressed
back against the train to work the white strangers. With nimble
jumps and turns they dodged the slashing sticks and whizzing
whips, ran a few paces ahead, and circled quickly back to return
to their working stations. "Bakshish! Bakshish!" Never ending:
"Bakshish! Bakshish! Lidy, Lidy, sank you, yes, yes!"*

*The train started to move, gained a little more speed, and
finally our tormentors were shaken off windows and doorsteps.
With a sigh that was part relief, part satisfaction, I sank back
into my seat, only to jump up again after a few minutes to join
the others at the windows.*

*Now the landscape of Egypt greeted us for the first time.
Here was the ancient ground of one of the first human cultures,
the home of ingenious discoverers and creators, the land of
Akhenaten and Nefertiti, his queen. I felt as if I were dreaming.
I leaned out of the window as far as I could, and everything that
flew past became a wondrous sensation: a hut, an ibis, a man
riding comfortably on a donkey while his wife walked barefoot
in a long black gown and veiled face behind him, carrying a
vessel on her head. A small group of peasants drove a herd of
goats and carried large baskets. A single rider on camelback
galloped along at an amazing speed. Tiny villages of mud huts
had straw-covered flat roofs. In a larger village in a grove of
palm trees two blindfolded, skinny horses were tethered to a
long pole that extended horizontally from a well in the middle.
They seemed to be walking around and around in a circle, maybe
pumping water or grinding something. I could not tell.*

*We were all very excited. Baedeker could not contain himself.
He had to sing "Celeste Aida" at the top of his voice, in spite of
his friend Ebermayer's dutiful reminder off and on, "Mac, stop
it," or "Mac, shut up." It was to no avail. The singer was*

overwhelmed. Even the modest young man who had been sitting in his corner up to now roused himself and put his book aside. He introduced himself: Lieutenant von Kleewitz, pilot. I don't know why, but later we invariably referred to him as Kleewinkel. At first we treated him rather cautiously because of his Lieutenant status. But we discovered, by and by, that he was not infected with Nazi germs. So we became good friends.

Toward evening we arrived in Cairo. We said a temporary goodbye to the three men, who left us for a few days to see Cairo and then Memphis and Sakkara with another group from the tour. They were not going as far as Aswan, as we would.

We realized again how hot it was when we changed trains at the station. Full of foreboding of the night ahead of us, we entered the stuffy sleeping car that was to take us along the Nile to Aswan. It was unbelievably crowded. The first thing we did was to install Mother in the almost completely occupied dining car to save a seat. Then Pappi and I went on a search for our baggage, which was finally thrown into our compartment through the window by a very upset handler, with considerable fury. We had no idea what had made him mad. Then, for the first time, we were served dinner by brown, turbaned, long-gowned Egyptians, while the train slowly started to move.

We were on our way!

I thought of a book title, "Deep in the Heart of Egypt." Corny, certainly, but not to be disputed.

Later, we stood in the corridor and talked to our travel guide, a measly, baldheaded individual, and his Egyptian interpreter and colleague, an older, roundish man with a fez, who tried obviously to be entertaining and intelligent. At first he tried to flirt with Mutti, then with me, and winked suggestively when he saw that we had sleeping compartments next to each other. "You idiot," I thought, and retired.

But said idiot made himself known once more. I had undressed, lain in bed, studied the excursion plan for the next day and then put the light out when, lo and behold, something scratched at my door. I thought at first I was mistaken, but when I realized that I was not, I sat bolt upright in bed and put the light back on. Look here! The handle of the connecting door to the neighboring compartment moved slowly up and down, and again up and down. Then it was quiet for a moment, as if someone tried to listen. Again the handle was pressed, this time a little less carefully, as if he were quite sure of what he wanted. I thought this was almost romantic, grinned from ear to ear, turned my behind to the door and went to sleep, although, I must admit, not without turning the light on again a few times and checking the handle. It was a little uncomfortable, after all. "Rape on the Orient Express!" Some lark. I wished I could have told Ursel and giggled about it with her.

March 13, 1937

They woke us very early the next morning. The train had stopped in the middle of the desert. The sign on the tiny station house said "Edfu." Only a few huts were to be seen. Walking down a winding, sandy road we passed a school, a small building that was not really a house, but which had a floor, a roof, and partial walls. All of the children came out, yelling and waving at us. The teacher, a friendly and nice looking young man in a snow-white European suit, laughed and chased them back inside, wielding a bamboo stick.

The sun was burning down on us and even in our shoes the scratchy sand found our toes. Each one of us carried a whisk that was made of long strands of some animal's hair attached to a bone or wooden handle. We had learned to swish the strands across our faces, and alternately from one shoulder to the other chasing away the droves of ever-present flies.

And then all discomfort was forgotten. Before us lay the wide river, the Nile, the river of history, the river of legend. There it was, flowing calmly and slowly as it had for thousands of years. My own smallness grabbed me again. Where did I belong in all this immensity of time?

We could vaguely recognize stands of palm trees and clusters of what looked like low-slung houses on the shore across the murky yellow-gray water. Fragments of broken walls and pillars could be seen here and there, distanced from each other by flat stretches of sand and low shrubs.

Small, shallow boats with strange sails that spread above them like huge wings expected us. White-sleeved brown arms lifted us on board. We sat on wooden planks that served for seats and held onto each other. There were too many of us on each vessel. Getting dumped into the river and eternity, even if it was through the waters of the Nile, did not feel very appealing.

Right in front of me a young boy of about eight or nine years old stood on one of the benches holding onto the mast and the lines of the sail. He seemed to be part of the crew. He wore a little green and white woven cotton cap on the back of his head and a striped long sleeved shirt that reached his ankles, protecting him from sun and insects, I presumed. He did not seem to mind that flies were crawling over his sweaty nose, half open mouth and lovely dark eyes as he scanned the waters like a professional sailor. The sail's giant sheet of cloth unfolded along its ropes and poles above him, piercing the sky with its sharp triangular wing and carried our little boat below it like a bird of prey would grasp its quarry.

Palm trees and dwellings were sliding by. We passed small, narrow tongues of sandy land that cropped out of the shallows from which barefoot women scooped water into vessels. Robed in black from head to toe, some had their garments bunched up to their knees. They were wading and maybe just washing their feet. We were gliding along so gently that there was no cause for worry. Even my mother sighed a deep sigh of satisfaction and scanned the sky and shore, smiling with delight.

A pack of donkeys awaited us on the opposite bank. We were pulled onto their backs by a horde of wildly screaming drivers, who had great fun scaring us by making their animals gallop at top speed through the desert and the village of Edfu.

"Good donkey, good donkey, slowly, slowly!" Grinning, my man reassured me and gave his animal an extra whack on the behind with his cudgel, sending it racing in a cloud of dust, with me on its back, down the main street of the village. A group of young boys, riding on donkeys without saddles, dashed wildly by, their naked feet on the animals' necks, barely holding onto their ears and manes. The ground shook. It was incredibly hot, but all the sweating was well worth it.

To stand in front of the façade of the powerful Horus temple, to feel the might of past history in this gigantic complex was absolutely breathtaking. Our guide, Effendi Abdullah, the one with the crippled arm, did a very good job of telling us about past times in Egypt. With beating heart I walked silently through the enormous portals into the small rooms of the inner court. It was so dark that Abdullah had to let his flashlight shine over the walls to reveal the bas-reliefs and inscriptions that completely covered them. I put my hands against the rough walls to convince myself that this was all real.

When we attempted to remount our donkeys, a wild fight broke out among the drivers, who attacked each other with fists and cudgels like veritable devils. I am convinced that they would have turned on us also if the police had not arrived with sticks and rifle butts, flailing ruthlessly into the crowd. It was an incredible scene. Mutti's smile vanished for a while.

Back on the train we sank gratefully into our seats and had time to recover a little. After a two-hour trip, we arrived in Aswan. Longing for a good shower and a change of clothes, our wish was granted at the plush Cataract Hotel. Adjacent to a wide terrace, with a view down to the cataract of the Nile's waters running around and over large, black granite rocks, we had lunch in the relatively cool dining room. The waiters were incredibly phlegmatic men in turbans and long white robes. They did not allow themselves to be bothered in the least by the exasperated headwaiter. He, in turn, ran around in desperation from one to the other, trying to get them going. A tough proposition.

After lunch, we went down to the banks of the river and were taken, by sailboat again, to the isle of Elephantine, accompanied by a horde of small Egyptian boys. They paddled along on the wide and deep water in little metal buckets and wooden boxes and sang the never-ending song of "Baksheesh, Baksheesh!" They rowed using their arms instead of oars. Their shiny dark skin dripped from sweat and the churning spray of the water.

We saw ancient Jewish ruins that were very unexpected in this landscape and fascinated me enormously. I must say, though, that I became less enchanted when a snake charmer began to blow his flute, and I thought that I saw the black rocks moving. I also moved, but in the direction of the boats, carefully putting one foot in front of the other.

After dinner, Mother and I sat on a bench under the terrace. We were dead tired but relished the magic of the hour that brought a short twilight and its rapid descent into night. Was it the smell of jasmine that surrounded us? The stars glistened above us and from the water's edge came the voices of a group of women. They were singing. It was so beautiful, I felt like crying.

Completely exhausted from the heat and all I had seen, I threw myself on the bed, naked under the mosquito net, too weak to wash myself, in spite of the fact that the thought of lovely cold water almost made me groan. Nevertheless, I did not fall asleep for a long time.

March 14, 1937

It was five o'clock in the morning when I woke up. It seemed to be a little cooler, or maybe it just felt that way because I had slept and had not moved. I got up, put on my nightgown and, still sleepy, dragged myself out to the balcony. The hills, the river, the palms that stood in isolated groups like people determined to hold onto each other, were all still dreaming in the translucent light that rose from dawn. The black granite rocks of the cataract below gleamed, forever washed by the water that gushed and swirled around them.

While I watched, a man appeared rising from high up over the top of a sandy hill, riding on a donkey and clad all in white. All of a sudden the sun rose right behind his back as he came riding down the hill, like a god emerging from a fireball.

Later, rowboats took us to the island of Philae in the reservoir and the submerged temple of Isis. In the afternoon, a four-hour train trip to Luxor, Hotel Winter Palace.

I wandered among the great ruins of the temples of Karnak and Luxor, gazing up at the immense columns that stood sometimes so close together that I felt I was walking in a forest of giant stone tree trunks. Broken pieces of sculpture lay on the ground here and there, as if they had just tumbled down. Walking up a few sandy steps and turning a corner, an over-life-sized Pharaoh seemed to stride towards me, one foot extended slightly, ready to disengage from the wall that held him. In his god-like aloofness he paid no attention to me or to his small delicate queen who clung to his side, reaching no higher than just above his knee. A large stone beetle, a scarab, rested on top of a tall pedestal that was obviously carved just for him. He was complete, unbroken, a symbol of a determination that the memory of a vital culture of the past should not be forgotten amid its ruins.

Thebes, the Valley of the Kings, the graves of Tutankhamen and Ramses, and the Colossos of Memnon. Five day old camel and three little girls at the river. From Luxor to Cairo via sleeping car. Ebermayer, Mac and Kleewinkel joined us again at the Shephard's Hotel.

March 18, 1937

In the morning, arrival at Haifa. Mac is getting sick. We drive past Mount Carmel, through wide fields, slightly hilly stretches of majestic, lonely land. No house, no village is to be seen. There are a few fields being tilled by Arabs in flowing gowns. The earth is dry and terribly stony; one marvels at the people working on it with obvious industry and determination. We pass Jewish youth colonies. Boys and girls in shorts ride tractors and hay wagons, horses and donkeys. We see very modern-looking courtyards with walls around them, probably for protection. Nazareth—a nice, little, enchanted place. Stopped at Maria's Well, two rusty old pipes surrounded by newly set stones, nothing else. Mac is getting worse. Drive on via Canaan to Tiberias and the Sea of Genezareth, below sea level. Back to Nazareth. Lunch, then Church of the Annunciation and Joseph's Workplace. In the courtyard was a little Jewish boy. That's how Jesus could have looked. Evening in Jerusalem at the Hotel King David.

March 19, 1937

At night disturbances in Jerusalem, as well as in my stomach. The city declared strict curfew. My dear father, disobedient as always, was not to be deterred from seeing what he wanted to see and returned in the afternoon from a thorough jaunt through the town, including the Old-Town Bazaar. When knowledgeable people at the hotel heard of this exploit, they almost fainted. "You could have been killed," they said.

I developed a fever that rose steadily, and I sweated so hard that the water dripped through my mattress. A Dr. Frank administered medication.

March 20, 1937

Sick. Tea in bed and furious because of lost time. That's what I came to Palestine for!

A surprise. Two people called on us, Klaus and Alberta Halberstedter, who were our neighbors in Berlin-Dahlem and went to school with my brother Ralph. Their father, Dr. Halberstedter, is now a much-revered professor at the university here. Strange how people have been dislocated and spread all

*over the world and sometimes connect again with each other.
Each time a miracle.*

March 21, 1937

*Ebermayer decided that, sick or not, I just had to see
something of Jerusalem before we left, so he took me quickly to
the Jaffa Gate and the Bazaar this morning. After all, he is blond,
not a Jew, and does not look like one. It was safer with him.
Then we were taken to Haifa, via Jaffa and Tel-Aviv, under
protection of machine guns. What a feeling to travel surrounded
by soldiers in jeeps. Back on board of the Milwaukee.*

March 24, 1937

*Arrived in Beirut. Drive through a lovely springtime
landscape. The trees were in bloom, fields of rich, brown earth
with snow-capped mountains in the background. Quite heavenly.
A herd of goats with many babies. The Roman temples at
Baalbeck, dedicated to Jupiter and Bacchus. Am very weak and
tired.*

March 23 and 24, 1937

In bed and at sea.

March 25, 1937

*At six in the morning the ship went through the straits of
the Bosphorus around the Black Sea and the Sea of Marmara.
Went on land at Istanbul. Drove over the Galata Bridge to the
old Seraglio, which was very neglected and deteriorated. Fantastic
view down to the Sea of Marmara, the Golden Horn and the
harbor. The harem with a courtyard that is so closed in that
only the sky can be seen from inside. Small rooms with large*

beds. Eunuch's apartments and a prison. Drive back via Pera, dead tired. Lunch on board.

Again by car to the National Museum. Walk through the streets. Little outdoor cafés with water pipes. Men carrying terribly heavy loads like animals, ragged black women, pretty students, music. The Blue Mosque, a festive room dedicated to rest and spiritual cleansing in the presence of beauty and serenity. A place of real peace. Two more mosques. The Hagia Sophia, marvelous vaulted room, dark, splendid, and mysterious. Also the Suleiman Mosque.

The Bazaar, dusky, covered walkways bordered by stalls that run on and on like a rabbit warren. Colorful carpets, sparkling jewelry, water pipes, junk, scarves, honey, etc., and in between one can also find real antiques, if one is knowledgeable. If you show an interest in any of his wares, the owner of the stall will offer you a cup of strong, sweet Turkish coffee, and a seat. It is truly very hard to resist such hospitality! Father bought two shadow-play figures.

March 27, 1937

Arrive at Phaleron, the harbor of Athens. Pappi resurrects his school-days language studies and reads a Greek newspaper with help from the driver to find out what he could see in the Greek theater. As if there would have been time.

In Athens at the National Museum, the fragment of the figure of a young boy, riding wildly on a horse, that had been fished out of the ocean. Jewelry from Mykene, signet rings, two goblets in the form of bull's heads.

In a dark side room I looked at a sarcophagus, and a grizzled old guard, who must have been a member of a secret society that was dedicated to scaring foreign female tourists came up behind me. With a finger held to his lips warning me of imminent danger, he proceeded slowly, slowly to raise the lid and reveal a rather ghastly mummy within.

He may have expected me to shriek, but certainly not to run away before a few coins had been dropped into his palm. I almost disappointed him on all counts, but relented on the coins. He looked so ragged.

The Acropolis. Exhilarating, majestic. Climbing the high, broken steps, it felt as if the columns lifted me and my eyes and breath reached the sky.

The temple of Zeus. The temple of Theseus. The street of the graves, peaceful, and romantic. White marble, radiating light. Children in native costumes, boys in pleated skirts and shoes with pointed, upturned toes. Tiny Byzantine chapel. Lilac bushes. Drive back to Phaleron. Wonderful sunset at the ocean. Back on ship.

March 29, 1937

At noon we arrived at the volcanic island of Santorin. Another cruise ship, the French Champollion, occupied the only place near the island where an anchor could be dropped. Our ship had to wait in deep water. We had to be transported in relays by boat to the little harbor at the bottom of steep cliffs that reached down to the spare strip of flat land, where we disembarked. From there a long, narrow, winding road clawed its way zigzag fashion up the rocky lava wall. Ebermayer and Mac chose to walk, not realizing how far it was. It took the rest of us over twenty minutes to reach the top on the backs of the trusty, sweaty, fly-enveloped donkeys and in burning sun, looking alternately down to the Aegean Sea and then up toward the snow-white roofs of the small city far above us.

Climbing up and down steps on narrow, stone-paved streets, whitewashed houses, blinding in the heat of the sun, nestled close together, leaning against each other for protection, steadied by walls and arches that held them fast onto the steep terrain. The shutters, the steps, and the gutters were painted light blue and everything looked clean and happy. There was a terrace at the bend of a road. We stood and looked down to the sea, so very far down. The water was steel blue and almost iridescent in the sun.

Curious, friendly children gathered around us, healthy, happy faces, Greek noses, and sturdy little bodies. Toothless old women nodded to us.

From high up over the top of a wall a brown girl with long, shiny, black braids, red cheeks, and sparkling teeth laughed down to me, and behind her the blue sky framed her as if she had just flown out of it. She waved goodbye and kept laughing.

Coffee at a small inn, the Volcan Hotel Santorin. A cool room with a tile floor, wooden tables, and chair. A nervous young woman, round and inefficiently bustling, succeeded in creating confusion and delay upon receiving our modest request for a cup of coffee. Two children joined us at the table where we sat with Mac and Ebermayer. Trying to talk and play with them filled the endless wait for our refreshments.

My parents decided to start back down towards the harbor. The rest of us wanted to do some more exploring.

Turning away from the city, we moved toward the opposite side of the island. The land flattened out, level stony paths wound through fields, past old gnarled grape vines, and meadows. No house, no hut was to be seen. Once in a while a rider on a horse or donkey passed us. A little boy ambled behind us, singing quietly to himself. From around a bend in the road a herd of sheep came towards us with tiny fluffy-white lambs among them. They had black borders around their eyes and long, drooping ears. The youngest of them were carried by children, carefully and lovingly. We hugged them all, the children and the lambs.

We came upon a lonely little chapel, standing at the edge of a field where the cliffs plunged down again towards the ocean. It was obviously not much used to visitors, for the gate growled in annoyance when we opened it. In all probability it got company only when one of the islanders had departed from life and came here to rest in the little cemetery that dreamed in the sun, carefully embraced and watched by a low white wall and two cypresses. We did not talk. We just stood there and drank in the peace and quiet that surrounded us.

Slowly we walked back until we stood again at the other side of the island that dropped deep, deep down to the sea. Below us was the bay with the stubborn "Champollion" and the sulking "Milwaukee" that lay much farther out in the water, deprived of a place to drop its anchor. We moved down narrow, stony streets, under archways, passing people's windows at eye level and occasionally caught a glimpse of a smile or a frown from within. A little tethered donkey was scared of us. Gradually the sun started to slant towards the horizon. The road now was partially paved with large, round stones that were so smooth that we slipped and slid, holding onto each other until we reached the start of the long zigzag road of the final descent. Groups of our fellow passengers soon joined us and when we came to a small plateau at one of the downward curves of the road we gladly sank onto a round stone bench that had obviously been placed there just for us. There we waited until the last of the chatting crowd had passed. It was still too early to go on. Our ship lay as far out in the ocean as before.

Four little girls joined us. As dark brown eyes evaluated us thoroughly, small fingers touched our arms and jackets. Like all the children there, they wanted to give us their hands. We shook them energetically, and they laughed with delight. We were then their friends, and we all were happy. To their amazement though, I picked some pieces of pumice out of a low wall next to us and put them in my pocket as remembrance of the day. Good for ink-stained fingers, I tried to convey to them. I don't know what the word "crazy" is in Greek, but I am sure the children thought of it.

The ships down below started to breathe thin streams of smoke into the sky. The Champollion pulled the last boat up its side and steamed away. The victor left the field. Slowly the Milwaukee moved in, preceded by a swarm of hurrying boats.

We went on our way again, trudging down and down, endlessly
down. Finally we arrived. Ebermayer bought a bottle of wine,
and we were back on ship.

March 29, 1937

At sea. Captain's dinner in the evening with caviar. Then at
the grill bar dancing with "The Boys."

March 30, 1937

At noon we arrived at Gravosa, Yugoslavia.

Colorful, small harbor with sailing ships and cargo boats,
wildly romantic-looking seamen smoking pipes on deck in front
of their tiny cabins. Some wore wide, bulbous pants that looked
like bunched up knickerbockers and sported earrings and bright
red fezzes. There were many poor-looking people in rags too,
and skinny, dirty children all over the place.

We walked to Ragusa. What an enchanting place! The huge,
old city walls with their enormous watchtower jutting out to
sea, invincible and built for the ages. The steep streets have steps
built into them, as in Naples, but are cleaner. Delightful stores
sell embroidered jackets, woven purses and carpets and many
things made from leather. Mother bought me a white wool jacket
with light blue embroidery on it. It is just beautiful.

We bought a belt and a brooch, decorated all over with small
flowers that were made entirely out of leather, also a cognac
service, a bottle, and six glasses, equally adorned with bright-
colored leather. Return to ship via streetcar, sitting across from
a blue-eyed, shrunken and dried-out pseudo vamp. Poor thing.

At night dancing with "The Boys." Kleewinkel gave me a
book about the actress Tony van Eyk, which was very nice of
him. Unfortunately, I felt so self-conscious on the dance floor
that my knees shook. My parents went to sleep. I went to the
bar with the others. Kleewinkel, as we still insisted on calling

him to his understandable chagrin, started to talk about his attempts to write a novel, hesitant at first, but rather more courageously after several drinks. Our good friend Ebermayer, an accomplished writer, was just barely polite enough to conceal his complete lack of interest. But he was too drunk to be entirely charitable. I left at midnight. I don't think my presence was comfortable for them anymore. With me around they probably could not talk the way they wanted to, or drink as much as they wanted to.

March 31, 1937

Packed our suitcases. Farewell coffee hour with everybody. Landing in Venice. It was ice cold. Five trunks had fallen into the sea. Thank God, not ours. We ambled slowly through the streets with Ebermayer and Mac and then said goodbye to them at Quadri's restaurant, after feasting on scampi and great sandwiches.

April 1, 1937

In Venice. Hotel Luna again.
Went shopping with Mother. Since she heard that clothes are so much more expensive in the Untied States she went on a buying spree in Venice that was beyond belief. Standing on the upstairs floor of the elegant couturier establishment I had to try one piece of clothing after another, whether I liked it or not. What I really liked was discarded immediately and I was too tired, hot, and grumpy to put up much of a fight. Mother, of course, was in seventh heaven and so were the sales ladies.

CHAPTER ELEVEN

Letters from Berlin

On the sixth of April we were back in Nice. Soon afterwards Mother went to Berlin again to check on Ralph, and Father received this letter from her:

April 27, 1937

Dear George,

I found Ralph looking better, which made me feel more assured. His tutor is on a short trip, and I will talk to him when he returns. Ralph swears that he will now go into the examination in earnest, and I will not leave here until he does.

The trip from Zurich was very strenuous, since I was not able to sleep in my compartment that was situated over a coupling and the washstand stank like a toilet. It is cold here, and I am happy to have my fur coat.

I talked to Miss Schneider, the American consul's secretary. She was very nice and researched your data out of old books. You were in the States in 1907 for a few weeks, also in 1923, in 1924, and in 1926. So you can write that for your passport and also mention the ships you used.

She likes Ralph very much, but she has no more patience with him. She says he has to get out of Germany and to America before he goes into a decline. She agrees with us completely. Ralph is such a great boy. I tremble for him.

Today I met Ilse! The first one that I like. Just a comrade, he says. Hmm! It is good that he has someone. Don't mention I told you.

I hope you don't stay up too late. How was the English lesson? You should go and play tennis with Fe. She must get exercise. Greet Mama, Franz, and Josephine.

My father's answer from Nice:

April 30, 1937

Dearest,

Received your letter with much pleasure. That you are satisfied with the fact that Ralph looks well is a relief. You should not have been surprised that an Ilse was already on the horizon again. Where does she come from; what does she do? Send photo, if available. The description "comrade" I translate only into No Impending Marriage, for a change. With him, of course, that could also mean exactly the opposite. Tell him that I did not get his letter yet because it probably waits for him to put it into the mailbox. A reasonable deduction!

Be careful in that climate there. It is not warm or very cold here, but very windy. During my English lesson I rehearsed getting questions from the American consul and answering them. You know how important rehearsals are before a difficult performance! This afternoon Fe and I will go to the university to hear a lecture with slides about the Greek theatre.

I so hoped to have heard already that Ralph has reported for his examination. I do not understand why a few days will make any difference. He just imagines everything to be so difficult. The month of August is not too far away. I don't think it would be good for him to travel right after all of this hard work without a little rest.

Mother's letter was written on the same day in Berlin.

April 30, 1937

Dear George,

Ralph's work is gong very well, and he is very diligent. Someone told us unofficially that as a result of his research certain safety laws for the bakers trade will be changed, and if he were German, his work would have been graded "excellent." Since he is of another nationality and on top of it of unpopular racial status, he only received a grudging "good." One of Ralph's colleagues told me that he, himself, did not know half as much as Ralph does when he made his States Exam and passed it.

This time our son does not drive himself crazy with Ilse, thank God. She is a very nice, intelligent girl from a good stable. "Just a Buddy," he says.

Yesterday I saw Albrecht (her brother-in-law). *He would very much enjoy spending his short vacation with you in Nice. I would rather like him to. Since 1920 he has had no vacation and is sixty-five years old. If only Mama would be sensible and behave when he is there! Remembering past times I worry about that.*

Tomorrow is going to be a big day here. Everything is decorated with flags. Today I saw the Fuehrer in a parade, really close up. His car had stopped right in front of me. Also Goebbels rode with him. Quite an experience!

Love!
Alice

I remembered Uncle Albrecht only vaguely as a tall, skinny man with a flabby belly sagging over his belt buckle and a pince-nez balanced on the tip of his nose. His thin hair was parted in the middle and glistened from copious applications of brilliantine. When he spoke, and he held forth incessantly, his voice was high and unusually sonorous. He was a singer, I was told, and had even appeared with the opera chorus.

Father writes from Nice:

May 3, 1937

My Dear Child (to his wife),

Schickeles and Marcu were here for a visit and just left. René is suffering from his asthma attacks again.

Yesterday I went to Monte Carlo to see the Russian Ballet. Since the rain came down in buckets Fe and Mama refused to come along. When I got there it was sold out. I was just going to leave when the director appeared in the lobby, recognized me and conjured up an extra ticket right out of his pocket. It was an excellent seat and free. The performance of **Don Juan** *by Gluck was very worthwhile indeed, surprisingly strong. The décor and the costumes were perfect.*

The weather is unpleasant, cold, and wet. We did not leave the house today.

Saturday, the Joskes, Pilles, and Kernecks were here for coffee. The Joske's children picked all of the strawberries in the garden, the ripe ones and the unripe ones.

On top of such effrontery, you want to invite houseguests? I did not believe my eyes when I read your letter! It is completely out of the question! Fe said immediately, "In that case, I'll just retire to my room," and Mama raised her hands to heaven and rolled her eyes in horror. I'd wish for him to have a nice vacation. Poor Albrecht deserves it, but I could not stand him around, even if both our ladies here had been delighted. Don't forget that I will be in this Paradise for only eighty more days. This time I want to reserve just for us alone together. When a stranger, especially Albrecht, lives in our house, I have not a quiet minute, no privacy. With friends of our children it is different. I do not have to engage with them. Do not accuse me of being egotistic. I am acting out of self-preservation. Now, I ask you not to mention this matter again in your next letter that, I hope, will arrive speedily.

What you write about Ralph's work pleases me much. Where is his promised letter to me? His date is getting closer and closer.

What is happening? Write to me in detail about where and what you eat and whom you meet and talk to. The films you see and how they were, you do not have to tell me. That does not interest me in the least. By all means go to the theatre. I am very interested what the quality of performances is now. That is more important to me right now than the kinds of plays they show. Go especially to the Deutsches Schauschpielhaus.

Today I got the answer from the Theatre-Congress in Paris. They reserved my hotel room.

Kisses to you and Ralph

Alice writes from Berlin:

May 7, 1937

Dear George,

I am impressed and pleased that you are writing so often. I'll send you the passport, but please return it as soon as you can. I just feel safer here when I can carry it. Sunday evening I'll go to Fulda's. Monday I saw the Wesseley film together with "The Boys." I have not been to the theatre yet, but will go soon. Ralph I see only at dinner. He studies. He is so sweet!

Your Alice

From George in Nice to Berlin.

May 9, 1937

Dearest,

If your letter had not arrived by today I would have phoned you. Fe and I find this communication from you pretty meager. You must improve in the future! We are expecting more from you. Summer has suddenly burst on the scene and since

Wednesday we can eat lunch in the garden. Cherry harvest has begun. Everything is in bloom, and the thought of leaving it all so soon is twice as sad.

Today we went swimming. Since Fe seems to get bored with her old father we asked the Kernecks to come along. The water was still quite cold. Fe decided that her swimsuit was too big and only sunned herself. We had coffee at Juan les Pine and were home at 6 o'clock.

We still did not mail the packages to Theodor, but will today. I have not been able to start on the driving lessons. Just the thought of doing that is pure torture for me! Send the passport immediately!

Now let us talk about the most important thing: Is Ralph still waiting for his tutor, or what for heaven's sake is keeping him from going ahead? Are they still not giving him a date for the examination? Time is running out! Write to me in detail! I am so very worried.

In the meantime I received the prospectus from the Panama Pacific line that will take us from New York to San Francisco through the Panama Canal. High season starts on the first of December and is more expensive. So we must leave New York on November twenty-seven. They have three steamers at 32,000 tons each. The photos look very elegant. There will be time to see Havana. We stop there for one day, the same in Panama City, and a half-day in Acapulco, Mexico. The price of $200 per person for the seventeen-day trip is not bad, not to be compared to the price of a ticket to New York with the Manhattan. The hotel Murray Hill in New York, where Mrs. Alexander lives, is old fashioned but centrally located and a double room with bath costs $65 per month, or $1 a day per person. Very reasonable. I am amazed at the sale prices of homes in the environment of New York. A five room, two bath villa in Long Island goes for $3,000, a seven room house with it's own beach, for $6,300. Unbelievable! From the center of Long Island to the center of New York takes fourteen minutes by train. No more than from

Dahlem to Berlin. I read in the paper that it is 30% cheaper to live in California than in New York.

I wish we would know already where we'd end up. I think the climate is probably best in Los Angeles, but the movie atmosphere less enjoyable. Although the people who have recently settled there are Max Reinhardt, Arnold Schoenberg, Stravinsky, Korngold, Oscar Strauss, and Otto Klemperer. Not bad company! Did you tell Ralph that Kokoschka got a professorship in San Francisco?

I do not worry about availability of good housing any more, but the problem of household help seems to be greater. I presume the home prices are so low because people move to apartment-hotels to save on those terrible prices for help. Living that way would be unthinkable for me.

Fe's poem is really very good. Theodor Wolff and Schickele are of the same opinion, but unfortunately it is so very sad. She claims she wrote it at some other time, earlier, and just reworked it. She really suffers from the fact that she is so alone, without companions of her own age. Richard left already with the Manhattan.

I wrote another phenomenal article in the meantime and even sent it off. Fe and I consider it enormously gifted and are especially pleased with it. So much for humility! Supposedly articles in the States are well paid, a little story gets $50. Maybe I'll try to translate some things from the **Theatre Arts Monthly** during my English lessons for the sake of practice. I now have four hours per week, that is all the time the lady can give me. My vocabulary is bigger than I thought, but sentence structure gives me a lot of trouble.

This would be a good time for you to write to Eugenia in Portland and to John in San Francisco (our American Cousins). You do things like that better than I.

The play Reinhardt directed in New York was supposed to run for two years but had to close within weeks. Four other performances that were successful in Germany and also in

London turned out to be complete flops in the States. Before I touch any kind of theatrical production I plan to study the American taste thoroughly. After all, new serious American plays have great success. Dr. Ullmann is supposedly very unhappy over there. That does not mean anything. One has to get acclimated for a while and give it a chance. You can see that I am already thinking about how I can busy myself over there. That much more do I worry about Ralph's situation.

I am amazed how long this letter has gotten to be, especially in comparison to your last short and skimpy one. Shame on you!

Pappi

One month later, in early June, Ralph left Berlin and came to Nice. He had given up. We all realized that the final date for his examination was just not forthcoming, a mean and subtle trick to hurt a foreign Jew. The August deadline to avoid cancellation of his passport was near.

I wrote in my diary:

June 21, 1937

Early this morning Ralph left for Paris. I took him to the train. I tried so hard to look cheerful when we hugged and said goodbye, but it was to no avail. The tears started to come and when the train pulled out of the station I really broke down. At least he could not see me anymore. Later, at home, we were all in a terrible mood, and I cried all night.

Ralph's girlfriend Ilse came to Paris to say goodbye to him. She was not Jewish and could travel without any difficulty.

This evening the Veendam sails from Boulogne to the United States with our Ralph on board.

June 30, 1937

Ralph's birthday. This morning I went to Dr. Blum because of my tonsils. Last week I cut my bare foot on something in the garden, and it still hurts. So I asked Blum to have a look at it since I was at his office. He tortured me. He poked and dug around and finally pronounced that I had a piece of metal in my foot and dragged me to the surgeon, Dr. Bassac. After two anesthetic injections they cut several rusty metal pieces out. In the afternoon I got an anti-tetanus horse-serum injection into the abdomen.

Ten agonizing days of excruciating pain and swollen glands, fever, and an itching rash from the top of my head to my toes followed. I tried so hard, if not to grin, to bear it. My dear Mama did not help that resolve. She sat on my bed and wept copiously.

I wrote in my diary:

July 11, 1937

Pappi declared that nothing, come hell or high water, would keep him from seeing St. Moritz one more time before leaving Europe. I am getting better but am still very weak. Washing my hair, let alone packing suitcases, is exhausting.

CHAPTER TWELVE

Good-bye St. Moritz

July 14, 1937

Left Nice by car in the morning. Dinner in Turin, in Italy. Auto-Strada to Milano. Stayed overnight. Hot. Exhausted.

July 15, 1937

Milano to Varenna. Lunch at a hotel under the branches of a giant, ancient chestnut tree that reached down to the lake over old walls and benches of stone. A wonderful place, deeply still, a bower of peace.

Via Chiavenna to the Swiss border. Coffee in Castasegnia, where I put on stockings and an undershirt. It's getting cool. Maloya Pass, Sils Maria, St. Moritz. Gray, but not cold.

July 16, 1937

When we arrived we found a letter from Ralph, a diary from aboard ship. He had fog and storm and also beautiful days. Got acquainted with young American men and is delighted with their personalities and their level of education. So much for his previous prejudice and his fears about crude and uncultured American people. Thank God! A good beginning! At the same time he sent a one-word telegram, "CALIFORNIA," it said.

He had arrived.

Amazingly enough, we received our suitcases on time this afternoon. Found a letter from Ebermayer at the hotel, announcing his presence here, which pleases us very much. Made an appointment with him to meet at Hanselmann's, which did not happen because a terrific thunderstorm broke out and then it snowed throughout the night. I checked the calendar to assure myself that it was really July. It was.

July 17, 1937

In the morning still deep snow. Ice cold. Afternoon met with Ebermayer and Mac at Hanselmann's pastry shop, then, with both, strolled in the village, buying books at Wega's. After that Ebermayer drove us in his car to Sils Maria, along the lakes, then to Maloja. Toward evening the sun still appeared a little and glanced across the new fields of snow on the mountains. The lake gleamed like metal and the air felt raw.

July 19, 1937

Read in the morning: "The World and Ideology, The Primitive Man," by Engelhardt. Had coffee in my room in the afternoon and finally got to write.

July 20, 1937

Worked very well this morning. Afternoon read Engelhardt again. Went to old Frau Gasser with my parents for coffee. It started to rain again. Pappi read to us about prices in restaurants and hotels in San Francisco. Amazingly cheap! Rents for homes are about the same as in Nice. Strolled to the pharmacy and to the Newspaper-Schmidts. Spoon-fed Cream of Oats to Bella for her upset stomach. Heavy thunder in the evening.

July 21, 1937

Read Engelhardt with mounting interest and enjoyment, up to "The Subtropical Man." How right Collins was when he said that I should go to a university to study. How can I? So I will try to study on my own and will succeed. In the afternoon I went for a walk by myself, picked flowers, and sat on a bench reading the works of Jean Paul. Had coffee, went home, and wrote further about my Egypt trip.

July 24, 1937

Wrote a poem. Called it "Summer Morning." Afternoon again, a sudden rainstorm. Played Ping Pong with Pappi. Won consistently. Finished letters and wrote to Schickele. Got a letter from Ursel.

July 26, 1937

John Altman and his family, our cousins from America, had embarked on a European tour and were going to come to Stresa, Italy, to meet us for the first time. So we traveled south from St. Moritz to Menaggio, had lunch, then coffee in Laguna. We sat outdoors at our old coffee house at the main square and relished it. Again and again the same question: Will I ever be able to return here? The promenade at the lake, the broad trees, the arcades in the old streets, the little steamboats—all unforgettable! Driving through Brissago we saw Hartung, another of Father's displaced colleagues. Sometimes the world seems so small when we unexpectedly meet old acquaintances in other countries, footloose emigrants all, just like us.

The dining room of the hotel in Stresa was suffused by the light of the bright sky reflected from the surface of the sea outside the many tall windows. We felt a little anxious.

What would these cousins be like? We thought of them as official envoys from our new country.

When we entered they were already seated at a table, and got up to meet us. John Cecil, the father, unlike my own father in stature, was slim and sun-browned, but in his features there was a noticeable kinship. He had the same high forehead, the same firm nose and mouth. My Father was a passionate artist and a scholar, an independent thinker and a man of knowledge, who also loved to joke and laugh and have a good time, aside from sticking tenaciously to certain self-made traditions. John was a successful lawyer, a man who followed social rules and decorum. Coming home from his office at night he would shower and then dress in a fresh shirt and tie and another dress suit before coming down to dinner. He lived in the fashionable suburbs of San Francisco, in San Mateo, with his wife Bess and his children, Betty and John Jr. Bess was tall, elegant, restrained and very proper. She was not pretty, but decidedly handsome. She could give you a friendly, warm smile with her nice, large eyes, although something in the composed expression of her narrow face and the straight-backed aristocratic bearing of her slim figure kept you at a polite distance. Somehow intimacy was not ladylike. She was sewn into the formality and tradition of her wealthy, influential, San Francisco families, the Greenebaums and the Koshlands. Only later, after many years, did I learn that cousin Bess could really be quite human, when she got to know you and dared to let her guard down.

The children, Betty, who was about my age, I think, and the younger John Jr. seemed to me like people from another world. They were so much more self-possessed than I was. They moved and spoke freely and without hesitation. They used expressions I had never heard before. Somehow the word "cute" sticks in my mind especially.

For some reason I found it puzzling when Betty came out with it, which she did most frequently.

I remember Betty as a fresh-faced buxom girl with exceptionally long lashes over beautiful large eyes. Her hair was soft and wavy, her coloring lighter than that of either of her parents, whereas young John had his mother's long and narrow face and very black hair. When we lived in San Francisco later on, we visited them once in a while, but not often enough to establish a bond. Somehow they always remained the relatives from across the sea, from another world, another culture. Of course they could not have found me, their new silent cousin, particularly engaging either.

Returning from Stresa we spent one more month in St. Moritz, a month of waiting, of hovering between two worlds, about to leave Europe yet not on the way to America. The time was spent hiking on the mountain trails, visiting with equally footloose friends over endless coffee hours with political discussions and worried contemplations about the future.

I buried myself in books. I read the Trilogy *Joseph and his Brothers* by Thomas Mann, poems by Friedrich Hoelderlin, and devoured as much of Herrmann Hesse's books as I could get a hold of, especially *Siddharta* and *Narziss and Goldmund*.

Father taught me to play tennis. He was an excellent player himself and had won quite a few tournaments in his youth. We had fun on the court, and I like to think that he felt as close to me then as I felt to him.

On August 27, 1937 we left St. Moritz for good. The Hotel-Schmidts, the Book-Schmidts, and Hairdresser Fahr assembled in front of the Metropole Hotel to say farewell to us. I quickly grabbed my camera and took a picture of this very special moment. It represented the end of an era in our lives. We also said goodbye to old Mrs. Gasser and the jewelers Scherbel. A sad wave in the direction of the

Konditorei Hanselmann and then the drive towards Italy and home to Nice began.

A note in my diary:

My mood is quite melancholic again. I am haunted by Betty's words in Stresa. "There isn't anything very old in America," she said. Assisi! Varenna! Soglio! Will I ever get to do more than sadly, longingly, briefly pass through my favorite places, never staying?

One night and one day we spent in Turin on the way. I remember standing for a long time in front of a small Rembrandt painting at the museum there. It was called: *Vecchio Dormiente* (Old Man Sleeping). Could I paint like that? I wondered.

CHAPTER THIRTEEN

Good-bye Europe

On August 29, 1937, we arrived home and started to sort and pack our personal belongings. Two weeks later a professional packing crew took over, wrapping and crating the whole household for the trip overseas. Bella ducked and cringed amidst all that upheaval with her tail between her legs. I picked her up, held her under my arm and wished that we could both hide somewhere.

On September 21, 1937, we left our house and moved into a hotel on the Boulevard Victor Hugo. Two sad weeks followed. I did not want to leave. Only then did I realize that I had actually taken root in that town without knowing it.

All kinds of reports about the United States were presented to us from various sources. The traffic was terrible, the people cold and hard, everything depended on money, and the state of general education was deplorable. Well-meaning friends tried to buck me up by pointing out that a great new adventure was awaiting me.

At that time a great wind, the Sirocco, blew across the sea from the African desert. It covered Nice and much of the coast, bringing sand and nervousness to all but the most impervious. There was talk about the China-Japan conflict and half-hidden preparations for war throughout the world.

Mother went wild again in a frenzy of clothes buying. She was convinced that everything was much more expensive "over there," and furthermore, not of good quality. She dragged me from dressmakers to hat and shoe stores, and I slouched numbly along, too depressed to resist.

My parents still preferred to consume their main meal in the middle of the day, or at least not late at night. This was a habit that stemmed from their life in the theater in Germany, when the mornings were taken up with rehearsals and the nights very often with performances or various social functions. These early main meals were also the custom in many German households, when the man of the house came home for lunch and returned to work afterwards.

Of course at this time in Nice there were not many dining establishments that would serve big meals at odd hours, but we had discovered a place that was just right for us. It was on one of those late afternoons when the little hole-in-the-wall restaurant was not yet open for service. We knew that all we had to do was to tap on the glass of the locked front door. We were recognized by a cautious eye peering at us around the lace curtain from the inside and were immediately admitted with open arms. We ate often at the restaurant of the Scheerer family. Mama and Papa cooked and the son, who had been a successful lawyer in Germany, did the serving.

This pale, slight little man stood next to our table and said, "It is amazing how one's whole personality can change with the position in which one finds oneself in daily life. Believe me, I never bowed to anyone in my former profession. Now I find myself scraping and smiling with a most servile demeanor, just like a waiter would. It just happens, unconsciously. It gets in your blood." He set the

table for us, flicking the napkins before spreading them on
our laps.

Papa Scheerer had been a well-established businessman
in Frankfurt, where his wife used to give dinner parties for
their friends, the food prepared by her cook and served by
two maids. Here she peeked out of her steamy, small kitchen,
wiping her hands on her apron and waved to us. Her cheeks
were sagging, the red of her dyed hair remained only at
the ends of its strands, which hung limp around her
sweating forehead.

"*Hammelfleisch mit Bohnen* (lamb stew with string-
beans)," she called, "It's just ready! Or would you rather
have a *Wiener Schnitzel?*"

"It was wonderful when you invited us for coffee to
your home the first time we met," Herr Scheerer pulled up
a chair and joined us for a few moments. "We just don't
get out much, being so busy here, and we don't know many
people. It was such a treat seeing all the art and books in
your house and then sitting in the garden with you. It must
be hard leaving all that now."

"How about that sweet little cat you had? What will
you do with her?" Frau Scheerer called from the kitchen.

"Would you like it?" I held my breath.

"Oh, yes, I'd love it! I want her to sit on my lap, and she
can even come to work with us."

There went one of my worries. I was so happy.

It was September 30, 1937. For the last time we were
together with some of our friends at the Café Monnot. There
were Hans, his parents, René Schickele and his wife, the
Theodor Wolffs, and Valeriu Marcu, who sat next to me
and gave his chair an extra push to lean against mine.

"I have a present and some good advice for you," he
said. He put a book into my hand, *The Iliad* by Homer, a
very nice edition with good illustrations. "And now comes

my special advice." After throwing a quick glance at the other end of the table where my parents sat, he leaned even closer to me. "Be sure to take a lover first, before you even *think* of getting married."

I looked at him, quite taken aback. Nobody had ever spoken to me so unashamedly and personally. I studied him for a minute. A middle-aged Faun with a wicked grin on his sunburned face. Was he making fun of me?

He shifted his pipe from one side of his mouth to the other, pushed his French beret to a more rakish angle and kept looking at me. His expression changed, and he seemed to contemplate me almost regretfully, like one looks at a lost opportunity. I was shocked, amused, and secretly flattered.

(Three years later, in 1940, Hitler crashed into France. Even the gentile Schickeles from Alsace, having been granted French citizenship, felt it safer to flee to the small city of Vence in the Provencale hills, where René died shortly afterwards. The Theodor Wolffs were caught by the Nazis, shipped back to Germany, and killed in a concentration camp. Their two sons escaped. I met Rudolph many years later in New York. Hans Schickele I found again in San Francisco. Marcu escaped via Spain. Whatever happened to all of our other friends, the Joskes, the Kernecks, even the Russian Abelmanns, I do not know.)

On October 4, 1937, the day of departure from Nice arrived. It started with hurried last minute packing and general confusion. Two jackets that were delivered by the dressmaker did not quite fit, so back we went to try them on again and wait for the alterations.

For the last time we went to the Scheerers' to buy sandwiches to take along for the drive up north. It was a very sad goodbye. We all had tears in our eyes, and Papa Scheerer actually sobbed openly and kissed our hands. I suppose that in the depth of depression, decorum has no more importance in one's life. We were the only people who had shown friendship and compassion to them, he said.

Finally, while our Franz paced up and down beside the car in front of the hotel like a racehorse waiting for the starting bell, we more or less successfully tuned out Oma Marta's multiple complaints and objections and bundled her safely into the back seat with Mutti, me, and Bella on my lap. Further confined by small baggage, blankets, and picnic gear at our feet, we were unable to move, while Pappi, of course, was comfortably enthroned next to Franz in the front seat, studying his trusty Michelin travel guide.

The weather was wonderful. The air sparkled. Everything conspired to make leaving more difficult.

After spending one night in Digne and the next in Geneva, we arrived in Zurich on October 6. We stayed for four days, specifically for Mother to make financial arrangements at her bank, transactions that were complete mysteries to me and, I dare say, to my father as well. In this respect, as in many others, she was the head of the family.

An entry in my diary.

October 6, 1937

We had lunch at the famous old "Zimmerleuten" restaurant. We had roast deer-back with small, square pieces of lard inserted into the meat, which is done by threading it through with a larding needle, I am told. With it came a sour cream sauce and lingonberries. What a treat! The writer Kesser joined us. Among other profound pronouncements he came up with: "Women only write well when they have confessions to make."

Is that true?

We were so used to heat in Nice, now it is ice cold. Left Zurich early in the morning, drove via Basel and Belfort back over the border to France. We stayed overnight in an ugly, unfriendly little hotel in Chaumont that was kept by an arrogant Madame wrapped in a shawl and a still more arrogant Mademoiselle in a knitted wool jacket. We are freezing miserably.

October 10, 1937

Drove through Troyes to Sense in the morning to see the beautiful gothic cathedral. Everywhere hunters and hounds walking through drifting fog over the fields. Brown earth and autumnal forest. On to the castle at Fontainebleau.

October 11, 1937

Toured the castle, drove on to Chartres and the overwhelming cathedral. The sun came out a little; it warmed up. Through the forest of Rambouillet to Versailles.

October 12, 1937

Visited the grand castle of Versailles in the morning and the large and small Trianons in the afternoon. I so regret not knowing enough of the history of that period. I guess I should have been aware of our itinerary and done some special studying ahead of time. Everything seems to be happening so much at random, one looses the impetus to plan.

For a high price of admission we were allowed to view Marie Antoinette's little private theater. Father would not have left without having seen that. How often in our travels did we have to drive out of our way to examine a stage or theater building in some unlikely place, so, of course, this famous edifice was not to be missed.

Walked through the unbelievably beautiful park. The paths were covered with fallen autumn leaves from the mighty trees overhead. There were little humped bridges. One slips on rotting foliage. Charmingly playful, the Hameau, the doll-and-love-village of the queen and her court, the elegant ladies and gentlemen playing shepherds and shepherdesses in powdered wigs and crinolines.

Walking back along a broad chestnut avenue I ran through the rustling leaves, kicking a shining chestnut and jumping around like a fool. To finish this bit off, I bought a red sucker from a very fat woman and proceeded to slurp it slowly with great enthusiasm.

Late in the afternoon we arrived in Paris and our Franz maneuvered us with death-defying skill through the incredible traffic. The city was teeming with visitors to the big French Colonial Exhibit. Even in our Hotel Corona, in the usually quiet Cité Bergere we had to spend the first night in one dark little room, the three of us together. Only Oma Marta got a room to herself.

A great part of the following week was spent at the grounds of the amazing exhibit. Every French colony had its own elaborate life-sized building in the style of its origin, often presenting people of that region demonstrating crafts, ceremonies, or dances. Animals of their lands were brought in and plant life, foods, and examples of industries were shown. It all stretched out in a huge park-like area, and we explored everything to the point of exhaustion, relishing the festive atmosphere.

Dinner at the small Auberge du Père Louis in the city. There again we had met the Bechers. A large spit roasted our delicious chicken. There were strawberries with whipped cream for desert. The room was quite dark, except for the candles on all of the tables. We spoke of many things but not of worries, such as the Japanese invading China, Hitler's growing strength, or the destruction of Guernica in Spain. Without mentioning it to each other we had decided to tune it all out for once and let the warm and friendly room and candlelight help us to forget for just a little while.

We saw the Greco exhibit at the Faubourg St. Honore. It was the first time that I could study Greco more intensively, and the impression was very strong.

The diary:

October 21,1937

In the early morning I went to the Palais d'Arts Moderne by myself to see the very great Van Gogh show. Then I took the Metro and went for a stroll at the Quartiers Latin, meandering slowly through the narrow streets.

I was saying goodbye to Paris on my own. The weather was beautiful. I took a bus for a lengthy ride down the teeming avenues, my face close to the window, gazing at the sidewalk cafés and the hustle and bustle of the crowded streets that celebrated the festive mood of the grand exhibition.

Tired from the constant running around during the last week and, to top it off, today's excursion, I landed at the Rond-Point of the Champs Elysees, got off the bus with shaking knees and headed happily for one of the many inviting benches looking out toward the Place de la Concorde. For a long time I sat in the sun. The trees were almost bare; their long spiky shadows weaved a net across the shiny streets. Golden leaves blew down on my hair and shoulders, blew across the square, and danced above the shimmering spray of the fountains. I said goodbye to one part of my life and perhaps, finally, to my childhood.

I then met my family at the Café de la Paix, and we drove to the train station with Oma Marta, mountains of baggage and, of course, Bella. We arrived at Le Havre and left Europe on the ship "Manhattan" at midnight on the twenty first of October in the year of nineteen thirty-seven, for me a moment in history.

My irrepressible mother on board the cruise ship Milwaukee, 1937

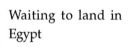

Waiting to land in Egypt

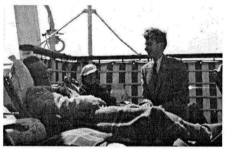

Erich Ebermayer, Mac Baedeker and I at Sea

FAY ALTMAN
Her Own "Dog-naper"

POODLE KIDNAPED

The crime of the voyage was told by its perpetrator, Miss Fay Altman, with obvious relish and no regard for consequence. Miss Altman, the daughter of a New York playwright, described the desperate measures she took to insure the proximity of her French poodle during the voyage.

With infinite stealth the poodle was kidnaped from the boat deck doghouse of the ship and stowed away in Miss Altman's cabin during the entire voyage.

Arrival in San Francisco, 1937

View from my window on Russian Hill, painted in 1941

Stage set for Rossini opera "Signor Bruschino,"
1942

Ralph and Pat's Wedding

Last picture of Oma Marta, died 1943

Werner and Elisabeth Philipp. 1942

Self portrait in New York, 1943

View from Christel's balcony in
Greenwich village, 1943

Christel and Baby Andrea, 1944

I return for Father's birthday

Engagement photo,
September, 1944

Such a "Nice Young Man"

The Wedding party. Clockwise from upper left: Father Gilbert, Gil, me, Ralph, Pat, my father, my mother, Mother Gilbert, Putzi in front

Chapter Fourteen

To Our New World

October 22, 1937

"Waves as high as a house," Mother called through my cabin door and lurched toward her own bunk. An ominous noise told me that she had crashed against the side wall before reaching her bed.

The passage through the much-feared channel had been quiet and nice, but right after dinner it started to rock. The night was bad. I hardly slept. I lay still without moving and contemplated my stomach. The ship sounded as if it wanted to crack.

October 23, 1937

Still storm! I stayed in bed, flat on my back, lousy nauseous and terribly bored. The whole day I lay like that and the whole night, eating nothing, only swallowing Vasano and counting the minutes. I tried to breathe calmly to hold my stomach in balance and moaned silently.

Towards evening Pappi threw up. Oma Marta had already done so earlier. Mutti followed suit.

October 24, 1937

A terrible night that was. The storm did not let up. I still could not eat. At lunch they brought me mashed potatoes and cold chicken. I swallowed two bites with difficulty. Again I lay stiff and could not move. I felt like dying. At night almost got thrown out of bed.

October 25, 1937

Storm. My God, it will never end. I could not even lift myself up.
"It will be over soon, Miss," Mr. Brugman, the steward, looked down on me and laughed. Later Mrs. Evans, the stewardess, who never laughed, came in and looked thoroughly disgusted. "Every one is sick," she said. Later in the afternoon the sea started to calm down, and I heaved a sigh of relief. Last night I slept deeply.

October 26, 1937

When I woke up the ocean was calm, innocently blue, and deceptively peaceful, as if nothing could ever stir up its fury again. Reeling and weak, I staggered up to the deck where the dog cages were kept.
There was Bella, still shaking with fear but whimpering with joy at seing me, pressing her little body so hard against the rungs of the cage that I had a hard time unlatching her door.
The dog deck was where I spent most of my time for the next three days, armed with a book and a blanket that became unusually bulky under my arm and heavy when I retired to my cabin at night.

October 29, 1937

Early in the morning someone knocked on my door. "We are landing in twenty minutes, Miss." Bella barked her answer from under my covers. I detected a puzzled silence beyond the threshold of my cabin. Then someone cleared his throat audibly and resumed walking to knock on other doors, probably shaking his head and frowning.

Very slowly the crowd started to filter down the gangplank as I came on deck. The famous skyline of New York was shrouded in fog. Everybody shivered. Mother was in stitches. She was sure I had been lost, shoved overboard, or at least raped in someone's cabin.

"Where have you been?" Father for once took the initiative and steered her toward the exit. When I was halfway down the plank with Bella firmly tucked under my arm there was a sudden commotion in front of me.

"Hey, you are pushing my wife!" screamed a big man elbowing the man in front of him.

"The hell I am," the other barked back, trying to keep his heavy suitcase from slipping.

More words were exchanged and suddenly fists were flying. Various pieces of baggage slipped under people's feet, everyone got pushed and pummeled and women shrieked. I stood and stared, incredulous, fascinated. Never had I seen adults hitting each other. Was that the custom here? The "Crude Americans," they had said in France. Was that what they meant? My first impression of the United States was devastating.

Later on the pier, in an ice-cold draft, I sat behind iron bars with Oma Marta and Bella. We were waiting for a customs inspection, and it was an endless wait. People who looked as cold and unhappy as we were milled about in droves. Bella squatted at the end of her leash among the piles of bags around us. I followed the resulting little stream with anxious eyes, praying that it would not disappear under a heap of packages and duffel bags.

Finally released and stuffed into a grimy taxicab, we were deposited at the Hotel Franconia on Seventy-Second Street, to a nice light apartment that was our home for the next month. It helped us to catch our breath.

Life became brighter from then on. We tried to explore the city by walking as much as we could along Fifth Avenue, in SoHo, and Rockefeller Center. We enjoyed walking in

Central Park and Bella especially approved. Riding in one of the many horse-drawn coaches that were parked for hire at the rim of the park seemed so utterly incongruous in this enormous, otherwise motorized city that it served to put us into a real holiday mood. It was fun. We took escorted bus excursions. Among other sights we were taken through Wall Street, Chinatown, and to a mission there, where pale white office boys arrogantly took it upon themselves to convert the heathens, as I wrote in my diary. We were taken to ghettos and to slums, but not on foot. It was very superficial and not at all enlightening.

One afternoon soon after we arrived, two young women knocked on our apartment door.

"Hello, I want to welcome you to our country," they announced to Mother. "My name is Gladys Loeb and this is my sister, Amy. I met your son Ralph when he was in New York on his way to Oregon, and he told us to look you up."

Black-haired Gladys, whose sincerity and warmth shone through her city-pale face, was somewhat older than I. Fat and short, pinkish-clean Amy was my age. We became good friends.

Gladys introduced her sister at least five times. "This is my sister, Amy." I never knew why she thought our foreignness would make it hard for us to grasp family relationships. From then on, whenever we mentioned Amy among ourselves, it was always as My Sister Amy.

I took off with them, and then I really got to see the town. That day and for several days during the next few weeks they showed me New York, not from a sightseeing bus, but mostly on foot, exploring the streets of this immense city. I had never walked so much in my life.

Late one afternoon we sank exhausted into our chairs at the Rainbow Grill high atop the Rockefeller Center. We found a free table at the wide ring of windows that ran around the curve of the whole crowded room. Elbows leaning on the table, I gazed down at the snaking procession of tiny people and cars so far below, among the mountainous buildings that rose like cliffs from the depths of their canyons. The sun had just gone down. The lights of the city started to come on, pouring a warm glow into the cold haze of the wintry air. Soon the dark of the night took over. Only little table lamps illuminated the room and the glass before me seemed to merge with the blackness of the sky and drew my eyes down through the now translucent air to a sea of blinking lights.

I held my drink carefully, sipping from it off and on. I had wine when I lived in France and whiskey in London, but this was my first cocktail in America, an Orange Blossom.

I looked at Gladys. We were all tired from running around, but she looked sad.

"Hey Sis, what's eating you?" Amy had noticed too.

"It's about my friend Stuart," Gladys said. "He's going to Spain to fight."

"Good for him." Her eyes blazing and her little round body almost rising out of her chair, My Sister Amy pounded her fist on the table. "That bastard Franco has to be stopped! Maybe I'll go myself."

"You'll get to crouch and shoot right next to Hemingway." That idea brightened Gladys' mood and in spite of her initial anger, even My Sister Amy had to laugh.

Many young people at that time went to Spain to fight and quite a few did not come back. Picasso painted his *Guernica*.

The whole world was restless around us. Japan's invasion of China, Hitler and Mussolini getting friendlier and friendlier, Britain's attempts to appease, and Germany's war machine revving up; how could we be oblivious to these events?

Even in New York, away from turbulent Europe, visiting the Metropolitan Museum, the Frick Collection, the theaters, and Central Park, the many teeming ethnic districts within the all-embracing city that brimmed with life and energy, the fundamental sense of insecurity and upheaval stayed deep within us, no matter how pleased and excited we were in discovering our new world.

"There is something that you absolutely have to see before you leave New York," Kaethe Steinitz paced back and forth in our apartment at the Hotel Franconia, waving a city map under our noses, like someone intent on directing traffic. "Here," she said, "One Hundred Forty-Second Street and Lenox Avenue, the Savoy Ballroom, in the black people's part of town. I'll take you tonight."

How it occurred that again and again we met old acquaintances from Europe in the United States I do not know. Kaethe Steinitz had been the wife of our physician in Hanover. She was a tiny, wiry woman of about my parent's age, always inquisitive, and so active that it was exhausting to be around her for any length of time. She was intensely interested in other people's lives and in art. She drew and read with enthusiasm and made it one of her missions to support talented young people, not only with money but also with her unflagging confidence.

In her home in Hanover one could find young persons congregating in the living room on any afternoon or evening of the week, having coffee and sandwiches, involved in animated discussions. They were not only her three daughters' friends, but young hopefuls of all kinds, including perhaps a few of the hopeless she picked up here and there. Art, personal aspirations, and certainly politics were discussed. The latter was decidedly one good reason why she and her family had to leave Germany at the earliest time possible, aside from the fact that they were Jewish.

I had seen black people here and there in London and Paris, but never in groups, dominating their surroundings.

The Savoy was a very large room, horseshoe-shaped and ringed by booths from which the action on the ballroom floor could be observed without getting pulled into the turbulence of the dancing couples. Yet at first getting pulled into it was exactly what I would have loved.

A group of people congregated next to the cloakroom when we entered through the main door. The music swung out at us through smoke and a whirlwind of movement and color. A tall, good-looking young man stretched out his hand, asking me to dance. Quickly Mother pulled me towards the booths, and my suitor turned with a shrug and grabbed another young woman, bouncing away with her as if he were rocking on the waves of the sea. My initial annoyance at Mother's interference quickly turned to relief. What a sorry figure I would have made among those incredible dancers and acrobats! I felt the rhythm in my bones, but that was where it had to stay.

I wrote in my diary:

November 27, 1937

We left New York and boarded the Pennsylvania, the ship that would take us through the Panama Canal to San Francisco.

November 30, 1937

The ship was gliding along slowly and peacefully. We stood under the canvas cover that shielded the deck. The air was hot and humid. The sun burned down on us, disappearing behind drifting clouds, giving way to sudden, short-lived, pouring rainfalls in twenty to thirty minute intervals that left the ship and the dense jungle along the shores steaming.
Sailed into the beautiful harbor of Havana at noon and toured the old part of the city.

Stopped for a short time in Cristobal and then sailed through the Panama Canal to Balboa. Went sightseeing and continued along the coast past Costa Rica, Nicaragua, and Guatemala to Acapulco, where we went on land again. Banana palms and a village of miserable huts in the midst of a clearing. Dense vegetation surrounded it. There were music and dancing and very friendly people living in abject poverty. I took photographs and fled the sight of a cockfight after snapping one dutiful picture. It was too awful.

December 11, 1937

When I got up at six o'clock it was still pitch dark as if it were night. The ship's bell kept ringing without interruption. That seemed strange to me. I was cold. I tightened the collar of my coat around my neck and went up on deck.

A chilly mist prickled against my face. We were wrapped in thick, heavy fog.

A shadowy figure coming toward me turned out to be the Egyptian night steward whose lengthy name I never could remember. "Better go inside, Miss; it's cold out here."

"When will we get to Los Angeles?" I asked, and he grinned and pointed down to the water. We had been standing still since last night. The anchor had been dropped, and the sailors sat fishing on the decks, looking like gray outcroppings on a terraced landscape.

Trying not to slip on the wet planks, I walked to the railing. Leaning there for a while, I looked back at the ship and the shadowy, floating shapes of masts and other faceless objects that loomed out of the fog, creating a painting like a Turner, done in his later years. It was scary, uncanny, but I stayed for a while because it was also somehow beautiful, like a dream. The foghorn sounded and a bell rang from time to time. The water below splashed rhythmically against the sides of the ship. After a while it got a little lighter, and the fog turned orange red.

Finally I went back to bed. It was seven o'clock.

The ship moved again when I awoke the second time and around noon we landed in San Pedro, the harbor of Los Angeles. We were taken to the city and then sightseeing by bus to Hollywood and Beverly Hills. The rain was pelting the windshield and the streets became rivers. We saw almost nothing except water and fog.

December 12, 1937

The weather was wonderful the next day. I sat on deck in the morning, sunning myself and brooding. Unusually large brown and white seagulls circled, and big heartedly permitted us to feed them, catching their loot in a dance of swooping wings. Two pelicans were the outsiders, rocking back and forth on the water with heavy beaks and gullets, content after a good meal.

As soon as we left the harbor in the afternoon, hefty waves started to shake us about again. The day before, a tornado had passed these shores, supposedly a rarity here. We were allowed to enjoy the aftermath. The night was not exactly pleasant.

December 13, 1937

After lunch the next day, San Francisco rose on the horizon like a fairytale city. Just for us, I am sure, it had pulled back its customary curtain of fog and cloud. The air was sparkling clear. The sun was streaming through the brilliant red tracery of the recently opened Golden Gate Bridge, creating a festive welcome garland, as our ship sailed underneath to the harbor. We felt completely overwhelmed by the indescribable beauty of it all.

Not even the ensuing turmoil of arrival, of going through the ritual of meeting with the immigration officers on board and muscling our way through hordes of photographers and journalists could erase the feeling of euphoria.

One eager young man with a mirror-reflex camera slung around his neck grabbed me by my elbow. "Please Miss, just a few questions. I am from the Chronicle."

He dragged me with Bella held tightly under my arm up to the sundeck, took my picture and fired a string of nosy questions at me, asking in the end how my dog liked the trip, since he knew that dogs had to be caged away from the cabins.

I laughed and confessed my misdeed to him. He was deliriously happy that he had a story. And so it was that Bella and I became celebrities, with picture and story published in the San Francisco Chronicle.

We truly had arrived!

On December 24, I looked down on the palm trees of Union Square from the window of my room at the Plaza Hotel. It was a cold, gray day, and the slight drizzle discouraged anyone from sitting on the benches around the fountain, except for a few disheveled men huddling in their ragged isolation. Brisk traffic swirled around the square, pouring in and out of the many streets that fed into it. One car suddenly ejected from the stream and landed right in front of the hotel with screaming brakes.

Almost colliding with the eager doorman who was trying to be helpful, a young man, coattails flying, dashed towards the entrance. It was my brother!

"I just had to greet you all," he grinned. "Portland can miss me for a week. I have to be back on the first. Merry Christmas!"

What a surprise it was. We had not expected him.

Up until that moment it had not felt like Christmas at all. We had passed the elegant stores on Post and Stockton streets, glittering with enticing holiday displays, and past the shivering Salvation Army stalwarts tinkling their little bells and assuring us of God's blessing, yet the spirit of the season had not taken hold of us. How could we have a tree in the hotel room? Just the three of us and Oma Marta, who could not care less, and—without Ralph?

So now, oh joy, the family was complete again!

The next week was spent exploring the city and its surroundings. The ferry took us to Berkeley with its university and the Greek Theatre. Some days later we went by train to San Mateo, where our cousins John and Bess Altman lived. There I met Pat and Nancy Benson, who were visiting from Portland. They too were our cousins. Their mother, Hazel, was John's sister, and Dr. Robert Benson, their father, had been instrumental in getting Ralph accepted to the university in Portland.

Pat was my age, nineteen, and just as Ralph had predicted, knowing me and now also Pat very well, she and I sat quietly during the general family chatter, not uttering a single word, either to each other or to the rest of the group. This mutual silence was surely proof that we were closely related. Little did we know that in three years time the relationship would be even closer.

A sunny December day in Golden Gate Park. We sat in the Japanese Tea Garden and Mother looked at me with slight disapproval. "Your brother thinks that you need a vacation from your parents. Is that true?"

I straightened my back and set my teacup down, ready for a string of arguments and accusations.

Ralph rescued me again. "I thought you might like to spend some time with me in Portland." He smiled at me. "I am kind of lonely by myself."

I tried to tone down my utter delight and felt that I still had to answer Mother's challenge. "I'd certainly like to. It would be nice, but what you just said, Mutti . . ."

Ralph interrupted me. "Stop, that's all we have to hear. It's a deal." With that he broke a fortune cookie in half and gave me the little paper slip. "Let's see what it says."

CHAPTER FIFTEEN

The Portland Family

January 1, 1938

Pappi took Ralph and me to the ferry in a taxi. Mutti stayed at the hotel with Bella, looking very pale and sad. Pappi almost cried when we said goodbye. Crossing the bay, we munched sandwiches on the ferry that took us to Oakland and the train station.

We ran into great luck on the train. All of the beds were sold out, so instead they gave us a whole compartment to ourselves. We closed the door in spite of the conductor's suspicious glances. A nice old porter made our beds up, and we went to sleep rather early.

January 2, 1938

At nine in the morning Ralph woke me, and I climbed down from my bunk. Great joy! We rode through the most beautiful winter forest that I have seen since Teufen. Tall, snow-covered pines, drifting snow clouds, off and on a little piece of blue sky.

Peaceful breakfast in the dining car. Scrambled eggs, toast and honey, and coffee. People obviously took us for newlyweds. I could tell by the way they smiled at us. Later we sat in our compartment, each with our legs across to the seat of the other.

We leafed through magazines, Story *and* Coronet, *talked a little and looked out of the window. Lonely snowed-in farmhouses, ice-crusted lakes, hills, valleys, again hills, again a farm, small frozen waterfalls, and forest, forest, forest.*

We arrived in Portland, and Ralph took me to the Elmwood Apartments, where I was going to live with him for the next few months. It was a big dark house, and the furnishings in our small place were as drab and unremarkable as our surroundings, inside and out. But never mind! I started immediately to rearrange the furniture in my room, as I had in every hotel room on our travels when we stayed for more than a few nights at a time. Whatever table there was got moved in front of the window and equipped with all of my books and writing materials. An armchair got positioned near a reasonable source of light for reading, and the sheets and blankets on the bed were loosened from the restraints of the mattress that would have prevented me from rolling myself up in them at night. I discovered a hideous ashtray and a ceramic flower vase that was shaped like a praying angel. They were both hidden away in the top shelf of the closet. Pictures of *The Sunset On The Nile and Purple Cows Grazing On Blue-Green Pastures* that Ralph had not paid any attention to were assigned a perfect spot under the bed. Only then did I make myself at home.

We led a peaceful life, the two of us. While Ralph was at the university, I would have my elbows on the window table, bent over a stack of papers trying to write a story, sometimes with success and, more often than not, despairing in the process.

"Now what's eating you?" Ralph was looking at me with narrowed eyes. It was early in the morning. He was about to leave for the university, his winter coat buttoned up over a heavy sweater, hastily stuffing papers into his briefcase. I was still sitting at the breakfast table, nursing a cup of already lukewarm coffee.

"Buck up. Why aren't you working on your story yet? Get some energy into your bones, for heaven's sake. You've got the talent, use it."

The door slammed. I got up, went to the window, and watched him rushing down the street. I took the dishes to the kitchen and then just stood there for a moment, quite inert, my hands on the cold rim of the sink. A mirror hung above the counter and when I slowly raised my head, a face appeared, and it was mine. I gazed at it, and then it spoke, and a poem was born. It was there within minutes, still in German and from the heart.

> *Ich kann mein Gesicht im Spiegel sehn*
> *und meinen Blick.*
> *Er laechelt mir zu*
> *und meine Nase she ich stehn*
> *recht gross und round*
> *und mein geschwungener Mund*
> *der sagt Du.*
>
> *Die Brauen ueber den Augen sind zu schwer*
> *und die Augen selbst wissen nicht was sie wollen*
> *ob sie lachen sollen*
> *oder besser weinen.*
> *So schauen sie ein bischen verquer.*
> *Du Gesicht dort im Spiegel,*
> *was willst du von mir.*
> *Du stoerst mich.*
> *Ich kann dir nichts geben.*
> *Ich lenk nicht das Leben.*
> *Warts ab.*

You, face, there in the mirror,
I see your glance.
What is it you want from me?
There is your nose, quite long and big
and your mouth says:
See, that's you.

The brows above the eyes are too heavy
and the eyes do not know what they want,
whether they want to laugh
or rather cry.
That's why they look so queer.

You face, there in the mirror, what do you want?
Your silly eyes long for something.
Your curved mouth longs for something.
What is it you want from me?
You bother me.
I can't give you anything.
I do not master life.
Just wait.

The dam was broken. I could write again. I did not show the poem to anybody for a long time, not even to Ralph when he came home late in the afternoon. It was too intimately mine.

A new story took hold.

I remembered the family doctor we had in Dahlem when I was a child who we met again many years later in Switzerland in nineteen thirty-three, the year of our emigration. He had become an old man and had managed to flee Germany. His long beard that used to tickle me when I was little as he listened to my chest was now white. His mind wandered, and it took patience to remain in his company for any length of time. A young girl like me would play a role in this new story. I saw it so clearly.

I wrote until Ralph came home, earlier than usual. He went to the closet, got my coat, and held it out to me. "We are having dinner with friends and maybe going to a movie afterwards," he said. "It's about time you got out a bit."

I liked all of his friends. There was Frank Perlman, Rob's assistant, a tall, handsome young man adored by cousin Nancy. But then, she adored every man who was good looking. Frances studied chemistry and did some tutoring for Ralph. Mary and Vivian were nurses. Two couples, the von Schmidts and the van Horns, who were called the Vons and the Vans by everybody, introduced me to their combined family of dachshunds who were responsible for my never-ending love of that canine breed.

During evening hours and on weekends we had plenty of company. Also, friends and relatives picked us up and took us places. We had no car, of course.

Several times a week we were picked up or went by bus to have dinner at the Bensons' home. It was a very old house, a grandmotherly house, commodious, leaning slightly sidewise, but not ready to fall for quite some time. Walking across the living room floor it felt as if one navigated on board a gently tilting ship. It was somewhat disconcerting to me at first, but then I got used to it. The house belonged to Dr. Robert Benson, Rob to us, who was a professor and head of the allergy department at the university, the husband of my father's cousin Hazel, and father of Pat, Nancy, and Bobby.

Dinner was being served there on my second day in Portland. We sat around the large polished mahogany table,

Rob at the head, towering, even when seated, over everybody, in size as well as in composure. He was tall, slim, and bony. His strong, narrow face was dominated by a large hooked nose, his expression one of dignity and reserve. His great grandmother had been of Ottawa and Chippewa Indian ancestry, and looking at Rob one could well believe it. Often he was stern and silent, but once in a while the sun broke through, he joined the company and the conversation, and one discovered that he had a fine sense of humor when he chose to display it.

Next to him sat his mother in law, Grandmother Eugenia, the mother of John Altman and Hazel, who was called Jutch among family members. I am not sure whether they did so to her face. She was born in Demming, New Mexico, became a schoolteacher, and told us often how hard it had been to ride a horse through dry and desolate countryside, in heat as well as in snow, to her one-room schoolhouse many miles away. When I was small, in Germany, letters would come from America signed by Aunt Eugenia. They were written in fluent German, studiously correct, with a teacher's precision. When and where she learned that language I do not know. Patsy and Nancy, her granddaughters, were always made to include little perfunctory notes to their nebulous cousins in an unreal land across the sea.

I remember her coming to Berlin-Dahlem to visit us once or twice when traveling to Europe. She had remained in my memory as an energetic, small woman with noisy shoes, a fur piece that had an animal's head with shiny glass eyes on one end of it and a bushy tail on the other, slung over her shoulders. She would hug and kiss me, always leaving a slight residue of moisture from her ample lips on my cheek as the fox's head would brush across my nose. I was immediately required to recite my alphabet and my numbers and show how many poems I knew by heart. Every time I heard her ever-cheerful voice I tried to hide.

So there she was sitting across from me, a bent and shriveled gnome with a slightly hoarse and weakened voice that nevertheless still knew how to lecture everyone around her. She expected excellent behavior.

Nancy and Bobby were the only other members of the family present at my first dinner in their home. Their mother, Hazel, was staying in San Francisco with Pat, who was recuperating from surgery in a hospital there.

Nancy was seventeen, two years younger than Pat and I. She was a brash young girl whose interests leaned first towards herself, then to the opposite sex in relation to herself, and finally to popular songs and beer. Unlike her older sister and younger brother she was not an intellectual. She was not happy, either. Something was missing in her life, and she made up for it by filling the emptiness with carousing and mischief.

Twelve-year-old Bobby, who was slightly darker skinned than the rest of his family, had shiny black hair and deep brown eyes. He was handsome, lively and impish, and could easily have been taken for a boy of Native American heritage.

With consideration and quite an air of fondness, two other members of the household were introduced to me. First came happy-faced Gunda, enveloped in the luscious aroma of onions and roast beef emanating from the enormous platter she deposited proudly next to the candelabra in the middle of the table. The warm light from the candles colored her round red cheeks even brighter. Thinking of Gunda, the word ample comes to mind. She was ample of body and ample of good spirits.

Behind her, Missy appeared from the kitchen, obviously eager to see the new member of the family in whose employ she had been for so many years. Her water-pale eyes looked at me over the rims of her wire-framed glasses with a questioning, searching look that said: Now let me see if I find you good enough to be accepted in this house. The wrinkled face relaxed after a few moments. The glasses were pushed back up the track of her long, skinny nose, some stray gray hair was brushed off her forehead, and with a nod and tentative little smile she stretched out her hand to me. I was accepted!

A little twinge of sadness grabbed me. I thought of Seusa, like Missy, practically a member of our family for many years, who had been more like a second mother than a nanny to me. She had to be left behind. We wanted to take her with us, but she was afraid of strange countries and people whose language she could not speak.

Rob, presiding at the head of the table, carved the roast with precision and elegance, his demeanor serious and concentrated. What followed was utterly incongruous.

"Now you will be introduced to a very important family ceremony," he said, turning to me, looking very grave and clearing his throat. I expected to have to listen to a formal speech or toast of some kind when he got up. Instead he stood very erect, scooped a large portion of mashed potato from a serving dish, raised his arm, ladle in hand, practically up to the ceiling and delivered its contents from that height to his plate with the precision of a basketball player sure of scoring a goal.

Everyone clapped and cheered. The eminent professor sat down again with an almost-noticeable grin on his face and a twinkle in his eye.

Dinner could begin.

From her golden frame on the wall over the mantelpiece Karoline Altman, the great-grandmother of all of us of the younger generation, looked down, most certainly scandalized.

When Ralph was not at the university he studied at home, bent over his books and papers. I could see the tension in his back and shoulders, the anxiety in the way he creased his forehead, running his hand through his hair from time to time. Days preceding a test were spent in fevered agony. He smoked incessantly.

Early one morning he carried his coffee cup to his desk. "I've got two hours before I have the test. I still have to go over some notes." He emptied the ashtray from the night before and lit the third cigarette since breakfast.

I nodded. "I'll be quiet," I said.

An hour passed. After brooding over my new story for a while I had just settled down at my table, ready to write full steam ahead, or so I hoped, when thunderous knocking shook the door.

Disheveled, Cousin Nancy burst into the room and threw herself on the sofa. She was very pale. The dark shadows under her small eyes did not enhance the otherwise pretty girl's appearance. Even her perfume could not disguise the smell of sweat and smoke about her.

"Boy, did I have a night!" She kicked her shoes off and settled back. "There were Betty and Sue and James and Roy and, of course, me and my Lionel. We drove up to Mount Hood at midnight. But then, you want to know what we did?"

She winked at us mischievously.

"Nanny," I said patiently, "Perhaps you'll tell us all about it tonight. Now we have to work. No time to visit."

I was talking to thin air.

"We had a whole bunch of six packs, see. We set them all out in the snow. They made a long, long row, and we drank them, one after the other. Isn't that just *too* funny?" She died with laughter and stretched her legs across the rickety coffee table, upsetting the remnants of our breakfast.

I started to get furious. "Nan, Ralph has to study. Please go!"

"Hey, what a goody-goody boy," she shrieked, and started to sing. *"Bei mir bist du schoen,"* on and on, over and over. I grabbed her arms to pull her up. She resisted.

Ralph finally threw his book down on the table in desperation, turned around and saw us furiously wrestling on the floor. It was he who was the winner. He threw himself into the tangle of arms and legs, pulled us apart, took Nan literally by the scruff of her neck as if she had been the proverbial puppy-dog, and transported her out the door, locking it behind her. We heard her tromping down the stairs, singing, "Hi Ho, Hi Ho, it's off to work we go." Snow White's dwarves would have fled. Never, ever was I able to hear that song from then on without thinking of Nanny.

"She is a Barbarian," I grumbled. Too late for more work, his morning ruined, Ralph dressed in a hurry and left.

We lived peacefully together. Ralph struggled with his studies, I wrote with varying success and bouts of depression or spurts of confidence and hope. Pat returned from the hospital in San Francisco with Hazel and was bedridden for a few more weeks. I spent much time keeping her company, and I am sure that she and Ralph formed an ever-tighter bond during that time.

I stayed with Ralph for nearly four months until I returned to San Francisco and the new house my parents had rented in the meantime.

CHAPTER SIXTEEN

The House on Russian Hill

Taylor Street climbed straight up the steep hill, allowed just enough space to accommodate a large house and small public park at the top, then plunged down towards Fisherman's Wharf.

Part of this house my parents had rented. It hugged the hill high above the city. We occupied the top two stories. Two other, smaller apartments could be entered lower down on the hill at the side of the building. An old lady, Dr. Esther Rosencrantz, a retired physician, lived in one of them, and a single young woman and her child inhabited the other, still further down the slope.

Stepping from the steeply inclined street into the shade of a pepper tree in the small courtyard that led to the entrance of our dwelling, one had to hold carefully onto an iron gate to keep one's equilibrium.

Above our spacious living room, Father's library, and the kitchen, there were two bedrooms, one of which was mine, outfitted with a sleeping couch instead of a bed. Since some of the Biedermeier furniture could not be accomodated downstairs, I inherited the desk and my beloved black flower carpet.

Standing at my window, I was suspended high above the city. A small, sturdy church raised its tower into the air like the mast of a ship sailing through the welter of the rising and dipping streets and courtyards of the Italian quarter, little Italy, below me. Beyond that the city sprawled out toward the water and our view swept across it to the Bay Bridge and the fog-shrouded hills beyond.

When you lived in a city long enough or intensely enough, it assumed a face, a character, a special identity. It was not just a collection of streets and houses, parks, bridges, and stoplights. There would be a particular street where you walked happily with particular friends, houses in which decisions were made or disappointments met. There would be a special park were you sat on a special bench and cried your eyes out on a hot summer morning.

There was the view that you waited for every time the cable car carried you to the top of the hill. You shivered in the drizzly air, held tight to the fog-damp seats, and gazed down toward the bay with its fishing boats and dark cloud shadows that brushed the glimmering water.

And then there was the park, wonderful Golden Gate Park, shaded by majestic trees, spreading like a slow-moving river along one side of the city.

We walked there one day, my parents and I. I had just returned from Portland a few days before. It was April and azaleas were blooming. Children and dogs played on the grassy hillocks, the fountain was splashing on the plaza in front of the aquarium, and a giddy young man was drawing figure eights on his bicycle around the wooden benches at the deserted bandstand.

We headed for the De Young Museum that sprawled across from the Aquarium building amidst lavish plantings of narcissus and crocus. A large exhibit of African and Oceanic ethnic art was on display. Father, keenly interested in one special mask that had a tower of many smaller faces rising from the top of its brow, asked to see the curator of the show.

Before we could see her, she announced her approach
by the slightly squishy sound her flat, rubber-soled shoes
made on the marble floor of the corridor that ran between
galleries of the museum. Coming into view and greeting us
with an outstretched hand and a welcoming smile, she
introduced herself: Dr. Elisabeth Moses. My parents were
more successful then I in suppressing any outward
expression of surprise, whereas my raised eyebrows and
half-open mouth gave away my shock and amusement.
Dr. Moses had a German accent that surpassed my father's,
and that was quite a feat.

Elisabeth became the first friend in our new life in San
Francisco. Middle-aged, fairly tall, and not yet corpulent,
but, as my mother would say, with a figure that was Well
Packed. Not handsome but imposing, with her eagle-sharp
face and her bright, intelligent eyes, she was not a person
one could easily overlook. We spent many a pleasant,
stimulating evening in her apartment getting acquainted
with a whole new group of friends and, most importantly,
with her brother Paul and his wife Li.

Paul was a physician whose specialty was the treatment
of ear, nose, and throat diseases. But the study of the influence
of mind and emotions on the function and use of the human
voice had come to be his main interest. He had also written
and lectured extensively on treatments and research for
various speech impediments, especially stuttering.

"You can tell so much about people," Paul would say,
"just by listening to their voices, whether they talk or sing."

He had already made a name for himself in professional
circles during the few years that he had practiced in this
country. Singers who came to perform at the San Francisco
Opera House, from as far away as the Metropolitan Opera
in New York, would consult him when the fog of the bay
area, a cold, or the rigors of travel were effecting their
voices. He treated them, soothed their worries, and more
often then not invited them to his home.

Li, his wife, had followed him in emigration, although she was not Jewish. She was a lively woman, very pretty, and quite a bit younger than he was. Her home was meticulously and tastefully kept. It seemed that her life revolved around the well being of her husband and young son, Stefan. She was a wonderful hostess and cook, loved friends, laughter and parties, and yet, as I later discovered, was not a completely happy person. She probably missed her homeland and her family. At Paul's urging she took up the study of textile and costume design. She had quite a flair for it, and she gained his approval, which she obviously craved. I liked Li. She was a nice, good-looking, and competent woman. Why was she so unsure of herself?

There was no reverse racial discrimination among the people we knew. We were all refugees, all in the same boat. There were many who were not Jewish, including my own mother. Kaethe Ostwald and Irma Engel, doctors' wives, and Dr. Karl Wieth, the museum-director from Cologne and his wife were gentile. I had met quite a few so-called Aryans since leaving Germany who had departed in protest or had to flee for political reasons. Still, that made them no less homesick for the country in which they grew up. Who could blame them?

An invitation to Paul and Li's house was always a joy. They entertained frequently, and I was often included. A whole group of immigrants gathered around them, not unlike the friends we had made in Nice, but there was a different atmosphere around these people: they were much more settled. A transient, uncertain way of life had been exchanged for a feeling of safety. Occupations and professions had been established, whether modest or substantial. We met several physicians, the Doctors Ostwald, Gassmann, and Gropper, all of whom, like Paul, had enrolled in medical schools in the U.S. to obtain American degrees. They all had thriving practices. Others, who had been bankers, lawyers, or in business, now were salespeople in department stores or worked in a bakery, became bookkeepers, or seamstresses. Never mind, they felt settled and safe, even though the trauma of having lost their homes and oftentimes family members and friends could never be erased.

Another big difference between the circle of friends we had in Nice and the composition of the group that gathered at the Moses' home: many new acquaintances were native San Franciscans. So unlike the exclusive French, who always kept us at arm's length, many Americans were drawn to us and we to them. We learned from each other.

Shortly after we arrived, my parents met Louis Levison, a retired businessman who made it his purpose in life to chaperone us and drive us all over town, the neighboring countryside and across the bay to Sausalito, where he had a second home, a bungalow at the water, and a boat. On many a summer morning he arrived to pick us up for a picnic, dressed in shorts that hung under his belly and a straw hat that kept his white hair down on his round head, like a dollop of whipped cream on his sunburned, cookie-brown skin. His eyes were bright blue and he smiled easily. I never saw him in a bad mood. We found out later that he had good reason to be unhappy and our admiration for his courage grew. He had a wife who hibernated in their big old house in the dark. She insisted that all the windows had to have their heavy velvet curtains drawn from morning to night. She never went out. So Louis, of course, was happiest when he could travel, roam freely around the landscape or broil at the beach in the sun. They had a son and two daughters. One girl was crippled by polio and in a wheelchair; another was retarded. Only the son was free of troubles.

Other early acquaintances were Emilia Hodell, an art critic at the *San Francisco Chronicle* and her husband Franz

Bergman, a painter and designer. Spencer Barefoot, a journalist at the same paper, was gay, a state of being that was still in disrepute in those days, but our friendship with him and his friends enriched us all. George Post, whose large, splashy watercolors I admired, reawakened in me a desire to paint. These were all interested and interesting people.

There was movement and action in our daily life in San Francisco, a big change from the feeling of numbness and brooding worry that had prevailed in Nice. People were busy and pursued or studied for new careers.

There were museum exhibits, lectures to attend, a good library, theatre performances, concerts, and friends with whom to share these treasures.

It had been a long concert and a very beautiful one. Alexander Brailowsky had played mostly Chopin and ended with a Mozart sonata. Listening to it, I felt I had been blessed, if such a description can be allowed an unreligious person.

We took the streetcar home. Paul, Li, and Elisabeth Moses were there, also my old friend Hans, who had appeared unexpectedly one day from Nice with a girlfriend, Gabrielle, and then Mother and I. Pappi hated concerts and had stayed home.

It was late, nearly eleven o'clock, a blustery October night. We still had to walk several blocks. Paul took the lead, as always, holding his wife's arm on his left. His arm encircled my shoulders on the right side, and I felt warm and protected. I looked up at him. He was tall, and his keen intelligence and intensely searching eyes made one forget completely that he was not a good-looking man. He had a long face and a prominent nose. His lips were always slightly pursed, as if he were just about to make a pronouncement. His hair was blowing, his big ears stuck out from the upturned collar of his coat, and his glasses glinted in the streetlights. He was as elated as we all were and hummed bits of the last sonata every few steps. We almost skipped, we were so happy.

"Alright, people," he turned back to the rest of the group, "Lets go up to our house and have a drink to celebrate."

My mother wrapped herself tighter in her coat. "Oh, but it is too late for my daughter; she needs her sleep. Another time, maybe. Thanks, dear Paul." With that she motioned me to follow her.

I had not been aware of the cold night until then. I clamped my teeth shut and stared at her. Paul's arm released my shoulder. He took a step towards her, looked at her over his lowered glasses and said, "Alice, you are too good a nanny."

With that, they all said good night, with regrets, and nothing was left for me but to listen to Mother's fury about Paul's ridicule and to feel my own seething anger.

Two days later I got a phone call from Li. "We'd like you to join us for a party next Saturday," she said.

"Great, I'll tell my parents."

"Oh no," she shot back, "We just want you by yourself. The parents will be asked another time."

I was ecstatic. They wanted just me, alone. I could hardly believe it.

So when I climbed the steep stairs up to the Moses' tall, narrow row house on Sutter Street the same old feeling of trepidation that had burdened me so often before grabbed me. A little girl venturing out on her own. It was ridiculous. Already the anger directed at myself paralyzed me.

"There you are!" Paul pulled me into the room. "Let me introduce you."

It was an awe-inspiring group that was assembled.

Two tall, full-bosomed ladies sat in opposite corners of the room. Either one or the other's sonorous voice could be heard unavoidably, off and on, above the general conversation. They were Elizabeth Rethberg and Kerstin Thorburg, both singers from the Metropolitan Opera who were in San Francisco to star in a performance of Wagner's *Meistersinger*. A deep voice complemented their higher register. It belonged to Alexander Kipniss, a bass baritone, I believe, who kept the guests greatly amused by telling very funny anecdotes collected during his career.

A quiet, wise-looking old man sat a little apart and leafed through one of Paul's books. I was told that he was Albert Bender, a well-known art collector and philanthropist. Later on I was seated next to him when Li called us to the table for one of her famous deserts.

"Oh, you must be the young lady Paul told me about." His little pointed beard turned away from a very chatty woman who had monopolized him relentlessly. "You like to paint, he said, and he thought that you were quite gifted."

I stared at him in amazement. Paul had seen a small painting of an imaginary theatre scene I had done some time ago. I never thought he'd remember it. Oh God, now I'll have to answer a lot of questions, I thought, and prepared to hear myself stammering and stuttering about in helpless embarrassment.

But no, old Bender proceeded to tell me about his love for art and his travels to museums all over the world. Little by little I managed to tell him that, yes, I had been to Venice and Florence too, and what I especially remembered. At the end of the evening he pulled a little jade elephant out of his vest-pocket and handed it to me. "To remember our nice visit," he said.

When I returned home, Father asked, "Well how was it? Did you have a good time?" Mother still looked peeved.

"It was alright," was all I said. Telling them about it would have diluted the feeling of pleasure I felt about the evening's experience.

From then on I was invited regularly without my parents, not only to Paul and Li's house, but also to Elisabeth's and other people's parties. Surely Paul had a hand in that.

Why I needed to have my tonsils removed I do not recall anymore. Paul, who had performed the surgery, sat at my bedside when I regained consciousness. He stayed by my side for hours and personally nursed me during the next days whenever he could spare the time. He fed me tiny ice cubes and funny stories, warning me not to laugh too hard.

A few weeks later he wanted to check my throat again. It was late in the afternoon and the end of his office hours. "It's healing just fine," he said. "I am done here. How about we have a cup of coffee at Manning's?"

I was so pleased and again overwhelmed that he really wanted to spend time with me. I looked up at him, and he took me in his arms and kissed me. Then he held me away at arms length and looked at me with great warmth and regret. "A pity you are too young for me. Let's go." With that he propelled me out the door and arm in arm we proceeded to Manning's coffee shop.

A note from my diary at that time:

A drive to the ocean. Hans is driving, Elisabeth sits next to him. Paul, another man and I are squeezed together in the back. Li has stayed home.

We drive along roller-coaster streets to the ocean. Dazzling, blinding light and the pungent smells of seaweed, sand, and salt. Honking sea lions on the rocks. Foaming clouds of water slapping over their slithery bodies. Wind and itching eyes. Clattering soles of sandals on the stone floors of the Cliff House Restaurant. Clinking of soda glasses, coffee smell, and rancid oil.

Poking through mounds of trinkets for sale. Giant seashells converted into lamps, little ones into ashtrays. Mermaids and fish in pink and blue, swimming on mirrors and boxes. I am relieved to see a small, expertly turned myrtle-wood bowl that is lost among plastic palm trees and a bag of marbles. I buy it.

Return drive along the coast in sinking sun. Red and deep blue light on the cowering water, waiting to churn up as soon as night falls. Paul's arm around my shoulder. I rest my head against it. I am sleepy.

Late one evening another spat with my mother. I rebelled, again. She screamed, again. She almost slapped me.

"I won't talk to you for a long time. You are just as ugly as your grandmother!" Again, words of hate. Her door slammed.

I lay in the dark on my bed, steeped in a black hole of despair. What was happening with my life? Where was I going? What was I meant to do? There was no hope, just emptiness and pain.

A small sliver of light that seeped from the hall through the threshold widened and a black shape appeared in the doorway.

"What are you doing?" my brother asked. I did not answer. "Remember, you'll enroll in school in the morning."

He had convinced me earlier that day that the place for me would be the California School of Fine Arts, which was very close, down the hill from us.

I still said nothing. He came closer and touched my face. "Why are you crying? You should be used to her by now." And then I broke out in convulsions of tears, utterly helpless.

He sat on my bed and waited until exhaustion set in, and I lay there, trying to dissolve into nothingness.

"Breakfast." He kicked the door open with his foot, carrying a tray with coffee and toast. It was a warm, sunny morning. "Get ready for school." I shook my head. I was bleary-eyed and slightly nauseous.

"I am leaving this house. I'll get a job and make some money. I can't go to school."

"You are going," he said, and threw my clothes on the bed. "Hurry up. I'll take you."

I stepped into a new world. The California School of Fine Arts on Chestnut Street was a lively place. The entrance, with its colorful courtyard and fountain, invited me in, and when I was presented with an extensive program of classes and studies my spirits rose.

Drawing with Mr. Poole. Plaster casts of Roman heads or a torso with hacked-off arms and legs confronted me. In my mind's eye I endowed them with flesh and blood, making the endless labor of rendering them more bearable, unless the object was a single ear, which remained a hunk of white plaster.

Painting with William Gaw. This was really exciting. Color became a language. A still life did not stay still; it developed a life of its own, speaking with color and shape.

Miss Hartwell taught design. It was fun to let squares and circles and triangles wander all over a sheet of paper, or to invent dramatic posters for toothpaste, a fashion show, or a circus.

Off and on a few of the beginners were allowed to sit in on a composition class given by Maurice Sterne, a well known French/Russian painter who was also a great figurative draftsman. This was really the highlight of my time at the school. When I progressed from plaster ears to Life Drawing he came in one day, stopped in front of my drawing, nodded his head, and mumbled something that sounded like approval. I was extremely happy.

I started to make friends. People talked in the cafeteria, the library, sitting in the courtyard at the fountain.

Georgia was a sweet, friendly girl who in class always wore flowery smocks over her freshly ironed blouses and plaid skirts. Her blond pageboy was carefully curled around her face, and paint never stained her hands for long. She was a warm and happy person, easy to be with, and I got used to having her near by in class.

So when, one morning in my second year, Allela occupied the easel next to mine in Figure Painting it was quite a shock. Our former peaceful, plodding pace had taken a turn. All of a sudden an aura of intense energy seemed to fill the room, a smoldering volcano had landed in our midst, threatening to erupt. It never did, except maybe in the form of paint that spewed with force against the canvas from her brush or palette knife. Even her blue jeans showed the effects of that intensity in somewhat irregular patterns. The big shirt that flopped loosely from her slim and lanky frame had often been used to wipe a brush when a rag happened to be out of reach. Impatient scissors had chopped her dark hair short around her neck and face.

I admired her work and her dedication to it. She was about my age but had already been painting for many years and joined the class solely for the purpose of using the model.

"You're okay," she said one day, scanning my canvas with a sharp eye. "Still a little timid, but you'll get there. Want to get some coffee?"

The cafeteria was empty. We sat and talked, and I felt at ease with her. There was no trifling chitchat; living with

and for art was our common theme. She was a poor girl
and was being sponsored by a very rich lady who had taken
an interest in her and was planning to send her to New
York soon for further studies.

We became good friends. We went to art shows and to
the museums in town. We drew and painted together and
had many sessions taking turns working on portraits of
each other. Not many words were uttered; the paint was
the language. Still today a little painting of a rather
thoughtful Allela hangs on my wall.

Months after Allela left for New York I was having my
lunch in the cafeteria, feeling rather forlorn. A fellow student
came up.

"Missing your friend?" He sat down, ready for a chat. I
just nodded. He looked at me. Obviously not much
conversation was going to be had from my direction.

"You know, of course, that rich dame of hers loved more
than her art." He cocked his head and looked at me
sidewise.

"What do you mean?" I said absently.

"Oh, nothing. Don't forget to see the Venetian Show at
the De Young Museum." With that, he drained his coffee
cup and left.

I was puzzled and then forgot about it.

The Venetian painting show was still mobbed, but not
as badly as on opening night the week before. Then San
Francisco had turned out full force, and it had been a party
for meeting old friends and making new acquaintances, an
event at which to be seen and feel important. People were
shoulder to shoulder; there were smiles, wine and
appetizers, light whiffs of diverse perfumes battling with
each other. There was some nasty little gossip whispered
discretely behind shielded lips.

I came to see the paintings, even though I could never stand looking at paintings with anybody at my heels, so to speak, anybody who would give me his or her reactions and opinions, regardless of whether they were negative or affirmative.

A rather substantial gentleman stepped in front of me and very close to the wonderful Titian I was admiring, and that had taken me over completely. He studied the surface of the painting with narrowed eyes, almost brushing it with his big nose, mumbling, "Hmm, hmm, hmm," to himself, wagging his head, which was topped by a black French beret at a rakish angle.

"You're obscuring my view, sir." Fury did not allow me to be timid. At the same moment, a stern guard tapped him on his shoulder, motioning him back.

"I don't hurt paintings. I am an artist myself." The offender was not in the least contrite. Ignoring the guard he turned a pair of big eyes, glowering under very bushy, black eyebrows at me to see whether I looked properly impressed.

"Werner, you should apologize." The woman who had been standing next to him laid her hand on his arm. "He is just so passionate about his art, Miss. He did not mean any harm."

This was the perfect introduction to two new friends, Werner and Elizabeth Philipp. He was the self-important, often bungling, mediocre painter, and she was forever shielding him and totally devoted.

Shortly after Hitler's threat became apparent in Germany, Werner had a chance to go to Palestine. He sold a painting or two there but soon ran out of funds. Elizabeth, an American lady, a buyer for a big New York department store, visited Jerusalem at that time. Soon, his soulful eyes under bushy brows won her lonely, already middle-aged heart. The two were married, and Werner was on his way to the United States with the help of Elizabeth's passport.

"How lucky for Werner, how convenient," little Spencer Barefoot would giggle, and he was not the only one. No matter, it was a good marriage for both of them.

Elizabeth gave up her job. Her husband's well being and the promotion of his art, which she considered to be of great importance, was what she lived for; her mothering instinct had found a target. Werner thrived under all that love and care. He treated her well and seemed so dependent on her that one could not imagine his ever managing anything without her. Yet I must admit that it occurred to me a few times that his appreciative eye had rather an intimate glance, and his handshake had an unnecessary warmth when he greeted the young female interior decorators who championed his wares to their clients. He was an amiable fellow, unless, you questioned his artistic capabilities.

Werner and Elizabeth both courted and charmed San Francisco society with great vigor. Elizabeth cooked and arranged dinner parties in their home, where Werner's pictures were shown for desert—just by chance, of course. No museum or gallery opening could be visited without also meeting the two of them. The result was that he became quite well known and was actually able to live by selling his pictures. This was amazing, considering how few artists were ever able to do so. His landscapes were pleasingly pseudo-French Impressionist, an image helped along by the wearing of his black beret. His many portrait commissions were executed either in a dignified though uninspired manner for male clients, or simpering and sweet for ladies. He was actually a fairly good craftsman; it was only his taste that was deplorable, and his inspiration that was totally lacking.

Still, they were both nice to be with off and on. They were kind, had a good sense of humor, and were pleasant company.

During my vacations from art school in the summer months Werner invited me to join him on forays around

304 Felicia Altman Gilbert

the city and its environs to do some landscape painting. *"En pleine air,"* he said, again doing justice to his French beret. That idea pleased me, since I would not have had the courage to work all by myself out of doors, lugging my paint box and in view of anybody that might be passing by. Anyway, I could still learn painting technique from him.

With his little old VW automobile stacked high with paint boxes, collapsible easels, lunch bags, and umbrellas to shield the canvas from the sun, we scouted the territory for suitable vistas until we came to a special place, of which there were so many around the beautiful bay. He would stop the car with a terrific rumble and a lurch that shifted all of our gear from the back toward our shoulders and necks in the front. He was a terrible driver.

Then he would get out, stand in the sun or wind or whatever there was at the time, sweep his arms wide across the landscape and exclaim, "Look what bounty lies before us!"

I would let him choose his special spot, wait until he was safely installed, and then move as far away from him as possible. Hunter's Point was one of our favorite places, with its wide view of the bay and many inlets to the hilly shore.

I always took a very long time to finish a painting, so we had to return to the same spot again and again.

There was a house on the slopes near the Golden Gate Bridge that I loved. It balanced precariously on the rocks over the water. It had a lush, wild flower garden with a white picket fence to one side. With the sharp cliffs around it, the bridge in the background and boats and seagulls constantly moving about, the composition could never stagnate. I observed the scene, kept changing the painting and improvised. Then one memorable day we arrived at my favorite spot and my house was gone. It had slipped into the sea.

This event followed the demise of a still life I had set up, thinking of the painter Chardin, that consisted of a loaf of bread, a jug of red wine, a knife, and a big slab of yellow cheese on a wooden board. The bread turned to stone, the wine sprouted a grayish skin of mold on top, and the cheese oozed, greenish, across the board.

"For heavens sake, don't go into portrait painting," Werner said, laughing uproariously. "Who knows what would happen to your subjects!"

I did subsequently paint portraits, because I was always interested in people. A little neighborhood girl from Mexico, Socorro, was one of my first victims. She was about eight years old and very sweet and patient. I dressed her in a colorful child's folk costume that my parents had brought back from Norway many years ago. Why couldn't a brown skinned, black haired child come from Norway?

When by chance another live subject for my fledgling efforts presented itself, it turned out to be even more incongruous. Old Dr. Esther Rosenkrantz, who was our neighbor in the other part of the house on Russian Hill, saw Socorro's portrait and fell in love with it. "Now I know what I want you to do." She put her hand on my shoulder. "Paint me and make me look like Angelika Kaufmann. Have you seen her portrait?"

She invited me to her home and stood in front of a gold framed mirror in her entrance hall, looking at herself, fingering the sagging skin at her throat and examining her face by turning it slightly from side to side.

"When I retired two years ago, the hospital wanted a portrait of me, to be displayed in the conference room. I just never got around to it. Now they shall get it." First she smiled at me triumphantly and then at herself in the mirror, pulling a few strands of hair closer to her forehead.

I looked at the old doctor. Angelika Kaufmann, the eighteenth century Swiss artist who painted a charming self-portrait? A lovely young woman with large eyes who could have been Jane Austen's friend? No, Esther, you are not Angelika and never were. I thought of a sumptuous portrait of Maria Luisa, the wife of King Carlos the Fourth of Spain. She stands in the midst of her royal family, seen through the pitiless eye of Goya, her utter lack of beauty and grace made even more devastating by the silks and gold surrounding her, and by the jewels and plumes in her hair.

Several mornings a week I set up my easel in Esther's living room. A dark green velvet wing chair was her throne, and she posed, sitting erect like a queen, a black lace shawl draped around her shoulders. Her red silk dress had puffy sleeves with gold-embroidered cuffs, and her hands rested in her lap holding an open fan. A large tortoise shell comb secured her iron-gray hair, piled up high on her head.

It was not the eighteenth century German Biedermeier period she embodied, but rather Goya's Spain. Had she read my mind?

We talked while I worked. I knew that as long as I could keep her attention focused she would not fall asleep. She talked about her childhood, her youth, and her career. I got to know and to really admire her. A strong woman and a bright one! There was not one word of being lonely or having regrets. Would I grow old like that, I thought, so calm and satisfied?

At midmorning the talk usually slowed down. The queen leaned back against her throne, the eyelids quivered and closed slowly. She sagged into her crumpling gown, and her jaw dropped in blissful relaxation. It was my time to concentrate on shawl and hands and light and color, my time to think.

It took months until the painting was completed with Esther's approval. The position of a hand was not quite right, a wrinkle here and a wrinkle there would absolutely have to be eliminated, and how about putting a little smile around the lips?

When I finally put my brushes down and heaved a sigh of relief, Esther rose from her chair and announced that now she would give a tea party so her friends and my friends could see the painting before it left the house.

Tiny cream cheese and watercress sandwiches and peppermint tea greeted the guests. After being duly overwhelmed by my painting, they were treated to a guided tour of the apartment and the complete histories of all of her antique furniture, piece by piece. The *pièce de résistance* was a truly magnificent four-poster bed that almost filled the small bedroom. Chinese peacocks and willow trees were embroidered on its silken cover and elaborately carved mahogany posts supported clouds of snow-white organdy billowing from a canopy overhead.

"My God, this bed deserves a better occupant."

Spencer Barefoot had followed me and now looked ruefully after the wobbling figure of our hostess, who had just left us, to show her portrait to a new arrival.

"You're mean," I said, but I had to laugh.

The great official day to unveil the historic masterpiece arrived. Dr. Esther Rosenkrantz was honored by a big and lavish party at the hospital. The portrait was greatly admired, and even my mother admitted that she was proud of me. I must say that I was pleased with the result of my labor. It was quite well painted, a good likeness; it had atmosphere, and it showed that I had enjoyed doing it.

The venerable doctor, who had performed surgery and attended to much illness during her career, was deathly afraid of mice. My brother was with us for a few days of vacation, and we were sitting in our living room one evening, just about to retire for the night. The phone rang. "A mouse, there is a mouse in my bedroom!" Esther was hysterical.

We ran to the rescue. We found her standing on her bed, holding onto the wall with one hand and clutching a broom with the other. Applying his best bedside manner and murmuring soothing words, Ralph led her out to the living room, leaving her in my care. He disappeared back into the bedroom.

For quite a while we heard the rustle and scraping of furniture being moved about, something that sounded like a carpet pulled aside, and then all of a sudden a terrific crash, a dull thud, and then all was quiet.

The wildlife hunter emerged, a large wad of toilet paper balled up in his hand and Esther dissolved in happy gratitude.

"Was it a big one?" I asked when we rounded the corner to our entrance door.

"A big what?" he replied.

"The mouse!" I said.

"Mouse? What mouse?"

The empty paper from his hand fluttered gracefully into the wastebasket, and the night passed in peaceful bliss for everyone.

In 1940 my brother Ralph and our cousin Pat got engaged, an event that pleased us all, except of course Mother, who had her reservations. I do not think that she would ever have approved of any woman her precious golden son would have chosen. Nevertheless, she made the best of it, and in place of enthusiasm presented her new daughter-in-law with one of her prized pieces of jewelry. On September 8th the marriage took place in Portland. Ralph and Pat took off in a little fire red VW car and drove down the coast to Santa Barbara for their honeymoon.

I had become very fond of Pat by then; we understood each other. Despite the differences in the ways in which we were brought up—in different countries and languages—there was a strong feeling of kinship between us. I was happy because two people I loved were together.

I was still alone. Would that ever change?

December 7, 1941. Japan attacked Pearl Harbor.
December 8, the United States declared war on Japan.
Germany and Italy declared war on the U. S..

The always-busy tempo of the city accelerated. The population grew and people moved from place to place, adjusting to the demands of war-related employment.

Because of his age, my brother Ralph was no longer on the first list of draftees. He went to work at the Bethlehem Steel shipyards in San Francisco. Following his last examination disaster, the result of his extreme nervous anxiety after his experiences in Germany, he had finally decided to give up on a medical career.

Reports came that German saboteurs had landed in Florida and New York and that U-boats were spotted on the California coast. Blackout was ordered and for quite a while our evenings were spent with tightly draped windows in candle light. There was the sound of sirens from time to time, and we all, my parents, Ralph and Pat, Bella, and I huddled together in one room, blowing our candles out.

The Post Office announced that it was looking for people with language skills. This was my chance to get into the action and out of the house. I applied for a job and was accepted employed by the Navy to censor letters sent to and from servicemen overseas.

I sat in a large room full of men and women of all ages. Bins and bins of mail were stacked in front of each one of us. I had to open and read letter after letter. Any references concerning the war to locations, equipment, rumors, even personal opinions I had to blot out with a big black pen. Sometimes I could not leave much more text than *Dear Suzy, Love and Kisses, Joe.* Reading those letters was often touching. I sometimes felt guilty, having to pry into other people's intimate lives and thoughts. I felt uneasy when giggles or snickers could be heard from other tables in the room in response to something read and often shared in barely suppressed whispers.

A few weeks had passed when I was called to a supervisor's desk. "It says on your application that you are a photographer. You are being transferred."

So from then on I sat all by myself in a dark little room perusing still photos and amateur movies for telltale signs of recognizable locations, ships, airplanes, or uniforms. Sometimes I was almost dizzy coming out into the daylight late in the afternoon, emerging from my dark cubicle. I was paid well, but most of all I felt needed and part of the concern shared by everyone around me.

Months passed, and I was called out to Administration again. This time it was to another floor, and the discreet little sign on the door spelled FBI. Two tall blond gentlemen received me and cordially invited me to sit on the other side of their desk.

"I see that you were born in Germany," the older man was studying the papers he held in his hand. "When did you become a citizen?" I launched into the lengthy tale of my grandparents births in the States and my registration at the American Consulate in Berlin, and my family's reason for leaving Germany.

"Your supervisor gave you excellent recommendations," the younger of the two smiled at me approvingly, "However," he cleared his throat, "I am afraid regulations are such that we will have to let you go immediately."

They both got up and shook my hand as if they were congratulating me for something. No further explanation was given. My coworkers out in the offices looked at me with wonder. Some shook hands and expressed regret. I did not talk to them for fear of breaking into tears. I felt humiliated, in spite of understanding the circumstances.

The thought of becoming independent never left me. I tried many avenues. When we still lived on Russian Hill, I became acquainted with the young woman who resided in the downstairs apartment. Her name was Gary. She had a two-year-old child and lived on welfare. I never saw her do any work, although she told me that she was an accomplished seamstress. I liked her, but always felt that there was something strange about her. She started to come upstairs to visit me more and more often. She professed to love me, maybe sometimes too intensely, and admired my work. One day she made a proposal. We could go into business together. She would make aprons and smocks and I would decorate them with colorful stencils of my own design and we'd sell them to stores that she had entrance to. Now that sounded pretty good to me. I asked my parents for a loan. Mother was delighted that I showed an interest in making money and promptly supported us in this enterprise. A studio was rented downtown, material was bought, and we started to manufacture our wares.

What we produced was really quite nice, if of marginal use to anybody. A few pieces we sold to start with and then sales petered out. When I came to the studio one morning after we had been there for several months, Gary was not there. She did not appear after lunch either, but I found a threatening letter from our landlord on my worktable. Rent had not been paid for three months, and we were going to be evicted and sued. It had been Gary's job to keep the books and pay bills. My duties were supposed to be the artistic part of the enterprise. I called Gary's phone. No answer. I went home and down to her apartment. It was empty. She must have left at night, taking her few possessions with her. Subsequently, more bills arrived. Nothing had been paid. A bitter experience. I must give my parents credit; recriminations were kept to a minimum, and I was duly reinstated to the status of dependant daughter.

In 1941, during the month of April, we moved away from our romantic rented home on the hill. My parents bought a large three-story house on Clay Street, a spacious white stucco house, square and solidly build with shutters on the windows and a two-car garage. It stood on level ground, but still on a high rise, looking down on streets below. Walking one block to Sacramento Street, we could board the cable car that would take us downtown. It was a safe and established neighborhood with large homes like ours all around. It lacked the atmosphere and romance of Russian Hill, but the view, especially from my studio window up on the third floor, was as magnificent as before. I looked right down to the bay and the Golden Gate Bridge. I saw the fog blowing through its red stanchions, settling down on the water toward night, lifting again at mid-morning, leaving the dark trees of the Presidio wet and glistening in the sun. This scene I painted also, though no disaster came to the bridge or the coast as a result.

The Biedermeier furniture again had its own space and alcove in the front of the house, towards the street. Lace curtains were draped around the windows and a grand

If the parents couldn't take money out of Germany where did the money for all this come from?

piano held silver-framed photographs on its lid. They were mostly of mother in various roles on stage that my father insisted on displaying. A few childhood pictures were also shown, a big one of Ralph in a sailor suit and a smaller one of me wearing a big bow in my hair in which I was obviously reluctant to smile. French doors that were never closed led right into the living room across from the entrance hall, where a broad staircase extended up in stages through the middle of the house. On the second floor extensive changes had been brought about. A separate apartment for Ralph and Pat had been created, with its own entrance from the outside of the building, leaving only the master bedroom and bath for my parents on the other side of a heavily insulated wall. I cannot help but wonder whether it would not have been more sensible to buy something less grand for the older generation in order to treat the children to a modest little place of their own. I guess Mother's needs were better served the way she arranged it, having the whole brood under her wing.

A car was acquired and a young Filipino man with a sweet bright smile and sparkling white teeth joined the household. He was very short and stocky. His face formed a triangle from his high cheekbones down to his round chin, and his shiny black hair stood like a veritable helmet around his big head. His name was Pedro. He acted as cook, chauffeur, and general help around the house. Soon it became apparent that Pedro was in awe of my mother. She became the trusted caregiver and confidant who could be relied upon to listen to his girlfriend troubles with sage advice and stern rebuke. When he asked her to keep part of his salary and save it for him so he would not spend it or gamble, she complied graciously. Mother had another child to take care of.

Father at that time was not inactive; in fact, he never was.

He went to intertribal Indian ceremonies in Gallup, New Mexico and to many pueblos around Santa Fe. He visited Mesa Verde and other Indian cultural sites in Colorado and Arizona, collecting material and writing articles about them.

Some years later he was invited to the University of Texas in Austin to spend two months and give thirty-six lectures on drama and theater direction. When he did not travel or engage in other activities, he sat at his desk, wrote and studied, or went to the library, even if it meant braving rainstorms and crowded buses.

There were a few more occasions in his life when his great gifts as a stage director shone. In 1941 the University of California in Berkeley celebrated its 75th anniversary and invited Father to direct Shakespeare's *Twelfth Night* at the open-air arena of the Greek Theatre. It was a spectacular performance. On another occasion he did the stage direction for Offenbach's *La belle Hélène*, also at the Greek Theatre. A stirring performance of *Julius Caesar* at the Green Street Theatre in San Francisco followed, to rave reviews.

He taught groups of drama students that presented evenings of one-act plays at the Community Playhouse, among them Bertolt Brecht's *Mother Courage and her Children*, which made a great impression on me.

In 1942 the conductor Walter Herbert asked Father to work on the staging of Rossini's comic opera *Il Signor Bruschino*. It was performed at the Curran Theatre in San Francisco, and like several other shows of his, taken on tour to cities like Sacramento, Stockton, and Los Angeles.

When Herbert came to our house for dinner one evening he asked to see some of my drawings and paintings, probably just to be polite.

"You did these?" He held a watercolor sketch up for closer inspection and then leafed through a whole stack of fantasy figures and landscapes I had done. Shaking his head in astonishment, as if he could not believe what he saw, he turned to me.

"I have been looking all over for a designer who would give me fresh ideas for *Signor Bruschino's* stage set and here you've been all the time! Will you do it?" I was speechless. I looked at my father. His head cocked to one side, he seemed not to be too certain about this proposition. That helped me to make up my mind.

I took a deep breath. "I'd love to," I said.

I went to work designing the set with tempera paints and pen and ink. It showed part of a small town plaza in Italy, basking in great mid-summer heat. A rough-hewn peasant table and three chairs awaited occupants, and a narrow red and white striped guardhouse wore a tasseled nightcap instead of a pointed roof. Behind a low stone wall stood a row of cypress trees. They had very unhappy faces, obviously suffering from the heat and trying to shield their green eyes with parts of their bushy branches. A little man in period costume wearing a top hat shook his fists at a giant sun, whose face grinned mischievously down at him from the intense blue of the sky. A hazy sun-drenched Umbrian landscape led the eye into the background.

After the set was built, I painted the landscape, the trees, the sun and the guardhouse with its cap and tassel.

The first performance took place at the end of January 1942 and was a great success. The curtain went up, and the audience broke out in spontaneous applause. I had imagined that even old Rossini in heaven would have been pleased.

Herbert and Father's work got great reviews, especially by Alfred Frankenstein of the *San Francisco Chronicle*. At the end of his critique he wrote, "Finally, one must record Felicia Altman's delightful setting and its extraordinary effects of sun and shadow." Another reviewer said, "The setting was a particularly important asset."

My nascent self esteem got quite a boost and when Walter Herbert asked me to design another set for a performance of Mozart's opera, *The Abduction from the Seraglio*, I was really flying high.

The time to prepare for this performance was short. Taking ideas from Persian artifacts, particularly from carpets, tiles and buildings, I erected a series of arches and entryways of different sizes on both sides of the stage and painted them as if they had tiles of blue and white designs set into them. I hung a large rope net in front of a black velvet background curtain. I had designed thin flat plywood pieces that were cut into shapes of flowers and animals. I then painted them in the style and bright colors of Persian miniatures and they were set irregularly here and there into the diamond-shaped open spaces of the rope hanging.

Here too, the critics did not forget to mention the stage set particularly. Alexander Fried of *The Examiner* said, "The whole was intimately framed in a whimsical stage design by Felicia Altman."

Alfred Frankenstein of *The Chronicle* wrote, "Felicia Altman's simple imaginative setting was not the least significant thing about the whole performance." I personally think that Mozart's lovely music enhanced the ambience of the design immeasurably, and I remember it with pleasure.

On a warm autumn day in 1942 that felt much more like spring, Mother lured me to go downtown with her.

"Just a little window-shopping," she said. "Why should I have a daughter if I can't have fun with her?" She took my arm, and we ambled along the sunny streets chatting and giggling like two schoolgirls on vacation.

When she was in a good mood and nobody crossed her, she could be fun to be with. She was elegant and pretty, looking much younger then she was. She sometimes seemed to me like a willful and capricious child, lovable when she behaved well.

"Ah! Here is Blum's!" She acted as if she had just discovered it. "Let's have coffee and strawberry tarts." The love of pastries I definitely inherited from her.

"Now tell me," she pushed a few crumbs of her tart around on her plate, "You enjoy the time you spend painting with Werner?"

"Sure," I said, "I can still learn from him, and when we work outside it's nice to have him around."

"How nice?" She lit a cigarette and tried to look casual, examining the burned out match. I looked at her, puzzled.

"You know, men like that sometimes get ideas about young girls, especially artists. He is even married." That last remark certainly made no sense, and the rest was preposterous.

"Mutti, for God's sake!" Had we not been at a restaurant, I would have thrown my hands up in the air with exasperation. So *that* was the reason for the sweet mother/daughter excursion!

I reassured her that I was not about to be raped, nor was I desperately and hopelessly in love.

She gave me one of her worried looks that preceded expected catastrophes, got up, smiled again as if relieved and said, "Let's go to Ransohof's and look for shoes."

The art historian Dr. Karl Wieth and his wife Gerda came to dinner at our house. Of course, at the behest of

Mother, daughter had to pull out her paintings for expert evaluation, regardless of daughter's protests.

After dutifully examining drawings and canvas after canvas with sharply piercing eyes and wrinkled brow, the judge pronounced the verdict: "It's time to study somewhere else. Go to New York, young lady, find a good teacher. You need fresh wind around your nose. The Art Students League might be just the thing for you." Both parents looked shocked.

"You would not want to go that far away." Later, Mother made that statement of fact, she did not ask it.

A bright picture had risen in my head, and a devious strategy formed at the same time. "I guess not," I sighed, "I enjoy painting with Werner. I'd miss that." It worked!

The next day at breakfast Father had finished his rolls and soft-boiled egg. Setting his coffee cup down he prepared to pull out the first cigar for the day. He looked at me over the top of his glasses, a customary way of his, to make contact and get my attention.

"Your mother and I have been talking. We think that maybe it might be good for you to study in New York for a while. How would you feel about that?"

How hard I tried not to agree immediately and with overwhelming enthusiasm. Soon though, I complied.

Ralph contacted his former girlfriend Fuchsi Lederer in New York who was now married. She agreed to be my guide and help me to get settled when I arrived in my new world.

CHAPTER SEVENTEEN

Adventures in New York

October 1942

For the first few weeks I stayed with Ralph's friend Fuchsi Lederer, her husband, and small children high up in their highrise apartment near the Hudson River until I was able to navigate the city on my own. It did not take long before I ventured out in search of a place of my own. After all, that was my main goal. I had to be independent, to be free.

November 2, 1942

1 Sheridan Square was an apartment house of no particular distinction, except that it was situated in the heart of Greenwich Village and boasted an elevator and a doorman to operate it. The studio apartment I rented was unfurnished and quite large. A big window looked down on the square and allowed plenty of light to shine on my easel and on the few pieces of furniture I had acquired from the Salvation Army. There was a single, narrow bed, a chest of drawers, an under-stuffed brown velvet armchair with sagging springs and a kitchen chair. Best of all, there was a very large, rugged dining table, most of which I used for my paints and art materials. One small corner of it was reserved for my sketchy meals. Plenty of floor space was

left, and I walked happily about, feeling the space and the freedom of my new life.

I wrote my first two letters home:

November 5, 1942

My Dear Ones,

   Following weeks of running around to the point of collapse, I was finally, finally able to rent an apartment. You cannot imagine the shortage of available housing here. Consequently all of the landlords have gotten crazy and prices have risen accordingly. One cannot even get a furnished room without a one-year lease. I almost had to choose between going to a hotel without kitchenette for a lot of money or to a boardinghouse with a shared bath and kitchen. Both of these situations seemed impossible to me.

   On one of my extensive searches I passed the house where Lorraine lives with her husband and decided to stop in. Almost casually as if to pass the time of day, I asked the janitor in the elevator whether there was anything to rent in the building and, by God, he said yes. He showed me a large, beautiful room, freshly renovated with a giant window that filled the whole north wall. It has a small kitchen and a very decent bathroom. It is unfurnished and the light is fantastic! Of course, I had to take the one-year lease.

   I am convinced that I did the right thing. It does not make sense to spend money on a furnished room in which I cannot work and consequently have fewer chances to make some money. As soon as I have moved in with my trunks and a couch from the Lederers I will go and look for work and try to earn my rent, at least. It is $ 52.50 per month. The house is in Greenwich Village, one and a half blocks from the subway that gets me to Forty-Second Street in seven minutes, and in ten minutes to

Columbus Circle and the Art Students League. I am on the sixth floor. There is an elevator, a switchboard, and all the trimmings. The main attraction for me is the big window that lets me see across the rooftops of the surrounding houses to the fabulous skyline and the heavens above.

My rent starts on the fifteenth, but I can move in now. I am afraid I have to ask you for another fifty dollars. I am going to pay you back one day. Now I will get busy with a vengeance! Too bad it takes so long to get established. Please send me the following right away: the pictures and drawing pads that I laid aside and showed Werner and my bedding and two towels.

Lorraine, who lives in the house, is so nice to me and always asks me for dinner. Allela's studio is practically around the corner. Today I am babysitting the Lederer's children while Fuchsi and Fred go to a concert.

November 10, 1942

The money flies out the window! Transporting my two trunks, three suitcases, a couch, and a little table the Lederers gave me cost seven dollars. I bought a bed and dishes. Two months rent, one hundred and fifty dollars. Telephone, fifteen dollars deposit, three fifty installation and three fifty per month for sixty six calls. I would be isolated without a telephone. I won't go to the Art Students League right away to save money. Tomorrow I'll go job hunting. When I have a job I'll go to the League at night.

I have not felt like calling on anybody here yet. With all of the running around, there is no time or peace of mind. Now I start to feel almost at home in the Village. It would have been a pity if I had landed in another part of the city. I love the atmosphere. There are painters, writers, musicians, and even a few solid citizens to keep matters on an even keel. I do not know anybody except Lorraine, but the elevator man keeps me informed about what goes on in the neighborhood. A big market is directly across the street and plenty of little Italian restaurants are serving

*reasonably priced food all over the Village. I cook for myself
most of the time, though. I live very cheaply and am convinced
that once the darn start-up expenses are taken care of, I'll be
able to pay for my keep.*

*I wish you could see me here in my own household. I just
finished dinner, macaroni with ham, stewed fruit, and cake,
simple but hearty, cost, 25 cents. Now I am sitting at the
Lederers' old children's table among all of my furniture. There
is a second-hand wicker chair that I carried by hand for ten
blocks from the store and my couch with one of the brown trunks
as coffee table in front of it. From Allela I inherited an easel, and
there is another VERY luxurious wicker chair with a pillow on
it that I transported the same way as the other one. That cost,
$2.50! I purchased two lamps, $2.50 for both, and a set of glass
dinner dishes serving eight people, including vegetable and meat
platters, creamer, sugar bowl, cups and goblets, all for $2.99!
The other day I ran into Irma Bechhoefer on Fifty-Seventh Street.
She will visit me soon. She looked very chic and works in Beauty
Care at Bergdorf Goodman. On Sunday I went on an excursion
with Franzi, her husband and another young couple. We walked
for four hours along the Hudson on rocky shores, under
wonderful autumn trees.*

*Dear Ones, this is not a very good letter. I do not feel like
writing, not at all. To write means to reflect, and I feel more like
getting into action. I write first of all to report to you and secondly
to get mail from you. Until now you have been pleasantly diligent.
Even Ralph! As soon as I am really in the swing of things you'll
get more interesting missives.*

*I love you all and long for you already. By the way, what do
you now say to the news after all? Terribly exciting? Finally
something positive!*

Forgive these mixed-up scribbles. Love and kisses,

From your happy daughter,
Fe

I signed up for classes at the Art Students League. Wandering around the corridors and peeking into the various studios to get acquainted and find my way around, I came across a billboard near the entrance to the cafeteria. I found offerings of reduced price brushes and paints, rooms for rent, and requests for used textbooks and, among these, also a few announcements for various available part-time jobs.

I wrote home, "From next month on, you won't have to send me any more money. I can now take care of myself." This was, of course, totally reckless, since I had not yet made one penny, and no job was in sight.

I found out later that my parents were greatly distressed by this turn of events. They were sure that I was going to starve myself to death or get engaged in some unsafe or questionable enterprise due to my innocence and lack of experience. Maybe they were half right in that diagnosis, because from then on I lived mostly on canned soups, scrambled eggs, and spaghetti, cooked on my two-burner hotplate. From time to time, I treated myself to a meal in one of the small Italian restaurants in Greenwich Village where they served, again, spaghetti, but this time with onions and luscious browned chicken livers.

I eventually found my first job in a porcelain factory, where I sat for six mornings a week at a long table with other workers, decorating cups and saucers, candy dishes, and ashtrays with wreaths of flowers and clumsy looking cherubs before they were fed into giant kilns for their final firing. At first I was only allowed to do the leaves. I soon graduated to flowers, and two months later I was deemed sufficiently trained to add color to the fat little bodies of the cherubs. At twelve o'clock, munching a sandwich on the bus, I rushed off to the Art Students League and then attempted to quickly rinse the morning's tedium out of my brain by downing two cups of coffee at the school's cafeteria before classes began.

Of my day-to-day work at the League, of interaction with fellow students I have no specific recollection. I remember the milling of the crowd, carrying canvasses, back packs and drawing-boards up and down the broad staircase, the noise and clatter from floor to floor, and then the intense quiet that prevailed in the working studios. In those rooms I felt at home, my life made sense, everything else fell away.

Morris Kantor taught oil painting and encouraged me greatly to use my imagination and work in full color with broad brushes. He gathered small groups of students at a cafeteria near school after classes. I was always included. We sat in a large booth in the farthest corner of the room and discussed art, literature, philosophy, and matters of common or personal concern. Those evenings always left me energized, full of enthusiasm.

There was another teacher who taught more conventional painting. His name was Corbino. His own canvases were teeming with racing, rearing, heroic horses in dark and menacing landscapes that left you exhausted just looking at them.

Reginald Marsh was a very well-known painter at the time. I did not take his class because I could not stand him. Bald, pasty-faced, broad-shouldered, and underslung, he could always be found sitting in the school cafeteria holding court, surrounded by admiring, mostly male students who burst into bellowing laughter at each of his oft-repeated and slightly salacious jokes.

On the first day of the watercolor class, eager and curious eyes met the teacher who entered the studio. His name was George Grosz. We had all seen at least some of his work in books and reproductions: accusing, scathing, satirical drawings and violent anti-war paintings, statements against the brutality of battle and the corruption of German society after the first World War, as well as powerful outcries against the destruction and inhumanity perpetrated in that country at the time. As early as 1932, observing the rise of fascism and Hitler's obviously mounting influence, he had left Germany and settled in the United States.

What kind of teacher would he be? Was he going to be harsh and demanding, maybe sarcastic and intimidating? Surely he would be a formidable presence.

He stood in the doorway for a few seconds, his hands dug deep into his blue painting smock. He looked from one to the other of us with a friendly smile. Then he nodded. "Good afternoon," he said in his unmistakable German accent, "Let's get to work."

We were amazed. He turned out to be everyone's benevolent uncle. He was gentle and had a wonderful sense of humor. He wandered leisurely, aimlessly from student to student looking over their shoulders at their paintings, commenting a little here and there, and telling funny stories. I do not remember that he ever actively criticized our individual work. He encouraged us to experiment with our materials. "Make your own brushes," he would say. "You can paint with tooth brushes, feathers, cotton balls. Whittle sticks into pens. Try rubbing the paper with the cut end of a raw potato. Experiment, invent!"

What did he actually teach us? I don't really know, maybe independence of spirit. Maybe that was why he did not critique our individual work more thoroughly. He preached observation, awareness of the world around us, to which he encouraged us to respond fervently in our drawings and paintings.

January 7, 1943

Dear Mutti,

What a strange climate we have here. For weeks we had mountains of snow. Hail to my high galoshes. Fervent gratitude and prayer of devotion to your fur coat and my gloves. Then suddenly, a few days ago, it got so warm that I kept the widows open and turned the heat off. The snow started to melt, and it rained. Disgusting! Now it is getting cold again, the mushy mess in the streets is freezing over and one slithers and slides on stiff legs hoping not to end in the gutter. A terrible storm is blowing and today a metal "No Parking" sign landed on my shoulder, thank God not on my head! The air is clear, though. I find that I am very strong, efficient, and take care of myself incredibly well. When Henri Temianka told you that I looked well he did not lie.

I am still working with the woman who makes ceramic buttons, unfortunately not for the six days she promised, only for three. She is waiting for new orders. This is not enough money for me. I keep looking for a better job.

Ernst Freund came twice already and took me out to dinner. His parents and Peter have been deported back to Germany and he has not heard anything from them since. Outwardly he is quite composed. What goes on within, one can only imagine.

Recently I met a Russian lady, Alexandra Grinevskaja, who was at first an actress and then a painter and worked for a long time with a very famous Russian theatre, designing costumes and decorations. She and her husband Alexeieff were the first artists to make modern advertising films in color.

"My Sister Amy" went to Washington recently to be accepted into the Red Cross and now has an excellent position as a psychiatric social worker in a large hospital not far from New York that treats sailors who went insane. She is very happy. Unfortunately, she has to wear a uniform and will probably look even more like a round bowling ball than she does already.

Talking about bowling balls and round: Everyone around me is pregnant. I am getting an inferiority complex! Lorraine is expecting. Do not tell her mother, I do not know whether it is official yet. Her husband got drafted last week, and the baby will come in July. She will probably go back to San Francisco in the spring.

If I could only have the inner peace and the chance to really concentrate on my painting and to learn more about it. I am convinced I would be successful. I made quite a few good connections here but lack the wherewithal to use them gainfully. Please write to me honestly whether it would be difficult for you or would you not like to send me sixty dollars per month for the next three months. I can easily earn fifty extra with a part-time job. Then, when I can use the rest of the day to study without having to fight constantly with a bad conscience, I would be really happy

One day later. This morning my ceramic-button lady had a new plan. It looks like she will get a big order for mass production. She wants me to be supervisor of several girls she will hire and put in my studio to work. She'll pay my rent, of course. I would work half day and maybe some evenings. That means I could go to the League in the afternoon. Might be a possibility.

Midday I had lunch with Dr. Neugarten in his fantastic office. He lives there also, has ten rooms, two nurses, and a cook on the most expensive part of Fifth Avenue. I had to wait quite a long time because he still had patients. When he appeared we had lunch in a little room next to his office. There was a nicely set table with candles and flowers and all the trimmings. It lasted exactly one hour by the clock. He was terribly nice. He said too that he saw no reason that it would be impossible to live off painting, only one must really know one's art, work hard, and be on one's toes. I should always announce myself for lunch whenever I felt like it. He had no time to go to a restaurant.

Did I write to you that I took a little still life of begonias to the art director of Sloane's, one of the largest interior decoration and furniture stores on Fifth Avenue? He offered to take my paintings on commission and hang them in his store when I have enough to show. I just did not have the proper amount of time to produce much as yet. Now that I am earning at least a little and see the possibility of getting more work, I start to feel better. Can you help a little? I think maybe with all of those shipyard workers in the house that pay rent it might be easier for you.

Just now I am returning from Allela's sketch class, and it is late. I have to get up at seven. It is already past midnight. It is good that I did not start anything with Benno Frank. All of a sudden he got drafted because he knows Arabic.

Talking about the draft, I just read that plans are under way to draft women and also men who are not eligible for combat I can clearly see Pappi in a Navy office job, in uniform, of course, and Mutti could become moral advisor for fallen girls in the service, or something like that.

I kiss you!
Good Night

January 27, 1943

Dear Ones,

I am horrified by how much time has passed since my last letter to you. By God, I shall write every Saturday from now on!

There is a rather weak reason behind the long silence, though. I was waiting to tell you about a new job that would have been very agreeable. It went up in smoke again like others before it. The manager gave the idiotic reason that I was too gifted and too artistic and would probably leave them after a short time. It was a publishing house for pulp magazines and comics, etc., and I was to do page layouts and occasionally do small sketches for twenty-five dollars five days a week. A pity! I would have liked that.

Now I am busy job hunting again. Today I worked at a place painting wooden salad bowls with apples, pears, and stupid garlands. I could stay there, and they are very happy with me, but the pay is low, and my brainwaves would stop vibrating in the very near future, a heavy price to pay.

Tomorrow I'll try a half-day job decorating ceramic jewelry for seventy cents per hour. That's a little better. The thought that I am still on your backs financially is terrible. At least next month I will only need fifty dollars. Soon I hope there will be better news from me. Otherwise, I am well.

February 13, 1943

Mutti, Dear Pappi,

I do not have an answer from you, but since it is Saturday I strongly feel that I can afford to be magnanimous and forgive you.

Following several warm, windy, and rainy days, a change of pace occurred again with a violent snowstorm descending on us. It is ice cold. I am really pleased at how healthy I am. Not one time did I have a full-fledged cold when every one else was sick around me. I believe that my house is also responsible for that. It is so well heated. Poor Allela froze for one week without heat, and the Bruckners felt that they could not have guests because their apartment was so cold. God knows my comparatively high rent seems to pay off. Ralph's friend Edith has a furnished room that is half as large as mine without kitchen and pays sixty-six a month.

My meager furnishings acquired several siblings. I bought a huge red-brown mahogany table at the Salvation Army for five dollars, and Barbara Sutro gave me a very comfortable upholstered chair.

I have a new job since yesterday, and it will be quite satisfactory, I think. I found it through a notice at the Art Students League. My boss is a terribly nice Italian, a Jewish refugee who has an equally nice American wife. They produce typical Italian pottery and have already a big inventory. I am sitting in a very light and warm room together with two art students and an older Italian sculptor. We even have a radio to

*entertain us. I paint little people, animals, flowers, etc. onto
everything that gets into my hands.*

*Talking to the sculptor, I mentioned that I know an Italian
family, the Anconas, in San Francisco. She was flabbergasted.
The Anconas were old friends from Florence, and she had just
received a letter from them.*

*Here again the strange phenomenon we noticed now several
times: people one left behind and lost touch with in one country
turn up again in another country in the most unexpected places.
It is like some big genie stuffed them all in to a big sack,
thoroughly shook them up together and then scattered them
out again all over the world.*

*It is very nice that I can work part-time there whenever I
want. So far I am there on Monday, Tuesday, and Wednesday
from 9 to 5, and Thursday and Friday from 9 to 1. That leaves
Thursday and Friday afternoon and all day on Saturday and
Sunday for my painting. I am making $16 per week. It follows,
Highly Revered Patrons, that now I will only need $40 and
even that sum will be unnecessary soon, I hope.*

*The reason for my leaving the ceramic outfit is simple. I felt
that I could not afford to wait for her promised future success
like she wanted me to. My youthful enthusiasm just was not
there anymore. I prefer the sparrow in the hand to the dove on
the roof. Apropos, something struck me as funny when I received
my first ashtray, which I was to adorn with a baby chicken
sitting in green grass with an egg laying next to it. I discovered
the following saying of eternal wisdom already printed at the
bottom: Better An Egg Today Then A Chicken Tomorrow. After
that I grinned the whole day and everyone decided that I was of
a rather happy nature, if maybe a little addled off and on.*

*The nice thing about this job is that nothing has to be exact
all of the time. If I feel like giving a different expression to my
chicken's face once in a while and letting it change position, that
is, as long as it behaves decently, I can do that. This makes the
monotony of the whole procedure more bearable. I can also invent
some of my own designs, if the boss approves first, of course.*

Since last week I am taking night classes from 7 to 10 at the League again, life drawing, anatomy, and perspective. I enjoy it immensely.

At intermission on Wednesday I walked through the school gallery to study my fellow students' work, recoiling in horror at some of them from time to time.

Three men were sitting on the floor in a corner near the exit, obviously embroiled in a heated discussion. They called me over to join them. Two of them were students and one was older, a small Jewish-looking man of maybe forty or forty-five years of age. He was supposedly a well-known painter and as I discovered later had quite a vast education and an equally great amount of enthusiasm. Like Paul Moses, he likes to pontificate and give lectures. I find it very stimulating to be around him. The discussion that day was about how to best study art, with or without teachers, and with what kind of teachers, traditional or independent ones. We migrated to a cafeteria where we sat and talked until midnight. This was so interesting! I discovered that I had thoughts and opinions that I had never recognized myself, let alone voiced to anyone. One thinks more clearly when there is an echo from someone else.

We are planning to rent a model for three hours every Sunday in the painters' studio if we find two more people to share the cost. It is fun to be together with the two boys who are as much in the initial upswing towards their vocation as I am.

I kiss and hug you.

March 20, 1943

My Dearest Mutti,

My God, if only one could hold time back with both hands! It runs away from me, it skips around in front of me, jumps over me, turns me in circles, and is absolutely not to be grasped.

Especially now since I took my old job back, one week passes like two days. As I wrote you, when I worked for the Italians full-time I went to the League at night. That was just too much.

I always try again and again to be highly energetic, and every time I have to realize that after all I only have a certain amount of perseverance in me and no more. Finally, I am starting to manage my inborn strength and resistance instead of going from one extreme to the other, from wallowing in moping inactivity to a degree of crazy exertion that leads inevitably to complete exhaustion.

My old boss received me with pleasure. So now I have the same schedule as before: Monday, Tuesday, and Wednesday from 9 to 5, Thursday and Friday from 9 to 1, $72 per month. Monday 8 to 10 sketch class at Allela's, Wednesday and Friday painting in the studio of the painter I wrote you about. Also on Sundays we share a model from 12 to 3. It would be impossible to pay for what I learned already from this man and paradoxically it does not cost me a penny.

You ask about my social activities. I do not sit alone at all as you seem to think. I would die from homesickness.

I certainly would have liked to call on the Bulovas, but did not know how to do that. Ostwald had only told me in a vague way to call them up and to ask about the sister. He did not give me a written recommendation. It is probably necessary to have one for such a prominent family that is probably overrun by people's requests for jobs or favors. The recommendations that Pappi gave me are mostly for jobs with theatre people. Without being a professional stage designer or union member, those contacts are useless to pursue. If we did not have that damned war I could make some plans, but a lengthy study like stage design seems so senseless. The devil only knows what lies ahead of us!

The only definite choice for me is my painting. Art is really a matter of conviction, a view of the world and one's place and voice in it, not a playful luxury, not a game. Aside from that there is the matter of doing something to provide food and lodging and the possibility of enjoying life a bit without prostituting the real expressions of art in order to make money with commercial so-called art. It would be preferable to pursue a trade, maybe making hats, or whatever. Maybe I should study journalism.

Back to social activities. I visited Fuchsi, and Fred and was glad when the evening was over. There are always such boring German and Viennese Philistines, awful!

I went to the School for Social Research with Hans Schwerin for performances of some of Bert Brecht's work. Pappi would have torn his hair out. Such a complete lack of ability to organize the evening. Such an amateurish affair. Pitiful! Three or four people dressed in dark street clothes read short scenes on a badly lit stage around a kitchen table. Then there was a talk given by a pale young man who seemed drained empty of all zest for living. He had obviously chosen his life's work as a Brecht scholar by the time he was a pissing baby. With a voice overwhelmed and clouded by awe he espoused the superiority of Brecht over the Wordy, Beautiful-Sounding Shallowness of Werfel and Thomas Mann, who, after all, still fed off Goethe's work and were hopelessly old-fashioned. Cripes!

Following this a record player entertained us with badly amplified Spanish and Russian war songs in obviously wrong succession. It was always different from what got announced. Some of the songs I had already heard before, but never knew that their text was written by Brecht. They were actually very beautiful. At the end of the program Elizabeth Bergner, in a black schoolgirl dress, a prissy white collar and red hair, read The Children's Crusade. *It was not her fault, but it was really good. I mean the poem! Finally, Edward G. Robinson, again at the kitchen table, read poems and did it most effectively. God, what Pappi would have made out of this affair! Well, what can one say? The house was packed. Brecht himself was there, so were Bruckner and everyone from Berlin and Vienna, and all looked very intellectual.*

Last Saturday I met very nice people at the Schwerin's. A

334 Felicia Altman Gilbert

man, a Russian, had a leading position at Disney in Hollywood and is the one who made Bambi. After the war he is going to become independent and told of very interesting plans for developing further this kind of drawing film, not for children, not cute, but serious and dramatic. He talked badly of Disney. He said Disney was completely illiterate, has never drawn or created anything, was just a very wily businessman adept at letting others get the coals out of the fire for him. To hear this will disappoint you since you love Disney so much.

A German psychologist who teaches at the School for Social Research was also there with his girlfriend, who is a painter. They are almost my neighbors and very nice. To supply variation to this assembly there was a South American painter with his fiancée and a German aristocrat who was a violent anti-Nazi.

God knows there are enough people around me, but it is quite doubtful that you will get a son-in-law in the near future. The young men who are still here are either married, have dozens of babies, are expecting them, or are sick.

I am sad that Lorraine moved away. I have inherited quite a bit from her, especially a big blue leather armchair, although it is only a loan. Furthermore, I got dishes, silverware, canned goods, an ironing board, garbage pail, and wastepaper basket. Oh, and the most important, her radio, until further notice.

What do I want for my birthday? First of all I am costing you enough already. Secondly, I need stockings and one or two slips. Everything is in rags. Shoes I need urgently. Those I will have to buy myself, though. I'd like some corduroy slacks that I can buy here for $3, a subscription to Art News that I can get for student price and finally, darn it, the photos you promised long ago, including Putzi's. I have plenty of food and feed myself excellently. It has not happened yet that I could not buy meat. I am just not picky. Some kind of chops one can usually find. The choice in restaurants is not great, but one mostly gets what one needs.

I am writing this letter in three installments. It has to get mailed, finally. Today is Sunday. This morning I slept late, was at my friend's studio at 12, painted from a model with the boys until 4:30 and got home at 5. Then I was all pepped up, so much so that I started to work some more. Suddenly at 6 I was so tired that I fell asleep, and now at 7 I have to rush to meet the boys for Chinese dinner. Tomorrow is a busy day, job till 5:30 and then 8 to 10 drawing at Allela's. I won't get to write then.

Kisses for the whole family

In April I quit my job at the porcelain factory. The daylight hours I lost from my study time at school became too precious. Also, confronting the sickening cherubs every morning turned into an unbearable ordeal. I joined some of my fellow students who worked the evening shift at a silk-screen printing establishment upstairs in a large warehouse, not too far from school. Posters and reproductions of paintings were produced there but also trade names were imprinted onto various containers of all kinds, like cookie boxes or cosmetic jars.

In a huge loft with large grimy windows that nobody ever saw open, a string of exhaust fans were whirring, supposedly sucking the chemical fumes out, but not erasing the acrid smell completely. On one side stood long tables upon tables, extending the entire width of the building. The posters were printed there.

Not so fondly, the other side of the room was called Torture Lane, for all of the machinery that ceaselessly ground and clacked there. It was manned by students and people needing extra income, or by those who could not find other jobs. There were people from Mexico, there were African-Americans, a few people from China, unemployed shop girls, and young housewives who hoped their children were safely asleep at home.

There I sat four nights a week among a row of sewing-machine type contraptions that were operated by foot pedals, speedy hands and a sense of urgency, for the faster one worked, the more money one made.

I adorned lipstick cases with names like Rubenstein, Arden, and Revlon. Right hand puts case on spindle, foot presses down on pedal, activates paint, and prints. Left hand removes case onto finish tray, right hand reaches for next case, and so on, faster, faster, faster. Feet pump, hands fly, a certain rhythm develops, and once in a while I was even able to think about other things at the same time, but not very often.

Twice a night a whistle blew, and we could stop. Thermos bottles would be opened and sandwiches unwrapped, masquerading as dinner. There was Coke, the smell of peanuts, a secret can of beer behind a screen in the corner. People talked, laughed, stretched, and lined up for the toilet, hoping to get in before their fifteen-minute recess was over.

With my mouth full of a hastily obtained bite of apple I settled back on my seat, but not before sending an inquiring glance in the direction of my neighbor, a tall young man seemingly spun into the incessant click, click, click of his machine. He never looked at anyone, never talked to anyone. He was encapsulated in a sphere of isolation. He appeared at work promptly on time, sat down, and his fingers flew. He never rose at recess; he just let his fingers rest in his lap until it was time to work the spindles again. Sometimes I would hear a little monotonous humming coming from his direction, easily mistaken for the sound of the machines.

Where was that man, I wondered? He was certainly not there. But still, somehow, his presence was felt. When I was at my easel I felt like that sometimes, I thought, so intense, submerged. But otherwise I took part in life around me. I looked, I reacted, I relished. How could one live in such a cocoon?

"Who is he?" someone asked.

"His name is Pollock," was the answer, "We think it's Jack or Jackson. Supposed to be a painter." Several months later Jackson Pollock had his first one man show.

By accident I discovered one day that Christiane lived in New York. Skinny, lanky Christel, the young actress with whom I played tomboy games in Switzerland when we were in our early teens. We climbed up the mountains above St. Moritz, lay in the meadows, looked down on the lake and the village, chatted, and exchanged confidences.

Ten years had gone by since those peaceful times from 1930 to 1932. Through the grapevine from other German refugees I had learned that she became the wife of the writer Ernst Toller, in 1935, when she had just turned seventeen, and that she had followed him into exile. In New York in 1939, having witnessed the destruction of the German life and culture he had grown up with, Toller killed himself out of depression and despair, as Stefan Zweig would eight years later.

I had climbed the dark narrow staircase to her New York apartment. A different Christel opened the door for me. I stared at her in amazement.

This was not Christel anymore, this was Christiane. She was as tall and slim as ever, had the same light blond shoulder-length hair tucked behind an ear on one side and hanging almost over her eye on the other. The large blue cat eyes in her heart-shaped face were the same, but their expression had changed. Wide-eyed enthusiasm and good-natured mischief had shone from them when we were thirteen and fourteen. There was still strength, but I also detected a tinge of sadness and a certain weariness in them, in spite of the happy smile she greeted me with. She wore a large man's shirt hanging low over her bare legs, failing to hide her belly, an unexpected, rude little hillock on an otherwise graceful, level landscape.

It was the end of May, already very hot, unseasonably early, even for New York. We sat on her cramped little balcony. The night air was still very warm but more bearable than the heat of the day. We looked down on steep, dark walls tunneling into narrow backyards strewn with garbage cans, outside iceboxes, and broken bicycles. Here and there were pitiful and touching attempts to create little gardens, a little outdoor refuge with a bench, maybe a few chairs and a table for rest and relief from big-city life. Someone must have had a jasmine plant in a pot somewhere, for its scent unmistakably alternated with the smell of garbage when the slight breeze turned.

"It's been ten years since we were last together." I shook my head, "It almost feels like a lifetime has passed."

"Oh, but it has." A childhood hoarseness in her voice had given way to a husky timbre.

I looked at her. "I feel that mine hasn't even started yet." I was startled at my own words.

No more was said for a while. Muffled traffic noises came from far below. The breeze had settled down and heat and dampness were seeping into every fiber of my body. I folded my hands behind my head, leaned back in the rickety canvas chair and swept my eyes over the night sky. Moving shafts of city lights swept into the darkness, turning it into shadowy waves, undulating like the sea.

I felt so lonely. The first few months, the first giddiness of freedom had passed when I had not registered at the League immediately. I had wanted to prolong my explorations of the city and relish the sense of not having to account to anybody for my daily life.

What had come out of my mouth a minute ago? That my life had not started?

"Got a man in your life?" Christel brought a tray with ice tea from her tiny kitchen, letting the screen door click shut behind her.

I shook my head.

"Anyone in sight? No? Then tell me about a past romance."

I shook my head again. "None. There have been none."

"What?" She looked at me in horror, as if I had the measles. "Don't tell me you are a virgin? At twenty-four?" This inadequacy of mine was utterly incomprehensible to her. The smoke from her cigarette curled around her scowling forehead. "Something ought to be done about *that*," she said in a low voice, and added in her best stage murmur, "And it must." She sounded like a Sibyl in a Greek myth, pronouncing her oracle.

It struck me as so funny that I laughed, but deep down my sense of dissatisfaction with myself and my life only increased.

That night in my spartan apartment I sat on my bed leaning against the wall. I knew I would not sleep. The front page of *The Times*, propped up against my pulled-up knees, slipped to the floor unread. I was trying to check up on the news of the war, but could not concentrate.

A virgin at twenty-four. A spinster. Later, the proverbial maiden aunt. Where was the man who was going to share my life, the person to love, to end this dreadful loneliness? It was not to be. I just knew it. I had to make a meaningful life on my own, with my art and personal strength.

June 4, 1943

Dear Mutti,

I have just finished breakfast, slurped the last cup of coffee and feel sticky in my clothes, enduring it with peaceful resignation. In the last few days one could not call the temperature moderate by any means.

Last night I was forced to climb into my silk slip and the dark blue dress with yellow flowers so I would look presentable for the good, fat Schwerin, who had invited me to go to the Russian Ballet with her. It was difficult. The standard dress here in the village consists of short, wide skirts, broomstick skirts, the thinnest blouses available, bare legs, and sandals. Even I have my hair pinned up away from my neck. I shower three to four times a day and sleep naked, but otherwise it is bearable. At the print shop, though, it is considerably warmer, since we are not allowed to open all of the windows to let the air in for ventilation. The paint in the screens would dry too fast. On top of that, the table on which I work has a cute little light affixed to it with a metal cap that exudes heart-warming heat in addition. The assembled men and women look more like a hiking party than a work crew, half naked and barefoot. In spite of the heat I feel absolutely good here. The atmosphere is so nice and friendly and business is improving steadily, as they say. We have more and more work. I hope to get a raise soon. In the meantime, I am biting my nails again. I was offered another job for more money, 84 cents per hour, also in silk-screening, but it is farther to travel daily by subway, and it is also more tiring. I would have to stand the whole time.

June 8, 1943

Oh My Dear Ones,

I need a secretary, but not one that does my writing to you for me. I like to do that myself, with pleasure!

It seems I carried this thing of going barefoot too far. Aside from that, it was so hot and stuffy the day before yesterday that our shop rebelled and finally tore all of the windows open. A refreshing draft developed on one side of the space and everybody congregated there. Consequently, I ended up with a horrible cold.

My eyes are as small as keyholes, and my hearing is not too good either. The whole winter long I did not sneeze even once. Nevertheless, I'll carry myself with dignity! Now we had some wild thunderstorms, and it has gotten cooler.

Yesterday I checked my new job out. A friend of Alberta's works there. He too is a painter. It is in a small workshop in Queens that is affiliated with a big textile factory. Only four people work there. They prepare the screens from which the dress material will be printed at the factory. My job would consist of transferring the designs to the screens. Tomorrow I will begin three tryout mornings. After that I'll have to join the Union. They will then send me to the boss of the factory to be hired. Since I have experience, I will earn from 75 to 84 cents per hour. If I work full-time I could make $40.00 per week. Not bad, eh? All of my friends say I would be an idiot if I do not take that job.

When, please, am I supposed to paint?

Edith and Joseph invited me for dinner and a movie, **The Moon Is Down,** *on Sunday. They got married three weeks ago because all of a sudden Joseph, who works for the government, got reprimanded for Living In Sin! Investigators swarmed all over their house, and friends and neighbors were interrogated. Ridiculous!*

Speaking of government, the kind of interview Pappi went through has been repeated with me. I was called to a special investigator, who turned out to be a very nice and educated man. When I appeared before him for the first time he looked at me in astonishment and asked, "When were you born?" He then broke out in great laughter and crossed ten years off my files.

He promised to quickly resolve the matter and said I would hear from him and sounded very reassuring. I have not heard a word since. I just wrote him that I am moving and maybe that will expedite things.

Mutti, if I did not mention the purse in the last letter, it was not intentional. It is especially beautiful. Terribly elegant!

Alright, I shall write to Anita. She is a shit woman. What's the address?

I just noticed that you asked about Consul Schwartz in your last letter. He has provided me with one of the most devilish bouts of laughter of my life.

He appeared one afternoon to pay me an unannounced visit. He planted himself, heaving belly and all, in my armchair and proceeded to talk for a full three hours. San Francisco was his destiny, he said. He had been very ill some time ago and during his recovery he and his wife met a young girl who "helped" his wife off and on by keeping him company. He recounted it in these words:

"So it happened, what generally happens when a man and a girl find themselves alone. It became a great love affair, and you will believe me, my dear young lady, I was in great pain when she left me."

There was a sad pause. I tried with all my might to look compassionate. Then he sighed and continued, looking at me with a hangdog expression, "And you, too, are from San Francisco."

Oh, oh, now I could not stay on WAVE LENGTH COMPASSION, as hard as I might have tried. I could not help myself. My grin was broader and broader. I swallowed repeatedly, gasped for air and blew my nose with great intensity. I felt that I did not deserve this afternoon's performance all by myself. It was too delicious!

His Excellency the Consul continued to puff his big cigar, sending gusts of smoke and lust throughout my room, while his considerable belly was pulsing up and down. He proceeded to assure me that a very free soul lived within him that was attuned to the art of living life to its fullest, and where or how or whenever he could be of help to me . . .

Finally, I was able to convince him that I was immensely busy and that it would be better that I call him as soon as my schedule permitted. He is still waiting. If I were not such a master in ticklish situations? It was unbelievably funny.

Let's get back to your last letter. The young man who lived in my new studio throughout last winter swears that it is very warm. The move will cost me about $12.00

Unfortunately, I have not been able to paint recently. From September onward George Grosz will conduct drawing classes again at the League. That makes me very happy. I am thinking now of taking the $40 job for the next two or three months to save some money and to return to my old job with the Italians in September in order to have more free time. I'll see.

Did you get my night letter for your wedding anniversary? I composed it like a business letter and phoned it in to Western Union, whereupon I was told that it obviously was a hidden congratulatory message, and I should be ashamed of myself. I was ashamed and changed it to sound even more businesslike and tried Postal Telegraph. Here they informed me that they would first inquire at that address whether there was a celebration of any kind and if there were, the message would not be delivered. I had to pay, nonetheless. The great prize question, did you get it?

Your check was most welcome! It paid the last rent here. Many thanks.

I'll stop now. My nose runs quite precocious, my blowing sounds ferocious.

Much love!

July 8, 1943

My Dear Ones, My Much Loved Ones,

This city eats you up! In the morning I get up and start to work and think I'll get to write to you in the evening. In the evening I sit on a bench in Washington Square trying to cool off, or I linger after dinner in the garden of a little Italian restaurant imagining that I feel a bit of a minuscule breeze. I drink beer in desperation. It even tastes good now.

*How much I would love to see you! If I were rich I would
first come to visit you all and then take Mutti home with me to
spend the autumn here. Then I would ask Pappi to keep me
company during the winter months. Of course, I would invite
Ralph and Pat to come with me to Santa Barbara in the
springtime. I would NEVER think of making money.*

*Oh you funny Mutti! I can clearly see how you worry about
my relationship with Christel. I swear to you, since my finances
are most precarious to say the least, I can ill afford to lend money
to anybody. She has a group of people who help her. Two weeks
ago her baby arrived, who answers, or rather will one day answer,
to the name of Andrea Valeria Grautoff. A perfect product, blond,
blue-eyed, and sturdy. Already yesterday Christel started to
work again. She gets manuscripts from the Fischer Publishing
House and also from individual writers to type and to translate.
She thinks she will be able to live off that. She is so sweet to me
and would have given me money if I had let her.*

*For-Betters-or-for-Worth (my friend Howard Bettersworth)
has developed into my entertainment agent. Too bad that 1) he
is old, end of forty, 2) on account of love, completely unattractive
and 3) on account of all of the above, completely and absolutely
not in the running. He is touchingly nice to me. Nothing less
then broiled lobster and foie gras is ordered for dinner and the
taxi awaits me in front of the door. Two weeks ago we went to a
fabulous concert at the stadium with Joseph Hoffmann as soloist,
playing a* Schumann *concerto and the* Shostakovich Fifth
Symphony *that I love so much. It was wonderful! Mutti would
have enjoyed it. In addition, it was agreeably cool, and three
fantastic comets raced across the clear starry sky over our heads.
Heaven accomplished an excellent stage direction. Oh, how Pappi
could direct* Julius Cesar *in this place! Anyway, what a letter
he wrote me! For three days I had to use eye-drops afterwards,
it was so exhausting to read. Will the play be shown in Los
Angeles? Anita finally sent me the check and mentioned what a
great success your direction had been.*

Mutti, what a stupid question! Whether I want you! How utterly ridiculous! Did I not make myself clear in my last letter? Only right now you would die from the heat. I am sitting here completely naked having breakfast, cute little drops on my upper lip and a small itchy heat rash near the hairline at the back of my neck. Under these circumstances I have a hunch that you would not be too happy here.

Since I am always in favor of extending pleasures, I would like to suggest that Pappi should come here after you leave, as continuation to the story, so to speak, the next volume. The theme PARENTS contains too much and is too rich and convoluted to be savored all at once. Since I am a gourmet, I prefer to time my intake slowly, one after the other. Anyway, it won't hurt you to have a little vacation from each other once in a while either.

Is Ralph in Santa Barbara yet? Greet my grandma, The Ancestor. Tell her I am wearing her broach often, which is a lie, but it will please her.

Whenever I see a small dog I think of Putzi and get terribly homesick.

Kisses,
Fe

August 8, 1943

Dear Mutti,

Your letter finally arrived, and I am grinning happily in a peaceful breakfast mood. I have to announce something new again, and that is why I am answering so quickly, excited and pleased. I have decided to study stage design after all. It is just too hard to have a job and to study art and paint at the same time. I just have to realize that, as bitter as it is. I was incredibly exhausted recently. Since I am a crazy nut anyway, as we all know, the job was three times as strenuous because it was so stinking boring. I realize that I have to do something constructive that interests me so much that it carries me along in spite of tiredness. I just got off the phone with Condell, the stage designer I was in contact with last spring. He said he just finalized a big contract with Schwartz. Who is Schwartz? Does Pappi know? He will not have time to teach his regular classes but could take me as his assistant, maybe. He wants me to call on him on the first of September. He had told me the first time that I could be a costume designer in nine months and enter that union, much cheaper than the stage designers union. Now that would be in May. At least then I would have a definite profession. I would also learn an awful lot about other applied arts. I'll paint in any case. From the 14th of September on, George Grosz will teach again twice a week. I won't miss that! I realize again and again that my painting and everything I produce has a tinge of the theatrical or decorative in it. At this moment I am working on a screen that has a circus theme. I'll try to sell it. Don't you think that sounds good? On the first of next month, I will talk all of that over with Condell.

Now to your letter. A terribly long time will pass until the ninth of October. I expected you in three weeks or so. In October the weather can get nasty already, and I had thought it would be so nice to be able to sit with you outside at the Café Breevoord and to take you on a boat in Central Park. Since yesterday the weather has been just beautiful, warm sunshine, cool wind, and the sky is radiantly blue, although you can never be sure that it will stay that way. Tomorrow it could be gray, horribly hot, and one could be dripping with sweat. Of course, in October there will be a lot more going on, as far as concerts, exhibits, and plays are concerned. That will be important for you. I'll order the sleeping car train tickets for you. Which class? Or is there only one? I hate to have to think of your return ticket already! I am looking forward to your visit so much. I hope that Pappi will take your place after you leave. Why don't you all just move here? Everything would be so much easier. Ralph can work in a shipyard here as well, and Pat can train Mei-Mei to walk on a leash and promenade down Fifth Avenue, feeling glamorous. I have seen a woman with a deer on a leash, so why not Mei-Mei? Putzi would be in Pee-Pee-Paradise in Central Park and chase all the squirrels he wants. Seriously!!??

The photo made me look grown up? Don't believe it. But I have only gotten older. The folds around my eyes are getting more pronounced. That comes from the climate and from lack of sleep. I am following the example of my knowledgeable Mama and cream and massage diligently. As the poet said, "The years did not leave without a trace!" My skin, though, is in good shape, totally free of pimples.

I cannot imagine Pat with a hairdo like Susie's. Why do they go to Santa Barbara for only a week? How can Mei-Mei's children get born there? Or are they not on the way? Amazing!

About housing for you. The hotels are supposed to be very full, so I have to make reservations early. Question #1, what do you want to pay? Question #2, where do you want to be? It would be nice to have you close to me, and it is pleasant around Washington Square, but maybe you want to live more in the middle of town, closer to shopping and sights. Unfortunately, I'll have to leave you for some hours a day to go to work, so then you'll be alone. It also takes you ten minutes by subway from the Village to go uptown.

I can see us already ambling arm in arm along Fifth Avenue. It will be like Christmas!

Yesterday I got the birth announcement from Lorraine. Christel's baby is blossoming. I have become a diaper-changing expert. She smiles a lot and has huge blue eyes.

I don't see so many people right now except Bettersworth. It is just too hot. But now since you will be coming I shall call on my neglected friends, so you'll get to know them. My fresco painter disappeared into the army and is stationed somewhere in Massachusetts. Another got a job in Boston. I also hope to meet more people through Condell and also through Grosz. Do not say that I am doing too much again. I am!

Write soon!

Love!
Your Daughter

It was early autumn. Summer heat had passed. The trees along Fifth Avenue and on Washington Square were starting to turn yellow. A slight wind blew discarded newspapers across the pavement. One wrapped itself around my ankle. I picked it up. "Tokyo Bombed," it said. West Coast Japanese Moved Inland to Camps. I crushed it into a ball and threw it away. There was no escape from news and repercussions from the war. Young men drafted, casualty lists in the papers, radio reports of battles, blackouts on the coast, rationing of sundry commodities, these things were with you all the time. I tried to forget. I had come to explore the art galleries behind their large showcase windows on either side of the street.

I wandered through one heavy glass or ornate wooden door after the other. There was a show of Oscar Kokoschka and Max Beckmann, where I lingered a long time. Kokoschka's marvelous, expressive portraits especially fascinated me. That's how I'd like to paint, I thought.

A group show of American painters needed much study. There were Marsden Hartley, John Marin, Milton Avery, and Jack Levine, also Max Weber. At the Durand-Ruel Gallery, Toulouse Lautrec's inimitable energy and immediate eloquence confronted me and left me with a feeling of great excitement. I had seen his work before in European museums but never in as comprehensive a one-man show as here.

I boarded the double-decker bus on Fifth Avenue, grabbed the railing of the steep stairs and pulled myself up to the top. I was on the way back to my apartment on Sheridan Square. It was not dark yet, but the streetlights were already coming on. Rush hour was in full swing. I looked down on people and cars, brightly lit storefronts and blinking stoplights. When the branches of trees interrupted the view as we drove along, it looked like images from a picture book just glimpsed, barely seen, when pages are flipped impatiently.

Was New York in 1943 much different than Paris in the 1880s? How would Lautrec walk and work among us now?

Often during preceding weeks I had climbed to the top of the bus and just rode up and down Fifth Avenue for hours, from Greenwich Village all the way to the end of the line and back again, maybe two or three times in succession without getting off, watching the life of the streets below, a stranger, lonely, feeling lost. It was different today. Excitement engulfed me. I'll learn from Lautrec, from Kokoschka. I'll look at life around me, draw and paint what I feel about it, how it resonates, through my own eyes. Here is my passion, I thought; that's what I am meant to do!

It would not be the professional model posing for us in class, but the children playing in the park, the old men dozing on benches or busily swapping stories with each other, people rushing to work, or shopping at the market. These I will observe and draw. "Look at life around you, react and connect," George Grosz had said.

It was almost dark when I landed at Washington Square and the air seemed oppressive, warmer than in the daytime. A half moon was coming up behind the treetops. There was a hush in the air. Even the people that were obviously on their way home from work slowed down, stopped for a minute or two near the fountain, maybe set a purse or briefcase down at their feet to light a cigarette or just listen to the splashing water. I passed a couple snuggled tight together on a bench, with foreheads touching and eyelids closed. I was not conscious of the noise of traffic. A light appeared from behind the shield of trees across the square and slowly rolled along the path. It looked like a special little moon and in its midst the ice cream man pushed his cart and shook his tinkling bell as if he were blessing the night.

Just a few blocks were left to reach Sheridan Square. A Chinese market was still open. A group of students, books under their arms, swaggered along, smoking and kidding each other. A beggar or two, a horse-drawn vegetable wagon passed by. People waited for tables in front of Gianni's restaurant. The streets were full of life, and I felt that I was part of it.

"You sure look happy tonight, Miss," The elevator man smiled at me.

I switched the lights on in my room. It was nearly empty, but it was mine. The smell of turpentine confirmed it.

I was hungry. The remainder of yesterday's sandwich from the refrigerator would do. I opened a can of soup and then forgot about it. Settling down at my table I uncorked the bottle of India ink, inserted a shiny new pen into a holder and started to draw, trying to conjure up what I had passed on my way home. I drew the Chinese waiter leaning in his doorway, hoping for a customer and smiling a broad invitation; the tired, spike-heeled sales girl stalking by on wobbly ankles, her intricate hairdo about to come apart; the ragged beggar sitting on the sidewalk cradling a scrawny little dog on his lap.

And then I came to the image I had tried to avoid, but it would not let me, the lovers on the bench. I drew one version, then another, and still a third. None pleased me. None showed the feeling of intensity I was trying to convey. Tearing it all up, I threw the pen down.

The elevator took me down again, and I was no longer elated. I needed company, and Allela lived on Washington Square, only a few blocks away.

It had gotten quite late by now. The streets were quiet. I knew that Allela would still be up. She was a night owl like me. Already on the stairs leading up to her second floor studio the smell of linseed oil and turpentine were unmistakable. Frequently-voiced complaints from other inhabitants had been to no avail.

"Hey, you're just in time! I'm done for tonight." She stood at her easel about to scrape the paint off her palette.

I looked at her. The red in her eyes and the pale skin of her strong face spoke of lack of sleep. Obviously, she had recently taken the scissors and cropped her black hair even shorter than before.

"Sit," she said. "Want some coffee?" She stuffed the paint rag into the pocket of her jeans. Wiping her hands on her T-shirt she went to get water from the sink in the corner and plugged in her ancient hotplate. A whiff of fat, rust, and burnt crumbs reassured us that it was still in working order.

I flopped down on the skinny mattress that served as sofa by day and as her bed at night. She came and set two marmalade glasses with steaming coffee on the floor in front of us.

"Have a doughnut."

I shook my head.

She settled down next to me, pulled her legs up and hugged her knees to her chest, examining me closely.

"So, what gives? You look kind of blue to me."

"I guess I need company. I'm a little lonely sometimes." I shrugged my shoulders.

Allela kept looking at me. Nothing was said for a while.

Then I asked, trying to sound casual, "You don't have a boyfriend either, do you?"

She raised her eyebrows and I thought I saw a faint, almost sarcastic little smile around her lips that disappeared immediately. She did not answer, but lowered her legs, stood up and patted the pockets of her jeans, looking for cigarettes. "Smoke?" She offered me her pack and struck a match for me. "You have not seen my last painting, have you?"

She turned a large canvas around that had been leaning against the wall and set it up on her easel. "What do you think?"

"Oh my God!" I gazed at the large painting with fascination. It showed the seated figure of a woman, her elbow on her knee, chin supported by her balled-up fist, staring out at me with a dark and glowering look, fiercely intense, terrifying and despairing at the same time. It was painted with large brushes and palette knives, mostly in earth colors, sienna, umber, ochre, some orange, small touches of deep blue, emphasized here and there with strong black lines. It reminded me of Beckmann or Rouault.

"My self portrait," she said, her large eyes behind the horn-rimmed glasses measuring me intently as if my answer were a test of my integrity.

"Look, it's a terrific, strong painting," I said and really meant it, "But it is not you, not remotely, it's someone else."

Allela nodded. "Right, it's someone you don't know."

(This conversation came to haunt me. Many years later I learned that Allela had killed herself. She had swallowed acid and died alone among her canvasses.)

It was late at night. The moon shone, too bright, it seemed. The trees were bare. A light wind blew and ruffled my hair. A man's arm was wrapped around my shoulders. He'd said, "I'll walk you home."

I had been to a party on Bleeker Street, invited by a girl who left me in a dim and smokey room with a crowd of noisy people I did not know. Why did I come, I wondered?. I felt terribly alone.

"A hot toddy might help." He held the steaming mug out to me. We danced. The music slowed down. He held me tight and looked down at me with kind blue eyes. I felt he knew me through and through. His name was Boris, he said. His parents had come from Russia.

"I think you need a friend," he said, and refilled my cup. He was older than the crowd around us, had a strong face and red hair. We danced some more. I discovered that I was quite able to talk. A third hot toddy had loosened my tongue.

Again the moon was there, glancing off the wall in my apartment. Boris had me in his arms, and I beheld myself as in a dream. *This is it*, I thought, *this is it.*

But suddenly everything changed. Deeper feelings emerged and my fists flew at my hapless lover in blind revolt at just the moment when the desired end was about to be achieved. The romantic evening failed utterly in making a full-fledged woman out of me.

My knight, whose armor no longer shone, gave me one last hug and put his clothes back on. "I guess I am just not the right one for you," he said and left.

In the bathroom I collapsed onto the stone-cold floor and wept in deepest misery.

I stayed awake all night, and when it started to get light outside I stood at the window, my hands holding the sill and my forehead leaning against the cool pane. A delivery truck rolled by, and Mrs. Alliotto's little dog downstairs was let out to lift his leg on the fire hydrant. The sudden clatter of the metal gate being pulled back from the grocer's storefront across the street declared the day begun. It was a gray day, a cool and foggy day.

Times of great depression followed. For a brief few hours I had thought that, finally, real romance, maybe even love had entered my life.

I did not leave my room for a week. There were a few eggs in the refrigerator, some bread and an orange or two. I was not hungry anyway. Little by little I started to draw, aimless pencil scribbles at first, then reached for the pen. Strange faces and shapes appeared on my paper. With brush and washes in ink I filled page after page with wild tormented trees and black figures flying among and around

them with twisted limbs and flying hair. Monster faces
stared through threatening clouds and giant birds circled
and circled around each other.
    Enough! I threw the brush down. I ripped the paper
up. Anger replaced despair.
    Idiot! You Goddamned fool, I swore at myself.
    The phone rang. It was Irma, a girl I had befriended
years ago when we were both hotel guests in Switzerland,
and met again in New York, the city that had become the
irresistible magnet for so many wanderers from Europe.
    "Come have lunch. I don't work today."
    Suddenly I was hungry. We both could afford the corner
cafeteria. I stepped out, ready to live again.

    Elegant Irma returned from the self-serve counter
gingerly balancing a tray with crackers and a bowl full to
the brim with chicken noodle soup. That was quite a feat,
considering the crowded room and the risk of loosing her
equilibrium, sailing along on her extra high-heeled pumps.
She made it. Not a drop was spilled.
    Fishing the plastic spoon and knife out of the rolled-up
paper napkin, she laughed. "What a come-down. Last night
there was lobster aux gratin, wine, crepes Suzette, an
elegant escort, and now this. And you, my disheveled,
virginal friend. Now, now, just a joke," she said, looking at
the fork that had stopped in mid-air on its way to my mouth.
"You needn't raise your eyebrows." She took her compact
out to check the tilt of her little hat in the mirror.
    "Have you known him long? How did you meet?" I
knew of her previous escapades and did not really care or
want to know more, but felt it my duty to ask.
    "Just sitting on a bench in Central Park," she giggled.
"He took me to the theater, to dinner and yes, to his
penthouse. Don't frown. This time it's really serious."

I shook my head. I had heard her but had not really listened. Absently I gazed out the big window next to us and thought about having to return to my room. I did not want to go back there. I needed to move, I thought, live somewhere else, forget that whole incident. Forgetting it was easier said then done, of course.

CHAPTER EIGHTEEN

The Studio on Fifteenth Street

I found my new studio in a very narrow, old three-story house on Fifteenth Street. It was squeezed between two tall warehouses, a David between two Goliaths. Dilapidated as it was, it suited my state of mind perfectly. A creaky flight of stairs led up to the second floor where I had a good-sized room with a large dirty skylight overhead. It had a fireplace, a tiny bathroom, a refrigerator, and even a small stove with an oven. Below me on the first floor lived an old man whose younger woman seemed to go out at night and return drunk towards morning. Consequently, screaming, fights, and commotion broke out at least twice a week, shaking the wobbly rafters of the house. A single woman and her teenaged son lived on the floor above me. Their room must have been very small; it was set on the part of the roof that was not occupied by my skylight and a chimney. They were very quiet, and I did not get a glimpse of them until somewhat later.

I wrote home:

Sometime in 1943

I improved my financial status considerably by renting another studio that is much cheaper and quite satisfactory. Moving day is getting close.

I pack, wash, clean, sort out, and throw junk away. Every day I take some stuff over to the new place that is quite close to here, thank God. It is only ten blocks farther and on the way to work.

To answer your question, of course it is in a good neighborhood, six houses from Fifth Avenue. Excellent! My landlord is a painter who lives somewhere in Vermont. He wrote me a very nice letter to say that he will do anything to make my stay agreeable.

All my love,
Fe

The "good neighborhood" remark was of course tailored to allay parental anxieties. It was in truth a rather dismal street, mostly occupied by warehouses and old office buildings, deserted and not very inviting to walk at night. So when a gentleman offered to escort me home one evening after a dinner party, I gladly accepted. He had been sitting at the far side of the table, and I had not caught his name when he was introduced to me. Walking down the stairs as we left he mentioned something about music, and I said I loved the voice of Marian Anderson.

"Oh, I have quite a few of her recordings," he said. "I live very close to here. How about coming up to my place for a while, have a little cognac and listen to Marian Anderson. It's still early in the evening."

He did not look particularly threatening. As a matter of fact, I still can't remember exactly what he looked like, clearly unimpressive. He was intelligent and spoke well. The walls of his studio apartment were lined with shelves up to the ceiling, holding an immense collection of records. There was music from the early Middle Ages to Stravinsky and Shostakovich. There was jazz and folk music. I was impressed.

"Forgive me," I said, "We were introduced, but I did not catch your name." There was a sofa in the middle of

the room and I was just about to sit down when he handed
me a glass of cognac.

"I am Clifford Odets." Of course I was surprised.

"Oh, I loved your play, *The Golden Boy*. I am so pleased
to meet you." He put his arm around my shoulder and
pulled me over to a door that was half open. I saw a
darkened room with one small, lighted lamp next to a huge
round bed.

"We can listen to music from here," he said.

"Except that it's time for me to go home," I twisted from
his arm.

"Don't you know how famous I am?" He regarded me
with a stern look. "You should feel honored that I want to
go to bed with you."

"I don't." I headed for the door. Nobody could have
looked less enticing at that moment than he did. He followed
me down and hailed a cab, put me in it, and slammed the
door. My brush with celebrity.

It was at about that time that I met George. We got into
a conversation at the public library. He was two or three
years older then I. He had the face of a poet, sensitive,
handsome, and kind. Except for an occasional kiss and a
hug our relationship was, and remained, platonic. I had
acquired another brother.

On weekends or warm summer evenings we would
stroll around the Village streets, poke around in little shops
that sold ethnic wares, and sit in bars listening to poetry
readings. Later when it got cold we would sit in front of
my fireplace, drinking hot toddies and talking about books
and ourselves.

I made another friend. I do not recall where or when
I met Elizabeth Sheldon. She was tall and energetic, also
somewhat older then I, a medical intern planning to

become a psychiatrist. Her close friend was Dr. Oljeneck, a brain surgeon who was much older then she. He was a very quirky, bright, and lively man. Sometimes we called him The Brain, but mostly Dr. O. I did not see these two very often. They were busy, of course, but when we got together I had a wonderful time. I think Elizabeth felt that I needed protection, and Dr. O., too, seemed to be fond of me.

Early in October I received a letter from my father, announcing my mother's departure from San Francisco to visit me in New York. She had to make elaborate arrangements at home before being able to leave, since her husband was utterly incapable of taking care of himself, let alone of running the household.

In answer to the official request from the government to ease the overcrowded conditions in the city, Mother had rented all extra rooms on the third story of our house to shipyard employees or others involved in wartime occupations.

She arranged for Richard Betts and Minna Levison, who had been acquaintances of ours when we lived in France, to move temporarily into my former room in her absence. They promised to take care of the home, the renters, helpless Pappi, and Putzi, the canine successor of Bella. Bella had finally decided to give in to old age and all that traveling. She had put her head and paws down and called it quits. Also, Ralph and Pat were commandeered to pitch in since they, too, lived in part of the house. Mother felt that it took many people to do the chores that she alone was capable of managing.

Actually, for a spoiled woman who had never been in a situation in which she had to do any physical labor such as cooking or keeping house until late middle age, she adapted with grace and diligence, if not with great aptitude.

Finally came the time of her arrival that I expected with anxiety, but also with pleasure.

Father wrote to me:

October 5, 1943

Dear Child,

I just put Mutti on the train. I am happy for her, but I am in somewhat of a miserable mood. I know Pat will take good care of me, but the house is so crowded. Richard and Minna Betts stay in your studio, and all of the renters whirl around the house. Mutti will tell you more about that.

Now to your concerns. One important principle, especially for New York: Do not let anybody take advantage of you! I do hope that Condell will pay you and that you as co-worker will get recognition on the programs, unless that is against union rules. Do not be the fifth wheel on the wagon! Does Condell have so much to do, or does he want to make it easy for himself? Does he really need an assistant, or are you only supposed to do his dirty work? I am a little skeptical that he mentioned Schwartz, because I know that that gentleman lost everything to the Nazis. He had been the director of the Opera in Hamburg and is a very good old acquaintance of mine, a very nice person. He looks like an older, out-of-wedlock brother of Paul Moses. If you bring him greetings from me he will take you in his arms. He has a daughter of your age, I think, who is an actress.

You will talk your whole situation over with Mutti. We are very worried about you! Is it sensible to stay in that neighborhood when your job is uptown?

Be sure that Mutti rests and does not exert herself in any way. Under no circumstances allow her to cook or clean!

Did you read the critique about my Mozart direction at the Temple Emanuel? They termed it PERFECTION. I gave a terrific talk of twenty minutes before the performance and earned all of fifteen dollars. Let Mutti tell you about it.

I gave Mutti twenty addressed and stamped envelopes to take along. They are to be used for your letters to me, used by **both** *of you!*

A hug from,
Pappi!

Letter from Father to Mutti:

October 8, 1943

Dr. Gropper brought me his prescription for you. He broke his toe because he went around barefoot at home. Please mention this to Fe, who also tends to such extravagances. Anyway, the prescription is the reason for my writing again so soon without hearing from you. The one who goes away has to write first, remember?

The empty bed next to me strikes me as very peculiar, and I miss what it should contain very much already.

The distribution of duties between Minna Betts and Pat proves to be quite workable, up to now. Putzi is happy and gets spoiled by everybody. Write in detail about your trip and your first days in New York. I am anxious to hear how you found Fe, the state of her health and nutrition.

Nothing new is to be told about life here. Sunday evening I will go to the Scottish Rite Auditorium to see Molly Picon, the famous Jewish actress.

I went to the police to get my driver's license permit again. The first cop told me they only allow two permits, and since I flunked two tests I could not get another one. I punished him with one of my famous contemptuous looks, went to the boss who said, "I hear you were away on a trip," and immediately gave me a new permit for another six months. I told Pat that now she absolutely has to practice with me because we already spent so much money on the car.

Love,
Pappi

Poor Pat nearly suffered nervous breakdowns giving Father driving lessons. He was determined to succeed, and at the same time, so completely inept that success would not have been possible. Pat went secretly to the driver's license bureau. "If you allow this man to drive," she told them, "You'll release a menace on the world."

From Mother to Pappi:

Hotel Lafayette, University Place, Ninth Street
October 10, 1943

Dear George,

I landed here, the only hotel within reasonable distance from Fe's studio. The following will tell you all about how Fe lives.

Her studio is actually not too bad. It is a house such as you would find on Sacramento Street, very old with creaking stairs and crooked slanting roof. When one opens a window all of the dirt of past generations blows in, so even with greatest attempts at keeping things clean it is an impossible task. If you add Fe's lack of interest in maintaining a cultivated, civilized home the way it is supposed to be, you can picture the condition yourself.

On the other hand, she told me verbatim, "You know that for the first time in my life I look forward to the coming day when I go to bed at night." So I am really completely disarmed! How little one knows even the people who are closest to one. So much is left in the dark. Actually, she looks quite well, needs only fresh air, which is not to be found here. She is searching for a new direction in her painting. I hope I can bring some of it home. In the morning she goes to George Grosz's class, in the afternoon at one o'clock she comes to be with me. We both cried with pleasure when we saw each other again. Naturally, she would love to have us move to New York, but that would be impossible because of the climate. Even now it is partially oppressive, and within one hour, it is ice cold and windy. Greenwich Village is very charming, reminiscent of the Paris artists' quarter. Good restaurants.

The train trip was agreeable, expensive, etc. Am leaving here on November fifteen, arrive San Francisco on November nineteen. I am glad Minna and Pat are taking care of you.

Love,
Alice

Father to Mother from San Francisco:

October 14,1943

You took your time to write!

Your description of Fe's apartment did not surprise me in the least. I do not know of any clean surroundings in that dirt nest, New York. It blows through the city from the harbor. It is of course very nice to know that Fe is happy there, even though it is a catastrophe that we are so far away from her.

Why don't you write anything about her work for the theater? Did she get paid for it? What are her future chances?

It is absolutely important that she gets into contact with society and does not continue to live a bohemian life in the long run. That is only possible as long as one is young. She also has to think about the time when your and my ashes are scattered into the wind. Be sure to bring some of her pictures back with you. I am very anxious to see them. How do you like them?

Pat will have her birthday soon. Shall I get something here for her, from you? Even if you send her a book from New York it will take two weeks to get here. Mail is so slow now.

Mama had her birthday yesterday and was up and walking around in her robe and slippers. For presents she only asked for cotton, orange marmalade, and butter. Pat and I visited her, and Minna came later and brought her strawberries that delighted her. Now that she is getting better and stronger she feels very unhappy because she is lonely there and has nobody to talk to.

Love,
Pappi

Mother to Father from New York:

October 14,1943

Send my beige camelhair coat. Fe can use it here, and I don't need it. The days pass quickly. Fe introduces me to all of the bohemian haunts in the Village. She is experimenting with new directions in her painting. I do not see any goal and worry about her future. We made a big mistake by making everything so easy for our children. They never had to fight for anything. God knows what will become of it! I am very depressed, so no more of this.

We visited a new museum at the Hudson, the Cloisters. There were wonderful wood sculptures, Gothic, from Germany, France, and Spain. One figure had a label that said, **Collection James Simon** (Oma Marta's brother, an avid collector and art lover in Berlin).

It would be so good if you were here, so I could talk to you about what is in my heart.

Love,
Alice

Father to Mutti from San Francisco:

October 18, 1943

I am surprised that you still have not answered my question about Fe's work for Condell. Did he give her any kind of salary or at least a token amount for time spent, transportation, and materials? Is there any possibility of getting a solid job with him? I already wrote her to be careful. Young people can get exploited easily.

That you are depressed I can well understand, but I do not know what we can do about the situation either. At her age she has to know what she wants to do. We cannot force her into anything anymore. It is sad that life pleases her in that dirt nest.

I had a funny experience on Friday. I informed Pat that I would not be home for lunch, since I was obliged to go to the citizenship examination as witness for Walter Herbert. Pat was pleased because she, too, had to appear at the same place and time to stand as witness for Henri Temianka. Herbert's exam took only fifteen minutes. Henri got grilled for half an hour by a lady judge. I was only asked for my passport. Then we had to go upstairs to see a judge who actually had a sense of humor. He posed a question to me, but spoke so quickly and unclearly that I did not understand and had to ask: I beg your pardon? For some reason he thought this funny and repeated: had I ever been in prison?

Then we had to swear that we believed that Herbert would be a good citizen, and Mrs. Lilianthal got scolded for not removing her gloves during the swearing in. Elizabeth Philipp got the same rebuke. So you see it was all quite chummy.

I will next direct Pergolesi's La Serva Padrona.

It is touching how people try to take care of me, to console me. Louis came on Thursday evening and Dr. Phillips later, because they did not want to see me so alone.

As you know, I like nothing better then to be left alone with my books.

Yesterday, on Sunday, Pat cooked chicken for everybody. Minna and Betts talked without interruption only about things that nobody cared about, like gossip stories from Vienna. Betts goes on my nerves.

Everybody spoils the dog, who produces the biggest poops you can imagine.

What kind of impression do you have of the two coffeehouses, Éclair and La Coupole? Are they European with newspapers, etc.? Don't forget the Vienna restaurant Neugroeschl.

Does Fe have any companionship of young people? Has she even painted anything that could be shown? I wish for detailed information!

In spite of the fact that the house is filled with possible and impossible people, it is terribly empty without you. When I go to the bedroom at night the empty bed strikes me as an insult.

Love,
George

Father to Mother:

October 27, 1943

Dear Alice,

It is awful how long the mail takes these days. I have already been worrying and thought you might be sick. Mama keeps telling me that you have only thin clothes to wear and to admonish you to buy warm things. Here in the newspaper we read about dim-outs and air-raid alarm tests and streets that are pounded by rain and wind in New York.

On Monday evening, we had an earthquake from nine forty five to ten. The house did not shake, the windows did not even rattle, but there was a lot of noise. The windows at the city hall in San Jose were all broken. Pat and Minna Levinson came running in, both trembling and then laughing uproariously at me because I asked in all sincerity whether this was an earthquake. It sounded as if a huge load of crates fell off a truck. Ralph did not hear anything at the shipyard either. Anyway, that was the only time that I was glad that you were not here.

Now to the latest news. Mama burst into a tantrum and declared that she could not stand living with all those idiots any more and the food was awful. I should throw Tiu out. She wants his room here. I told her that was impossible, and she then replied that she was going to sleep on the floor in the Biedermeier room. I called Dr. Gropper for help, and he told me that there was a vacancy at a place owned by a Viennese physician in Berkeley. We drove right over and rented a very pretty corner room from the first of November on. Three Germans and three Americans are there also.

Putzi did not pay any attention to the earthquake and the cat was terribly upset.

Love,
George

Mother to Father from New York:

October 30, 1943

You are writing so well in detail about everything. I would like to do the same, but I am so busy moving about, since Fe wants to show me everything we do not have in San Francisco. Bad weather and rain make things more difficult. We were at the Spanish museum today and then at the Indian one. Tonight we hear a concert at Carnegie Hall.

Thursday evening we were at Schwerins, who live in a very elegant apartment. Too bad that their son is blind! I keep thinking constantly about Fe's future. What would she have left if you took her painting away? She is as obsessed by it as you are with your theater. If only she would meet a nice man! She complained that everyone she meets wants to kiss right away or wants even more. With it all she looks so pretty.

I am sorry Tiu is leaving. Don't rent his room until I come back. I like to look my people over.

Love,
Alice

Father to Mother:

November 1, 1943

Your letter just arrived, stamped on the twenty sixth, a full six days on the road! Your letters always disappoint me. They are so short. I have to know in detail what you see, whom you meet, with whom you talk, and what you eat.

I can only get your ration book on the eighth. The first term has long past. Read my last letters through again carefully and reply to all of my questions. I so hope that Fe will sell something. That would give her courage.

This afternoon we will take Mama to another boarding home in Berkeley. Let us hope that she will finally like it there.

Putzi also needs you. No matter for how long Minna takes him out on a walk, he always returns to me and has reserved a few drops so I have to take him out again.

I was invited to the Concordia Club. Dr. Ostwald belongs to it too and thinks I should join because it has a good swimming pool and that would be good for me. It costs $15.00 per month. That is quite a bit of money and is not worth it.

Yesterday, I heard on the radio that Reinhardt passed away. Unfortunately, he had already outlived his career.

I am sure it will not be easy to get tickets for Othello, *but try hard in any case.* Oklahoma *and* One Touch of Venus *are supposed to be excellent.* Tomorrow the World *and* Harriet *with Helen Hayes are supposed to be interesting. That is all there is. Bergner's play is terrible. Just don't go to the movies. Every cent is wasted on them. The intelligence level is pitiful!*

Love,
George

Father to Mother:

November 8, 1943

Since my troubles here seem to give you all reason to laugh, I shall supply you with some more grounds for your heartless amusement.

I have a very unpleasant and exhausting week behind me. This is what happened at the last dinner party I was invited to. Mrs. Billiter announced to one and all at the end of the evening that she was available to be invited for dinners, since she was alone. Everybody invited her immediately, which gave me no choice but to join in. I invited her and Frau Bremer for lunch downtown. I was lucky in so far that she got sick, and I had only Mrs. Bremer to contend with. I thought, thank God, I have to pay only for one, but that one asked me what I thought about going to the Palace Hotel! Horrors! I could not possibly say no. At least she was already enough Americanized to order only a drink, a crab salad, and coffee. I only ordered an omelet with oysters and mushrooms. It was excellent. Price $4.25.

On Friday, I went with Pat to Gropper's. Nobody else was there. It was terribly boring, as always, at Gropper's. On both evenings, they fed me chicken, so now I can't stand any more of it for a while!

*The next day, on Saturday, I went to lunch at the Philipps'
with Karfiol. In the afternoon I was going to retire to my room
finally and take a rest. It turned out differently! Betts expected
an antiquarian book dealer at six and planned to be home at that
time, but that hapless woman appeared a half hour early. I offered
her a seat in the hall, and she acted as if she had not understood
and plunked herself down in my library, commenced to babble
incessantly, and played with Putzi at the same time. Finally,
Betts arrived and released me. She bought nearly $300 worth
from him. Now I had peace for twenty minutes. Another antique
dealer arrived for Betts, and both fat women settled down in the
Biedermeier room on our beautiful, delicate old armchairs, while
Minna was in the kitchen preparing dinner. They just wanted
to see the Meissen porcelains, they said. I was just waiting for
them to ask me whether I would be interested in selling any of
them. I would have thrown them out immediately.*

*Soon after that the young people from Oakland came to Minna
and Betts for a weekend visit. They had liked it so much the last
time, they said. They stayed in Kenneth's room and paid $2.50. I
had peace at my desk for thirty minutes before it was lost again.*

*At seven, everybody had dinner in the kitchen and made so
much noise that further concentration on my work was out of
the question. When it was still going on at nine, I was so desperate
and overly nervous that poor Pat had to get dressed and take a
walk with me through the dark streets. What else can one do on
a Saturday night? We got home at ten, and thank God it was
finally quiet. Until twelve, I was able to sit at my desk and then
fell into bed completely exhausted. I slept for ten hours.*

*Sunday again was a day of horrors. Philipps visited Betts
to play bridge. I protested immediately. Out of principle, bridge
playing was forbidden in my living room. They could do what
they wanted in their own space. Fearing they would come down
anyway, I spent the whole afternoon at Ralph's. When I finally
went carefully downstairs, they had left. The air was clear. I
was still so nervous I could not even read. So I took Putzi and*

*walked with him around block after block for an hour. Then I
slept again for ten hours, and today I feel fresh and rested.*

*Next week promises to be more peaceful. On Thursday is
Pat's birthday, and I am taking her to the Geary Theatre to see
a performance of* Jane Eyre *with the excellent actor Luther Adler,
whom we saw in New York playing in* The Golden Boy *by
Clifford Odets. Sunday I'll have dinner at Fried's. I only hope
they don't serve chicken!*

*Have I given you enough reason to laugh now? So I can get
serious and repeat my question about a joint recuperation trip
when you get back. How about Mexico?*

*Love you,
Pappi*

Mother left in the middle of November, and I was
relieved and sad at the same time, feeling more alone then
ever. Away from her household and her real and imagined
duties, she had been nice to be with, especially when I kept
her too busy to worry about anything by running around
and seeing things. I made a point of disregarding the
occasional, unavoidable criticisms, so we got along fine.

I still had to laugh when I thought of her stories about
her trials and tribulations with Father and managing
household and food and wartime restrictions. The vagaries
of her various renters gave her a lot to talk about, especially
of one young man, a Mr. Gilbert, who came up in her
conversation frequently.

"He works for a company that has something to do
with transporting troops," she said. "He is such a well
brought up young man, clean, and polite. When he goes
out at night he will always tell me at what time he will be
back at home, and when he is delayed he calls me to let me
know about it. He is such a treasure."

How pathetic, I thought, but kept my mouth shut. About people, Mother and I seldom saw eye to eye.

"You mean to say that an Altman wants to work at Lord and Taylor's Department store?" The personnel manager was greatly amused. It was the end of November. I handed in my application for a temporary Christmas sales job and felt quite compelled to explain that, no, I was not a spy for Altman's Department Store, in spite of carrying the same name. I was in no way related.

In training for a week I learned to fill out sales slips and to smile engagingly at the lady customers. I was told to be helpful, discreet, and accommodating to the gentlemen, but not too accommodating, of course. I was to dress smartly, wear high heels, and put my hair up. By the way, when showing merchandise, the higher priced items were the most desirable, weren't they? I understood completely.

So they allowed me to sell lady's handbags on the main floor. My high heels sank into the deep, soft carpet. My feet ached. There was no seat behind the counter. Meeting and serving the customers was an edifying experience for me. I encountered many nice and reasonable people but also a number of nasty, fussy, arrogant ones. Then there were the colorful, quirky characters that contributed greatly to my amusement and interest.

The loaded atmosphere in the saleslady's lunch and locker room, the gossip, the little confidences shared, the small intrigues that were concocted fascinated me no end. The matters of men friends and sex were, of course, favorite themes of conversation. Needless to say, they were also uppermost in my mind. Therefore, I guess, the indignant outburst of one thin, tall, black girl stays in my memory.

"What's so great about sex?" She practically spat the despised word out past the coffee machine. "Makes me feel nothin'. Just a damn nuisance!"

I remember feeling sorry for her and for myself at the same time. I knew there was supposed to be more to it then *nothin'*.

Letter from me to Mother:

December 21, 1943

Dear Mutti,

I am sure you had a lot of work and excitement in recent days. I hope you prepare for a peaceful Christmas and try to support each other and make life happier. Aleady for Pappi's sake you should keep the best attributes of our family in mind and support us by creating an atmosphere of calm and peace, especially now around the Christmas tree. You must realize that we are blessed and are the luckiest of people after all that has transpired. Let's be honest about that!

I gave a party here yesterday. The old Temiankas, Henri's parents, came and entertained themselves grandly. They are both very small people, even shorter than I. The mother has a large head, a broad Russian face, a big nose, and lots of wrinkles. She presented herself most elegantly with a new hairdo and a tiny sort of top hat of black fur with a veil. Terribly funny. They brought me excellent candy. Then came Hans Schwerin, who is really a very nice man. We get together once in a while. I am always amazed how he gets around unerringly, even in traffic, just by tapping his cane against the sidewalk. Of course, George was also there and, instead of you, he helped me to take care of the guests. You always did it better!

At this moment I am munching on the leftover cake and gazing at my pitiful little Christmas tree that has started to loose its needles already on the second day I've had it. It cost me one dollar. Trees are SO expensive. In addition I pepped my room up with fir branches and red berries. My guests thought it very cozy sitting around the fireplace with candles and a howling storm outside above my skylight. Only the usual little draft remains near one side of the sofa. It is plenty warm in here, and the heat is now kept on until ten. Also there is more light in the street, a Christmas present for me from Mayor La Guardia. A nice man, eh?

Finally, today my bathroom fixtures were repaired. You see how one stone after another of your contentions gets rolled out of the way and pressed methodically into the ground to form a good pavement, in every sense of the word, upon which you will tread happily one day when you return for another visit. The sun will shine, and you will realize how unimportant all of these stones have been.

I went to a nice party at Elisabeth Sheldon's. She failed parts of her State Board examination and now is pouring over her books and papers again like crazy. A friend of hers, also a medico, failed four times and is supposed to be highly gifted. Tell Ralph that! She is now an anesthetist for Dr. Oljenek's operations. He, by the way, sends you his best greetings.

Oh, before I forget, I found the address and phone number of Putzi's future bride. I hope she has not cheated on him yet. As far as I know, she belongs to the sister of the woman I bought him from. You better finally make a grownup, respectable dog out of him so he will not get to harbor all kinds of perverse thoughts and spend his life skittering, whether on four legs or two, backwards through the kitchen door, a complete neurotic. The real purpose of life has to be made clear to him!

Almost by accident I saw a fantastic affair at Carnegie Hall. I had a very elegant dinner at the Russian Tearoom with Norman and Vicky. Norman left us afterwards, and Vicky and I planned to go to a movie. We then met a friend of Elisabeth's who said we should look in at Carnegie Hall. We found ourselves at a big

African Dance Festival given by the African Academy of Arts and Research, a newly created institution for the promotion of African and American relations.

Huge drums performed a greeting to America. After that rousing beginning a black Professor from Harvard University gave a short talk about the next act, a wedding feast that was completely authentic, performed by people who came directly from Africa. The dancing was beautiful and so were the dancers.

After that, four people marched on stage in a neat line, counteracting the movement and gayety that went before. Now came speeches by three black people and one white one, two men and two women. There was the director of the academy, with the beautiful name Kingsley Ozuomba Mbadive. Next to him stood a very proud man in a long gown and a turban, Prince Akiki Nyabongo. One of the women was a very imposing dark chocolate brown lady with snow-white hair on her temples, a purple evening dress and considerable girth. Her name was Mary McLeod Bethune, a communist writer. You may have heard of her. The other woman was . . . Eleanor Roosevelt! I usually do not like speeches, but I must say that I was fascinated.

The Professor, Mrs. Bethune, and the Prince, who was a top official of the Nigerian government, had come especially to America for this occasion. They all spoke freely and with great dignity, in wonderful English. Unfortunately, Mrs. Roosevelt could not hold a candle to them. She posed, recited in the style of a Fireside Chat, and I realized that being Mrs. President would be difficult and had to be learned and practiced. It was not inborn. She persisted courageously, though, and when she said, "Racial intolerance is nothing but ignorance," the whole house broke out in roaring applause.

She and Mrs. Bethune got presents from the Prince, and everyone was touched by the way he showed his obvious feeling of love and friendship toward them and all of his fellow human beings.

Oh, and there will still be pogroms and Jim Crow in this world for a long time!

More dances followed. They were so perfect that I knew it was great art: the control of the body, the beauty, and triumphant perfection of movement. It was a delight.

Now I have to dash to the post office. I hope, I hope this letter will get to you by the twenty-fourth.

My dear Mutti, celebrate Christmas and be sensible. Look around you with wise and clear eyes.

With great love,
Fe

From overhead florescent bulbs stabbed down on us. Piercing light, no shadows, nothing hidden. Jake Perloff's studio and I at my easel, carving heavy paint onto the canvas with knife and brush, fighting to make it glow like the colors of the red, yellow, and orange fruit that was draped in the blue-green cloth on the wooden table in front of me. It was a Friday night at the end of a very busy working day. Four hours had passed since I started to paint, and exhaustion was conquered by excitement. There was simply no room for fatigue. I felt feverish, consumed with the need to conjure all of the intense feeling that smoldered in me into the painting, letting it speak on the canvas with color and light.

"Enough for tonight. Rest." Jake switched the lights off. "Let's stop and go home before this chick kills herself," he said to the two younger men, and gave me a half smiling, searching look over his shoulder.

We walked home, the four of us. The streets were dark and deserted. It was late, the air quite raw. Jake walked ahead with a boy whose name I don't remember. I followed at a distance and at a slower pace with the other young man, Trubach.

He hooked his arm under mine. We talked little. Some fog came in, I shivered, and he slung one side of his coat around my shoulders and drew me close to him. My head leaned against his shoulder. It felt so good to be near someone, not to be alone. The other two were far ahead now. I saw them stop once under a streetlight way down the road, Jake turning to look for us. I think it was a look of regret when he saw us, but I may have imagined that. It was too far for me to read his face. They continued on their way, and soon they disappeared out of sight.

We leaned against the portal of a sleeping house and kissed, wrapped in his coat, a human cocoon, spun into nothing but our own existence.

We became good friends, Trubach and I. He was a slight man, light-eyed and rather pale, with a little sandy mustache under a broad nose. He, too, looked somewhat Russian, but he was of strictly Anglo-Saxon stock. We painted together, discussed each other's work, went to exhibits, to dinner. We hugged and kissed. There was no strain, no urgency on his part. He was biding his time.

February 21, 1944

My Dearest Family, All of You,

I will only be able to obtain your forgiveness for my silence by telling you the truth about my experiences in the past weeks, in spite of my fervent desire to cover them up in the darkest recesses of my extensive secret double life. The only explanation for my long silence is that I was all muddled up, in a mess.

The flu. Well now. I had decided that in these times it does not become one to be an isolationist and, out of idealistic conviction, joined the teaming masses and got sick. It was not very bad. My grocer supplied me with food daily and my Sir Galahad, George, took great care of me, very dutifully. It was comfortable and peaceful. It is already behind me and quite forgotten.

The following was more distressing.

Three weeks ago I returned home at twelve thirty at night and found to my horror that the window that I had kept locked stood wide open. To say "horror" is an exaggeration. In hindsight let us say it was upsetting. Nothing was missing. Jewelry and everything else was there. Since my friend Vicky, who had picked me up earlier to go to a movie, assured me that she had not touched the window, I collected some of my belongings, jewelry, fur, Leica, and spent the night at Vicky's place. Next morning, I went home and had breakfast. The sun was shining, and it was peaceful. Nothing had been disturbed.

Consequently, I sat and pondered. Could I have left the window open myself? Since there was no answer to this prize question I finally shrugged my shoulders and threw myself into my work with my usual well-known zeal.

Don't laugh!

Someone knocked at my door and the fifteen-year-old blond boy who lives with his mother above me on the third floor appeared and asked whether he could climb through my window. His antenna had fallen over. I eyed him sharply and asked whether he had already done so yesterday evening, etc. etc. He swore, "Absolutely not," looked very honest and blue-eyed and offered to nail the window shut for the night. We became friends and the end result was that now I had a model for fifty cents per hour.

Daily I worked on a large painting of his portrait, and he sat still without complaint. Progress was excellent, and I forgot my worries until the light started to fade in the evening. Then I started to feel uncomfortable again.

Vicky had a fallout with her landlord and moved to a hotel. She had already paid for her apartment through the rest of the month and let me occupy it in the meantime. Why should I be scared at night? I decided to accept her offer. At the same time,

I tried to go apartment hunting, and I discovered that New York did not have one single hole-in-the-wall to offer me. A week and a half passed, and the uncertainty still annoyed me greatly. What to do? Just call it all a figment of my imagination.

Again I returned home one morning to have breakfast and to work on my canvas. I stood in my kitchenette and felt puzzled. Something seemed to be missing, but what? Something was not there. A funny feeling. Quite a while passed until I found what it was: the canned fruit was gone. There was the proof and, oh horror, I had left my silver Moroccan bracelet on the table the evening before. It was gone!

I immediately phoned the agent of the building who informed me in a very friendly manner that yesterday evening there had also been a burglary next door, at a painter's place who lives on the second floor there. He lost cans of food. And paintings.

I was insulted! MY paintings were not taken! This thief had no taste. Now I was doubly mad at him. The search for another place to live was desperately speeded up. I could not stay with Vicky anymore, so I slept in a hotel for one night, two more with a friend of Edith's, and two at George's place. (Now, now, don't be upset! Exemplary chastity! No cause for heart attacks!) Finally Elizabeth Sheldon got wind of the situation and put me up on the couch in her living room. I suppose Dr. O. had to suffer a little under this arrangement, but he carried it off with dignity and humor, appeared every morning for breakfast and cooked eggs and bacon for us.

In the meantime, I tried with all my might to complete the boy's portrait. It promised to be really good. Bert sat for me, unshakable and immovable, almost a still life to behold.

A few days ago I was caught in a rainstorm and went home to get my umbrella. It was in the evening at seven o'clock. I tried to unlock my door. Look here, look here, it did not open!

My right knee decided that it was rather chilly and also my left one acquired goose bumps and started to shake. Since that made me mad I hauled out and pounded the door energetically with my foot, an enterprise that was short-lived, because SOMETHING moved about inside my room: it ran, it audibly threw drawers shut and seemed to be in quite a hurry.

That I can still jump like that at my age! In three jumps I was at the telephone of the sandwich shop outside and then it took several eternities until two patrol cars with eight huge cops appeared. Old Mr. Kahn, my neighbor, shuffled excitedly about. Bert came running and the cops, like Disney elephants, broke my door down with just their shoulders on the first try, after asking me officially whether I was ready to pay for the damage, which made me burn with anger.

It was just like in the movies. Of course, nobody was in the room anymore. The window that had been carefully locked and outfitted with special fixtures by a carpenter after the first burglary stood wide open. One cop climbed out, others surrounded the house, and I was interrogated. They telephoned for a special detective. It seemed again that nothing was missing. Suddenly Bert appeared with my silver cigarette case that I had been given by Seusa. He had just found this on the roof, between two buckets.

"Found it, eh? Come here, Sonny Boy. Let's see your pockets." I got very angry. These cops love to show how important they are. This is the most decent boy in the world. He too was very insulted and astonished.

"This here burglar got in through the door," said the cop. "Let's see your keys." They pulled a brand new shiny key out of his pocket, among much-handled old ones. What bad luck the poor boy had. Such a stupid accident. Even fit my door, that key. Too dumb.

"I ain't been here. I didn't take nothin'. Honest." The detective appeared as expected: cigar, hat pulled down almost over his eyes, collar turned up, directly from Paramount.

Now they grilled the kid and the sparks flew. "You found this here cigarette case between them two pails, eh? Well, there is no light up there. You couldn't have seen it. So you do not smoke? Well there is a pack of Luckys right in your pocket. Where did you get the key? You don't know. You found it. You had it made last year for a trunk. You have never seen it in your life."

The questions bombarded him. I felt so sorry for the boy, convinced of his decency. Such a blond, clean babyface, a little stupid, but I took that as the Nordic influence, heaven forgive me.

His mother was summoned and appeared, snarling, in her nightgown, but did not seem particularly surprised.

Finally after two hours, "Sonny Boy" broke down. God in heaven, he was the culprit! They searched his room. They returned items to me that I had not even missed: my silver belt, books, woodcarving knife, fountain pen, and then all of the costume jewelry I had left here, worthless, but pretty stuff anyway. Only the bracelet was not there.

"Felicia, come here," said the detective. He took me aside indicating that this was strictly confidential.

"Do you ever make drawings of nude women?"

"Sure," I said, "In school. Lots of times."

"Well, is this yours?" From under his jacket he pulled a large rolled-up oil sketch that I had made of a standing nude model. "This," the long arm of the law grumbled out of the corner of his mouth that was not occupied by the stub of his cigar, "This he had under his bed cover, masturbating on it, see?" In spite of all the upset and excitement, I had to pull myself together strenuously in order not to laugh. To all my friends I had complained that the thief had shown a disdain for my paintings and now this, if I may say so, triumph.

In short, as far as I can judge, my good little boy is slightly nuts. In my opinion he did not fully realize the situation, did not care. No emotion at all. I refused to sue him and agreed to let them refer the case to the Juvenile Aid agency.

"Yeah, I'll watch him," said the mother with a shrug that really said: Who cares? Leave me alone, you pests.

Two post-scripts to this story:

1. *At night following this adventure I got the shakes all of a sudden.*
2. *Several days afterward the mother appeared at my door to return several other things of mine, among them my bracelet. I then tried to talk to her and explain that I thought her son needed to see a psychiatrist urgently and also to get general medical attention.*

She squinted at me and gave a funny little snort through her screwed-up nose. "People like us are destined to die anyway," she said.

I tried to console her, whereupon she confided, "My dear girl, I met my spiritual deliverance years ago."

Then she pressed both hands to her bosom and straightened herself up as high as her scrawny self allowed and spoke thusly, "Don't you see that we HAVE to suffer? Can't you see that I am the Holy Ghost?"

At first I said nothing. Then I said "Oh. Well, we all have to be strong," and took pains to remove myself expeditiously. Of course, I notified my detective immediately of the resurrection of the Holy Ghost. He said there was nothing about that in the civil code, and it was probably not against the law. Higher authorities would have to be notified.

In any case, the landlord promised to put bars on my window and changed the door lock. Now everything is peaceful again. It was no picnic. Camping out with other people, hunting for a place to live, not feeling safe, everything piled up. The Devil can take it! Now I can work again in peace, thank God.

Since today I have a new model, the younger brother of George. Chapter George, to assure Mutti, is completely harmless and not even worth raising an eyebrow over. It is nicer to eat with someone else than all by oneself, and anyway people who

*like you do not grow on trees. There is no talk of love on my
part. He behaves touchingly and selflessly.*

Now I have to go to sleep. I kiss you all, one after the other.

Longing for you mightily,
Fe

April 1, 1944

Dear Mutti,

*You are unfair! Your poor struggling daughter is constantly
battling an ogre of conflict in her soul that, from morning to
night, keeps grabbing her around the neck in ever-changing,
flickering, chameleon-like shades of color. She feels utterly
neglected by you from the heights of your existence of secure
woman and motherhood. Shame on you! I know exactly what
lurks behind your miserable behavior.*

*You are now the one and only reigning queen of your
over-populated male harem. Pat probably has been subdued
and worn out already. What, please, are you going to do
when your daughter comes home in June, all fresh and full of
piss and vinegar? You see, I have your number. Unless you
sit down now immediately and write, I promise that I will
turn the whole household against you and cause a revolution
when I get home.*

*I will procure girls for your sailors under your nose, seduce
that Gilbert to learn tap dancing, and practice to the sounds of
Boogie Woogie that he will play from then on, instead of Mozart
and Beethoven. The old man in the basement will find whisky
on his bed table and will try to polish your staircase with acetone.
Do not tell me that I did not warn you!!*

*I now have Easter vacation. I will use it to get more sleep.
I am again in a whole period of sleepless nights. I don't fall*

asleep until nearly four a.m. It's awful. Of course I want to engender only pity from you with that confession. So write already.

Otherwise I am healthy and chipper and sociable. I see Elisabeth and the Brain often. Should I try to rent my studio out while I am in San Francisco? It would be cheaper than to move completely out and then look for something else when I get back. Should I put my fur in storage here? How about the bed covers? These considerations come a bit early, but they are proof that I am impatient to get home to see you all and to celebrate Pappi's birthday. If I did not have the university now I might have come earlier.

By the way, my teacher told me that I could get some sort of report card and a certificate stating that I studied at Columbia. Aside from that there are prizes, fellowships, and commissions, but not after one semester. He sounded very upbeat about my chances and predicted that I would become a very good artist. I fully agree with him! Just don't expect too much when I get home. I am learning. I do not look towards production. Otherwise, I would remain a sad amateur.

There is not much else to tell. I have to get dressed now. I have been invited by a Russian interior decorator for lunch. He is terribly nice to me and wants to introduce me to several artists.

Write!
Fe

Trubach and I were having lunch sitting across from each other in the garden of an outdoor café. There were trees, some in bloom, flowers in borders around grassy areas, sunshine and sparrows picking crumbs around our feet with industrious zeal. It was the beginning of spring.

"I'll have to leave New York," he said and shook his head regretfully. His eyes were swollen and a little wheezing sigh followed his words. "That damned allergy haunts me every spring. I have to get to the ocean, to Provincetown. There is a whole colony of artists."

He reached for my hand across the table, "Will you come with me, please? We'll have a great time."

I looked at his pleading face.

I did not love him. I liked him. He was a nice and considerate man, good company, easy to be with.

If I lost him there would be lonely dinners again, but I'd have more time to paint. Would I miss him? A little. He had a room on the fourth floor of an old apartment house in the village where we could climb out one of the windows and stand on the flat roof arm in arm. We would try to see the horizon that peeked through the open spaces left between the towering buildings of the city in the early morning. I would miss that. Our long and silent hours of painting together, the trips to the zoo, drawing the animals and buying popcorn and ice cream cones while discussing the merits of Edward Hopper or Graham Sutherland, both of whom we had recently discovered. I would miss those times.

I thought of his little bathroom that was papered from floor to ceiling with covers of the *New Yorker*. That made it actually pleasant to sit on the john, surrounded by vibrant color and sprightly designs.

There I had stood a few weeks ago, a cigarette in hand, examining my face in the mirror. A little pain, some blood on his sheet and his face smiling proudly down on me that morning. "We've done it," he said.

His hand now squeezed mine again across the table. "Say you'll come."

Leave my job, my classes? "Maybe in summer, when the League closes," I answered and did not mean it.

I felt disconnected, devoid of emotion. I had finally accomplished what I had planed to do in my battle for independence. It had not been a revelation. The world had not shook, as Hemingway described it in *For Whom The Bell*

Tolls. The only way life would have meaning for me is if I experience it through art, I thought.

April 10, 1944

Dearest Mutti,

Unfortunately, your birthday package will arrive late. You have to use your imagination and make do with these special-delivery kisses for now. I had ordered something for you and in spite of a promised early arrival, it just arrived here. Are you going to have a BIG CELEBRATION? At least Ralph is now with you in the evening, a pleasure we are not yet used to. I wish I could take a plane to California on the twenty second, my birthday. Like Seusa used to say so poetically: I've got a mind to.

Again, no letter from you, not even for Easter. Is that still supposed to be punishment? Enough already! Other people think of me. I got a pineapple from Dr. Oljeneck instead of an Easter egg and a bottle of Curacao. Elisabeth is waiting desperately for the result of her new exam and is convinced that she failed again.

We went to a nice French film together: **Bizarre, Bizarre,** *with Françoise Rozay, Jouvet, and Jean Louis Barrault. Go see it. Dr. O., the Brain, picked us up, and we stayed at my place for a while longer.*

This is not much of a birthday letter. I have an awful headache. The changeable weather truly honors the month of April. Last week, we had a tremendous snowstorm, today it is clammy warm, partially black sky, and cloud bursts, then again comes radiant sunshine. I am working a lot, otherwise not much to tell.

If I don't have a letter tomorrow, you know the consequences! Bad person, I love you!

> *Respectfully yours,*
> *Your Crazy Daughter*

Father's sixtieth birthday was on June fifteenth, a very important day. I was going home for just a short time to help with his special BIG CELEBRATION.

It was the 9th of June, 1944, a very warm, late evening on the platform of Grand Central Station in New York. Two tall, familiar people on either side of me held my elbows and, between them, I felt myself almost floating along in a happy daze, surrounded by whirling humanity, steam, whistles, and flashing lights.

I was going home.

Elisabeth and Dr. O. had decided that I was anxious and, therefore, had taken me out to dinner before my departure. They plied me first with a hefty martini followed by a glass of champagne with the food.

"Now be sure you come back," I heard Elizabeth say.

"We'll miss you." That was Dr. O. I felt myself wrapped in his arms and kissed with warmth and vigor. They must have stowed me in my compartment, but I don't remember. What I could not forget was Dr. O.'s embrace. Did he like me that much? For some reason I never failed to be surprised when I found out that people liked me.

The train ride was wonderful. Five days of just being carried along without having any responsibility, free of care. That is, if you could turn your brain off and stop thinking.

I slept, read, enjoyed the dining car, and tried not to brood, without quite succeeding.

I dreamt again of Kokoschka's paintings—the brush strokes that talked, the color that sang. Yes, I thought, yes, that's where I'll go, and I felt stronger and more confident.

So when I looked into my parents' smiling faces and fell into their outstretched arms at the Berkeley Train Station I was genuinely happy. I felt sure of myself.

"You don't look quite as bad as I expected." My mother's backhanded compliment did not deflate my euphoria. I laughed and then became aware of someone appearing behind my father. He was a tall man with his strong chin up in the air, a broad, handsome face, and eyes that smiled confidently down on me as if to say, "Look, here I am, the dream of every girl's heart and desire."

Immediately my hackles were up. Who does he think he is, I wondered? Well, you sure won't get *me*, mister.

"This is Mr. Gilbert, our boarder who lives in your room now. I told you about him, remember? He was so nice to drive us to the station to get you," Mother beamed. She always liked young men, especially when they were well spoken, polite, and admired her in return. This one fit the bill.

He wore a very conventional business suit and pointy highly polished shoes. Ugh! He had curly black hair, heavy black brows over eyes that seemed to measure me intently. What arrogance. I could not stand him.

CHAPTER NINETEEN

Such a Nice Young Man!

"My God, he even eats with us." I was appalled.

"That's the arrangement," Mother said, "And we enjoy having him around. He is such a nice young man. I told you about him, remember?"

How often did I have to hear about that? I groaned. Another annoyance was that he occupied my own room while I had to sleep in one of the little side rooms that happened to be vacant at the time.

Father's sixtieth birthday came and he got his BIG CELEBRATION with all of his family and good friends in attendance.

It was the middle of June and for the next few weeks Mother's star boarder seemed to be constantly near me when he was home from work. He showed interest in my painting aspirations, told me about some of his museum visits, and showed me some framed reproductions of Holbein drawings he loved and had hanging on his wall. Off and on his pronouncements about art made me chuckle and sniff a little, but I suppressed it discretely in order not to embarrass him. He had a large collection of records. He loved classical chamber music.

"Listen to this Boccherini quartet. Do you know it?" He asked me to his room, and I listened and had to admit how little I really knew about music. But I was ready to learn.

Mr. Gilbert became Gil after a while. Our friends liked him, and one evening, as it had happened several times before, he was invited to a party at the Gropper's with us.

The hostess asked Gil to take care of the bar and help serve drinks, which he was happy to do. One of the guests was a lady who had just come back from China and told very interesting tales of her experiences. Everybody sat around her and listened with fascination. I had a drink in my hand, and my attention was riveted on the storyteller. Ah, Gil thought, here was his chance. He thought he could get me a little tipsy and make headway. He filled my glass, and I drank without looking up. I took another sip and then another. He refilled my glass. He must have thought that I had a hollow leg. He refilled my glass again, but I never noticed and kept sipping. The party having ended, we drove into the garage at home. Now he thought he had me. He reached for me and grabbed thin air. I had already jumped out and waved good night from the exit door.

Oh yes, I was very cautious. No more upsets and disappointments for me. We kissed, but they were careful kisses, tentative getting-acquainted kisses. July came, and August. The atmosphere got warmer and warmer around San Francisco Bay and on the third floor of the house on Clay Street.

We went to Chinatown one night. Hand in hand we sauntered leisurely down Grant Avenue and examined the shop windows, looking at nice small ivory carvings or pieces of jade among a welter of paper dragons, porcelain tea sets, and embroidered kimonos. We discovered often that we liked the same pieces and had fun rummaging around the shops hoping to find some unexpected treasure. We took pleasure in pointing things out to each other in the street, be it a small boy munching on his sugarcane with earnest concentration or the rather daunting display of a Chinese butcher shop, with chunks of meat, pigs heads, sausages and furry and feathered things hanging from hooks over the counters of their open stalls. The smells of garlic and spices, rotting cabbage, and incense floated through the night air. Lights shone from the windows, and those that flickered from the stalls seemed to turn the grimiest tourist into a festive reveler.

I did not have the feeling that I walked into the small restaurant on my own steam. I was being steered, propelled through a crowd of milling people by my escort's strong hands on my shoulders. The light inside was dim. We slipped into the shabby booth. The plastic-covered seat felt sticky.

"There, we made it," he said with satisfaction, as if he had overcome a big obstacle. I looked at him across the table. I sensed then that he could steer me anywhere he wanted to, as he had maneuvered me through the crowd just now, and I would follow.

The skinny chopsticks looked rather incongruous in his big hands. I watched him stab at a slippery shrimp that was determined to evade his grasp. His dark eyebrows were pulled together and his lips pursed in concentration. He was determined to succeed.

We talked while we ate. He told me where he grew up, in the Bronx of New York. "I lived in a neighborhood of big apartment houses that were teeming with children of all colors and origins. My two brothers and I were friends with everybody. In many kid's homes we were welcome at any time. Antonio's Mama baked cookies. If it were lunchtime on weekends there were always mountains of spaghetti. My mom also baked cookies. They were awful, but her chocolate pudding was so good that I once devoured a big bowl of it, a bowl that was meant for the whole family. I got so sick. My mother beat me, not too hard though; I was the oldest and her favorite. When Paul and Nat did something wrong she really let them have it every time."

As if emphasizing his mother's fury, he lunged once more at his elusive shrimp, threw his chopsticks down, and called for a fork. Then he looked at me for a moment as if considering a possibility. "Don't you ever make chocolate pudding for me," he said. I was perplexed.

"We stole apples from the fruit stand," he continued. "We rang people's doorbells and then hid around a corner to watch their annoyance when they found no caller. Our playground was the street. We played kickball after school, and the competition was fierce.

There was this boy whose name was Elliot. He was quiet and timid and not very bright. Whenever we picked players for our teams Elliot was always the last to be chosen. I felt sorry for him and decided to take him under my wing. One day I took him aside. 'Elliot,' I said, 'I'll teach you to stand up for yourself. But the first thing we'll do is change your name. From now on your name is Biff.'

At the next game he was the first player I picked for my team. Well, he grew in everybody's esteem, especially in his own. A boy with a name like Biff, chosen by the captain of the team could not be overlooked. You should have seen how proud he was. I think it changed his whole personality. He became an excellent player, and everyone admired him."

It was actually Gil who then looked proud, and I who admired him.

When he took me home that night the kiss was no longer so tentative.

Even though the first week of September had just begun, it was hot. I opened the windows of my studio, looked down to the backyard and stared in amazement. The sun was beating down on the cement paving, and there was Gil sitting in Father's deckchair, his handsome face turned up to the sky, eyes closed, and one long leg crossed over the other. I could see the glint of light from the tip of his shiny black shoe boring into the shadow against the wall of the house like the eye of a small flashlight. It was only the middle of the morning. Why was he not at work? Being home, why had he not called on me?

We met just a few weeks ago, and every day since then, as soon as he got home from work, he sprinted up the stairs to knock on my studio door. He'd enter with a big grin on his face and wrap me in his arms like someone who knew exactly where he belonged. I was in awe of him; he was so self assured and strong. I was a bundle of uncertainties and doubts. Was he the carefree young renter toying with his host's daughter? He must have had lots of women, glamorous, beautiful ones, as handsome and worldly as he was. How could I measure up? Hold back, be careful, don't get hurt, I kept telling myself. And still I watched the clock every day at dinnertime and listened for sounds of greeting from the downstairs hall and his eager footsteps mounting towards my studio door.

What could have happened since, I wondered? Had he lost his job? Was he sick? Had I hurt his feelings, insulted him somehow? He is a stranger again. Why doesn't he come to see me?

The light staccato tread of high-heeled shoes announced Mother's approach. I quickly left the window. It would not do to have her catch me gazing down on him in Father's chair. I did not wish any comments or questions from her about my relationship or the extent of my involvement with him. After all, these were questions I could not yet answer for myself.

I was back at my easel as soon as the door opened. She stood in the doorway looking at me with a questioning expression.

"Now what do you think about *that*?" she said.

"About what?"

"About Gil being transferred, of course. That nice young man. I will hate to see him go."

"Well that's his job, I guess." I tried to look as cool and unconcerned as possible. "Look, I really have to concentrate on my painting now. I don't want to mess it up at this point."

I turned away pretending to mix more color on my palette, feeling the pressure of her unspoken questions and frustration at my back. She stood there for a minute or two, hoping I would turn around again and betray my thoughts and emotions about this situation. She probably suspected that I was not indifferent. Clearly defeated, she left. I could imagine her shaking her head on the way downstairs and muttering, "Can't ever get anything out of this girl."

I tried to take a deep breath, but it did not ease the tension. So that's it, I thought. He is going away and leaving me behind. Had I been a momentary diversion, after all?

I went back to the window and looked down on him again. He seemed to be reading now. His head was bent down. I could not see his face.

I'll loose him.

I can't loose him.

I must not loose him.

No other thought was in my mind.

I saw the open book sink to his lap. He reclined as before, and I could see his face again, eyes closed not only to the sun but also to anything or anybody who might attempt access to his private thoughts. He was all alone and seemed unapproachable. When finally he arose and went into the house I thought he would come up and talk to me. I waited in vain for the rest of the day, and it was a long day.

Dinnertime was over. He had not appeared.

At long last a knock on my door. "Would you come for a drive with me?"

The night was hot and muggy. A light fog was coming in, promising cooling relief. For a long time we just drove, we did not talk. Silence enveloped us like the stifling air. He looked straight ahead, expressionless, his face emerging from the darkness off and on, illuminated by city lights and passing cars. My teeth were clenched and I waited.

"You heard what happened?" He turned his head to me for just a second, long enough for me to see a look of deep worry in his eyes.

I nodded.

"I have to go. I don't want to leave you." His voice sounded tight, like a spring about to be snapped.

"I'd come along." Desperation alone got those words out of my mouth.

I saw his hands tighten on the steering wheel.

"I have thought about it all day," he said. And then he talked and talked about his future, how unstable his job was. He did not know what would become of him after the war when his assignment ended. He could not provide for me the way I was used to being provided for, and so on and so on. All the while we drove and drove, until my patience was at an end.

"For heaven's sake, I don't care about money. I don't care how we live. We'll make it somehow. I know how to work. I can adjust to anything as long as we are together."

We were now at the edge of Golden Gate Park. Abruptly he swung the car around, headed down one of the deserted garden roads, glided slowly onto the grass, and stopped the car near a massive stand of trees whose branches spread their dark canopies over us, shielding us even from the moonlit sky.

We tried to keep our plans secret at first but had to relent after a few days. Yet it seemed we unconsciously telegraphed our excitement, even to my withdrawn grandmother. Arch sidelong glances met us from all directions, and we decided to confess.

"I'll go and talk to your father," he announced.

It struck me as so old fashioned and sweet. I laughed. "Wait, I have to warn you. There is going to be a problem."

Gil looked worried.

"Father always said that he would never allow any man to marry me if he had not read Goethe's *Faust*. So, what are you going to do now?"

The grin I loved most reappeared on his face. "No problem," he said. "Is there an English translation? Where is the nearest bookstore?"

So with book in hand he descended to Father's library the next day. Immediately and without any further explanation he recited a monologue from Goethe's play that he had memorized the night before. Of course, Father recognized the meaning of this unexpected, impromptu performance and beamed with delight.

To my amazement even Mutti was happy, in spite of the fact that her future son-in law was neither a doctor, a lawyer, nor a banker. She had always liked "That Nice Young Man."

Gil's transfer to Los Angeles was to start the next year, on the first of January, 1945. It was already the beginning of September.

"I have to go down for a conference with my new boss," he said. "I would love it if you came along to meet my parents."

His family had lived in Los Angeles since his teen-age years. We drove up to the plain, comfortable-looking little house on 30th Street where he grew up, a little house like all the others that stood in a row up and down the street. I entered another world, another culture.

His parents greeted me with friendly smiles and outstretched hands. I felt that they needed to take their time to examine me. I probably seemed like some strange bird that had unexpectedly landed in their midst.

I too felt ill at ease, anxious to be liked and accepted.

We entered the small living room. An oval, highly polished table of dark wood stood in the middle of the room like a well-groomed receptionist. A bowl holding artificial fruit stood on its surface and chairs with tasseled pillows surrounded it. On one wall a chunky, waist-high gramophone cabinet supported a vase with fresh calla lilies on its cover. They obviously came from the narrow strip of plants that formed a border around the house. To water and nurture these plants was one of Gil's mother's few pleasures, as I learned later.

Through a doorway one went down a hall to three tiny bedrooms and a bath, and by circling the living room table one reached the kitchen through another door. The kitchen was really the heart of this house and family. It had a small alcove with windows on three sides looking out to the front and to the street. Here all of the meals were taken. Many a time I was to sit there in years to come and eat Granny's chicken soup and kreplach, or struggle with mountains of meatballs and cabbage. "*Ess, mein kind,*" she would say and refill my plate mercilessly. Here I presumed had also stood the famous chocolate pudding that had made young Irving so sick. Irving was Gil's first name, and he hated it. Was it because people called him Irv, or his mother's Jewish, New York accent made him an "Oiving"? An Oiving would never amount to much, he felt.

Fresh out of the business program of his high school he attempted to find his first job. After many rejections his counselor took him aside. "Look, young man," she said, "With the high recommendations from our school and your first-rate skills in stenography, businesses should be grabbing you. Do you know what stops them from doing that? It's your name, Gelbfish. Change your name, young man; you'll get a job in no time.

And so it was that Irving became Gil and Gelbfish became Gilbert, after much soul searching and helpless anger. It was a matter of succeeding or struggling endlessly. The rest of the family followed suit, the parents, and both brothers.

Gil's father's extended family, his numerous brothers and his famous great-uncle Sam, all shed the name of Gelbfish and became Goldwyns instead.

I was amazed to discover how small the parents Gilbert were. How had they produced such a tall son? His dad was taller than I, but not by too much. He was slight but wiry, his shoulders stooped from sitting at a workbench in New York for too many years. His job had been making wire frames for handbags at a large factory until some ailment, maybe in his heart or lungs, forced him to retire and move to California, to Los Angeles, on doctor's orders. He had a cigar and newspaper stand in a large office building downtown when I met him. Dominated by a large nose, his narrow face formed a triangle from the rounded chin running up to the broader forehead. There were very kind and intelligent eyes behind his wire-rimmed glasses, and they left a strong impression on me. He was a man who loved music, I learned. It was from him that Gil inherited his lifelong passion. Father and son went to open-air concerts in Central Park when he was still quite small and later on with standing-room-only tickets to the Opera house. They listened to recordings of Caruso and Gigli, Verdi operas, and Beethoven symphonies.

Mother Gilbert had no use for any of it. She loved the Yiddish Art Theatre where Sholem Aleichem's plays were performed. She would get to go once in a while on special occasions, perhaps her birthdays. Her main mission in life was to clean her house, polish and scrub from morning to night, and beat her children because it was good for them. She ruled with an iron hand, and her husband retired into quiet and philosophical docility.

She was a small, strong woman, nearly half a head shorter then I. And I was only two inches over five feet. To make up for her size Granny was feisty. God knows she had had to fight for herself since she had been orphaned in Poland, her parents victims of a pogrom. At the age of eight she became a servant and slept on the floor under a staircase. She never went to school, never learned anything formally, and couldn't read or write. The youngest of six siblings, she stayed behind when her three brothers and two sisters went to the United States and followed them when they were able to send for her. She was seventeen by then. Whether she married her husband at eighteen because it was a prudent and safe thing to do or whether there actually was love at first, nobody knows. I never observed a trace of warmth or sympathy towards him in all of the years I knew her. She blamed him for everything, especially for the horrors of childbirth that she endured three times, and that she considered entirely his fault. Her favorite name for him was "that old goat." And she hated sex.

She loved her oldest son, and I rather think she was fond of me in her own funny way. Somehow, I could do no wrong. When I looked at her broad, peasant face grinning up at me I could not help liking her and, at the same time, feeling sad for her. Someone had just dropped her on this earth and left her there without love or guidance, struggling to hold her own. It was not by accident that her sons called her The Old Battleaxe amongst themselves.

During the week we spent in Los Angeles I was alone with her much of the day. Gil and his father had gone to work at their different endeavors. So there was ample time to chat.

"Honey," she said, brushing non-existent dust off a lampshade, "My son is a good boy and so caring. May the Good Lord strike me dead if I tell a lie. Oh, how he loved that Lill." I knew that he had been married before and divorced six years ago, but that was all he had told me, none of the reasons or his feelings about it. I did not really want to know yet, especially not from her, but clearly there was no way out. "She was *so* beautiful, just like a movie star. You should have seen them hugging and kissing all the time. He would not let her out of his sight." She wandered into the kitchen, examining the drinking glasses for water spots and polished them where no polishing was needed. She shook her head and clicked her tongue against the roof of her mouth, click, click, click. It sounded like Morse code, inescapable stabs at my heart. "*Oy vay*, how he worshipped her!"

Was this malice or just plain ignorance? I would never know. The modest sense of self-assurance I had gained in these last weeks nearly went up in smoke. *She was so beautiful, just like a movie star*. I heard it again and again, even in my sleep.

"Here, let me show you," she said, munching on a biscuit that gave her considerable difficulty because of two front teeth that were missing. Her jaws busily moved back and forth. She refused to see a dentist. "Why bother?" was her response to any suggestion.

An album of photographs was spread out on the table for my further edification. There they were, the loving young couple, arm in arm, the glamorous Lill smiling at me triumphantly. The man I had fallen in love with, the first and only man I really loved, had his arm around her waist and gazed at her with obvious delight.

We were so careful with each other, Gil and I. I was willing, even eager to confide, to share my thoughts and emotions. I wanted to tell him about my life, the loneliness, the searching and confusion, the misery I had felt. But something in his obvious reluctance to talk about his own inner life held me back. He talked about his youth, his family and his work, the music and the books he liked, but never about his past, his first marriage and the feelings he had about it. I wanted to ask, "Tell me about your marriage and tell me about Lill. Why did you part, and most importantly, how much do you love *me*?"

He did not ask what had happened in my life before we met, and I wanted to tell him. I thought that he did not want to know. We lived in the here and now, very happy, but underneath I was never really completely sure of myself. I was not beautiful like Lill, I thought. I had a very good-looking husband who was admired by every female he came in contact with. He charmed them all. Did I measure up?

The day of our wedding arrived on October 28, 1944 at an important house among the many we had called home, the white house on Clay Street. It sparkled in the midday sun. I stood high up on the staircase and looked down on the little group that had assembled in the spacious hall below. Golden light was pouring in through the two tall, narrow windows on either side of the main door. They did not really need that extra glow that shone around them. Their smiling faces beamed up at me and illuminated not only the hallway but also spilled over into both of the festive rooms on either side of the stairs as I descended.

My parents were there. I was aware of Pappi's face: his smiling eyes were moist and the lips of his delicate mouth were pressed together tightly. Mother seemed to swim in happiness and relief. Finally her daughter was going to be taken care of. She had her son-in-law. Such a nice young man! She had known all the time that he was the right one. Wasn't it all her doing?

My brother Ralph was looking up at me with an expression of pleasure and bemusement. Our eyes met and we greeted each other silently with love. I knew what he was thinking: my little sister getting married? Does she remember the Armadillo and the Platypus?

There was Pat, his wife, who had become very dear to me. And then Gil's parents were there with a family friend who had chaperoned Mother Gilbert a few days earlier on the train from her home in Los Angeles to San Francisco.

Father Gilbert arrived on the wedding day because he had to work. All showed their pleasure without reservation.

Only one man stood a little aside, a weak, polite smile on his face, stealing a sidelong glance at his wristwatch. This was the Justice of the Peace who was to perform the ceremony.

Finally the bridegroom appeared. He looked a little pale, a little nervous, certainly, but not "Green with fear and shaking like a leaf," as his wicked brother-in-law loved to describe him at later gatherings of friends and family. I did not mind the tailored "Young Executive" suit, with the impossibly wide padded shoulders, and the shiny, pointed shoes. All I saw was the radiance in his face and the love in his eyes while he came up the stairs to take my hand and lead me forward.

There were two large rooms on either side of the hall. One held Father's library and desk. In the other the golden wood of my beloved Biedermeier furniture provided the perfect background for the ceremony that initiated my future life. No matter that the man with the wristwatch delivered a perfunctory little speech reminding us of love, trust, obligations, and duty, etc., etc. At least he stayed away from god and country. He applied his seal and signature to our documents, accepted his check and a glass of champagne, and departed. Then we all kissed, and Mother Gilbert shed a few tears when I hugged her.

A few days earlier a small incident during the first meeting of both mothers, two women from vastly different worlds, had given me new respect and admiration for Mother Gilbert. Here she was, transported from her little house that she had rarely left in Los Angeles to an elegant drawing room in another city, among people whose style of life she had never experienced. With the help of somewhat constricting undergarments she had changed from her favorite apron and long baggy pants into a nice, black afternoon dress. She had her hair done. Her heavy legs and swollen feet were supported by flimsy, stylish shoes that obviously gave her trouble. She was used to lugging heavy shopping bags from the market, doing her laundry and housework, and being on her feet from morning to night. Standing for any length of time in one place on soft carpets with a glass of champagne in her hand and saying polite things to people she did not know was very hard for her, but she bore it nobly.

Now my mother obviously either forgot or did not know that in strict Jewish households meat and dairy products could not be consumed at the same time. She had heard, though, that Mother Gilbert kept Kosher. She did not understand what that entailed, but she thought that her new relative might be anxious about what she would be given to eat. So just before lunch started she reassuringly laid her hand on the other's arm and said, in her most caressing stage manner, "Please don't worry about the food, Dear. I have prepared everything with great care. There will be chicken, cooked only in the purest butter."

Granny, as we later called her, did not faint. She probably bit her lip, held her breath, swallowed hard, and then smiled and actually ate some of the chicken when lunch was served. It was an act of tremendous courage and sacrifice.

The real festivity started later in the afternoon when our friends arrived. I was hugged and kissed and kidded. Broadly beaming, Gil was admired and got his hands shaken. A few of my parent's friends, trying to curb their customary European arrogance, eyed him with veiled caution, but most were happy for me without reservation and appreciated his charm and intelligence.

The rest of the day is vague in my memory. There were hugs and kisses, laughter, and champagne glasses were raised to speeches full of good wishes for the future.

Mascha Gropper's glass had been filled too often, as usual. She had to be pried off my neck while reciting a poem she had written just for me. Gil and I took great pains to assure Dr. Esther Rosenkranz that we were "just entranced" by the awful gift she had bestowed on us. It was a huge glass fruit bowl in the shape of a very long necked swan.

Paul Moses embraced me tightly and kissed me warmly on both cheeks. There was a strange expression on his face. I looked up at him, and he smiled a little wistfully as our eyes met for just two or three seconds. "Take care of her," he said to Gil, shook his hand and turned away abruptly.

At long last everyone lined up on the steps and outside on the sidewalk. They threw rice at us and cheered while we drove off.

We stopped for the night at a hotel in San Mateo. It was already quite late, and only a few guests were left in the dining room. The light was subdued. We looked at each other across the table and the little candle between us. We held hands, relished the quiet, and had no need to talk.

The end of the meal arrived, and to our amazement the waiter approached and lowered a festive candle-decorated cake between us. "The management wishes to congratulate you," he said, and the smile on his face could not have been any broader.

"How did they know?" I was amazed.

Gil smiled and reached over, touching my face. "That's how," he said, retrieving some kernels of rice from my hair.

Felicia Altman Gilbert, 2004

2/2017

You write incredibly well &
already did so as a teenager,
judging by your letters.

You can be funny,
sad, sentimental, but
also keenly observant.

Also:

Stage set design

Your descriptions of
houses, apts + people
are vivid.

I'm sorry that
Germans rejected you when
the Nazi policies were
started.

BVG